THE THEOLOGY OF
KARL BARTH

An Introduction by

HERBERT HARTWELL

LL.D. (Erlangen), D.Phil. (Oxon)

GERALD DUCKWORTH & CO. LTD.

3 Henrietta Street, London, W.C.2

Printed in Great Britain by Richard Clay and Company, Ltd.,
Bungay, Suffolk

To my wife
without whose loving care and patience
this book could not have been written

PREFACE

In accordance with the purpose of the 'Studies in Theology' this volume is primarily intended for theological students. The aim has therefore been to expound Barth's theology as basically and as simply as possible and to indicate both its achievements and those aspects of it which are open to criticism. I hope, however, that the experts too may find something which is of interest to them. For in the Anglo-Saxon countries, at least in the past, no continental theologian has been more widely misunderstood and misinterpreted than Karl Barth. One only needs to read the article on Karl Barth in *The Oxford Dictionary of the Christian Church* to find ample proof for this statement. Professor T. F. Torrance's book on *Karl Barth, An Introduction to His Early Theology, 1910–1931* (1962), appeared in the course of the writing of this volume and Professor A. B. Come's *Introduction to Barth's Dogmatics for Preachers* (1963), was published when this volume had been almost completed. As far as possible, I have tried to take account of these two books, though for technical reasons this could be done mainly only in footnotes.

The authorized English translation of Karl Barth's *Church Dogmatics*, edited by Professor T. F. Torrance and Dr. G. W. Bromiley, has been used in all references to the existent twelve volumes of that work. In quoting therefrom I have however used my own translation from the German original whenever I found this necessary to render the true meaning of the latter. I pay tribute to the magnificent service rendered by the translators of this monumental work, but must add the warning that a translation which for a number of reasons, as will become evident in the course of this study, had to face great difficulties cannot be expected to be free from inaccuracies and even serious mistranslations, some of which have been pointed out in this volume.

London, September 1963.   H. H.

ABBREVIATIONS

1. The following abbreviations are used for some of Barth's writings:

Anselm	*Anselm: Fides quaerens intellectum*
Bultmann	*Rudolf Bultmann—An Attempt to understand him*
CD	*Church Dogmatics*
GF	*The Gift of Freedom*
Gifford	Gifford Lectures 1937/38: *The Knowledge of God and the Service of God*
GL	*Gospel and Law*
IET	*Evangelical Theology: An Introduction*
KD	*Kirchliche Dogmatik*
Philippians	Commentary on *The Epistle to the Philippians*
Romans	,, ,, *The Epistle to the Romans*
TT	*Karl Barth's Table Talk*

2. Other abbreviations:

ET	English Translation
SJT	Scottish Journal of Theology

ACKNOWLEDGMENTS

My thanks are due to Professor Barth who has authorized the writing of this book for the Studies in Theology series.

Quotations from the authorized English translation of *Church Dogmatics*, and of H. Gollwitzer: *Selections of Karl Barth's Church Dogmatics*, are included with the kind permission of the publishers and copyright holders, T. and T. Clark, Edinburgh.

H. H.

CONTENTS

xiii

I.—GENERAL INTRODUCTION

1. Preliminary Remarks

ANYONE interested in the movement of human thought in the realm of theology will be fascinated by the way in which man's thought is determined and shaped by his reaction to other thought forms or particular conditions and events of his age. H. R. Mackintosh[1] rightly points out: 'The progress of thought, at least in theology, is rather apt to proceed by way of what is called "the swing of the pendulum". Its movement is of a "zigzag" kind, sometimes with violent dashes from one extreme to the other.' We only need compare Barth's theocentric mode of thought with the anthropocentric theological writings of the nineteenth and the beginning of the twentieth century, in particular with Schleiermacher's theology of feeling, Hegel's theology of speculative rationalism, Albrecht Ritschl's theology of moral value-judgments and Ernst Troeltsch's theology of scientific religious history, and further with the theological systems worked out in our time by Rudolf Bultmann and Paul Tillich on the basis of or in conjunction with existentialist philosophy, to recognize the truth of this statement.

As far as Barth's theology is concerned, we must go even further. Though many theologies have been developed in the course of the history of Christianity, of only a few of them can it be said that they have accomplished a real turning-point in man's theological thinking, let alone, to use another metaphor, have turned the helm through an angle of 180 degrees. This, however, is precisely what Barth has done, taking his stand on a new point of departure for the whole problem of theology, a point of departure diametrically opposed to that of most of

1

the other Protestant theologians since the Reformation, so
that his theology may be said to represent a Copernican turn
in the history of human thought. It is therefore not surprising that Dietrich Bonhoeffer in a lecture on '*The Theology of
Crisis and its Attitude to Philosophy and Science*', delivered in
1931,[2] warned his hearers that he did not see any other possible way for them to get into real contact with Barth's
thinking than by forgetting 'at least for this one hour' everything they had previously learned concerning this problem.
Though, since then, Barth's theology has developed in new
directions and has become more widely known, this warning
is nevertheless still relevant.

Within the scope of this volume it is not possible to expound
the whole of Barth's teaching. For his theology has not only
been hammered out over a period of more than fifty years
but is embodied in (so far) twelve weighty volumes of his
Church Dogmatics and in many other writings, large and
small, the knowledge of which in some cases is as important
for a true understanding of his thought as the knowledge of
the *Church Dogmatics*.[3] For the same reason even a brief
synopsis could not be undertaken without distorting his
teaching or without laying it open to serious misunderstandings on account of the severe condensation required in that
case. All that can be attempted here is to introduce the
reader to the main thoughts which have guided Barth in
working out his theology. Even an introduction limited in
this way is faced with difficulties of one kind or another. For
we are here moving in a realm of ideas which in many of its
aspects is so different from that of other theologies, and, in
particular, because of Barth's uncompromising rejection of
natural theology and philosophy alike as a basis or even a
partial basis of theology, is so alien to the philosophical way
of thinking of Anglo-Saxon theologians that a full understanding of Barth's position as regards the one or other aspect
of his teaching would require a much more detailed exposition
of the latter than can possibly be undertaken within the
space at our disposal. Here the reader will continually be

referred to the relevant sections of Barth's *Church Dogmatics*
or to other writings of his for further study. Again, Barth's
theology has been and still is so widely misunderstood and,
consequently, misinterpreted by many of his critics that a
clarification of his views on these aspects of his teaching is
imperative. These misunderstandings and misinterpretations
have therefore constantly been borne in mind in the exposition of the leading thoughts of Barth's theology. Within the
limited scope of this volume it is however not possible to
deal with them separately, let alone in extenso, though they
will be particularly referred to whenever such a reference is
required for the sake of clarity. For the same reason we must
refrain from discussing the many factors which have contributed to these misunderstandings, though some of them will
be dealt with in this chapter (par. 4, 5) and others will be
pointed out in the course of this study. If the account, here
attempted, of Barth's leading thoughts will enable the reader
to find the right approach to his theology and to attain to a
first true apprehension of the main trends of his theological
thinking, this volume will have achieved its purpose. From
what has been said so far, it will be evident that it cannot
serve as a substitute for the study of Barth's own writings.
On the contrary, its aim is to encourage the reader to turn
to the latter for a fuller exploration of our subject.

2. ORIGINS

For the true understanding of Barth's theology as a whole
it is essential to grasp the situation in which the latter took
its rise. It was the peculiar situation of the preacher who is
called to proclaim the Word of God but instead is in constant
danger of speaking the word of man. During the twelve years
of his ministry, first in Geneva (1909–11) and then in Safenwil
(1911–21), the young Swiss pastor, born at Basle in 1886,
wrestled with the problem of how he could genuinely preach
the Word of God, in other words, how he could prevent his
sermon from being merely his own word. In a later address[4]
he expressed this problem, which every minister has to face,

B

in these words: 'As ministers we ought to speak of God. We are human, however, and so cannot speak of God. . . . For to speak of God seriously would mean to speak in the realm of revelation and faith.' These few words already contain in a nutshell what Barth was going to develop in his theology. Moreover, he was constantly perplexed by the conflict between the problematic nature of human life and the content of the Bible. In a famous passage of his address on *The Need and Promise of Christian Preaching*[5] he said: 'Often enough these two magnitudes, life and the Bible, have risen before me like Scylla and Charybdis.' Thus, to find an answer to these problems, he began to search for the Word of God, and that search as well as the responsible hearing and expounding of the Word of God has since then become the constant motive force and the guiding principle of all his theological labours.

To find the Word of God he had to turn to the Bible. For— here we encounter the second motive of his theology—he came to realize that not only the leading theologians of his time, such as his teachers W. Herrmann and A. v. Harnack[6] and also E. Troeltsch, but most of the theologians since the Reformation were of no help in that respect, that, on the contrary, they had to a larger or lesser degree substituted the word of man for the Word of God. It must suffice to point out here quite summarily[7] that in the eighteenth century, which saw a revival of the sixteenth-century Renaissance,[8] man optimistically thought that he could master life, its problems and riddles, by means of his own understanding. It was the age of the Enlightenment, the century of 'absolute man', as Barth terms it,[9] 'who discovers his own power and ability, the potentiality dormant in his humanity, that is, his human being as such, and looks upon it as the final, the real and absolute'.[10] The rationalism dominating that century put human reason on the seat of judgment and demanded 'that every Christian doctrine must undergo trial in the court of reason'.[11] In the realm of philosophy this anthropocentric thinking of man reached new heights in the philosophical

renascence that followed the Enlightenment, in the philosophical Idealism of Kant, Fichte, Schelling and Hegel.

In the theological field it found its most marked expression
in the Protestant theology of the nineteenth century.
Schleiermacher, whose theology was dominant in that century, made man's feeling of utter dependence, that is, the
feeling of his connection with God, in other words, man's
religious consciousness the basis, the theme and the criterion
of theology.[12] Moreover, in his view the kingdom of God is
identical with the advance of civilization since religion in
general and the Christian religion in particular is to him the
highest value in life, and civilization without religion, without
the Christian religion, is incomplete.[13] Again, Hegel's theology[14] was entirely speculative or metaphysical both in
origin and in content, having its basis in abstract general
reasoning. In it religion, in essence, was man's imaginative
response to the universe, and philosophy was the supreme
court of appeal also with regard to the Christian Faith and
its tenets. Jesus was not the Godman but according to
Hegel's rigidly monistic thinking only the first man to perceive a great (speculative) truth, namely the truth that God
and man are one. God had reality only in the minds of those
who believe in Him. Barth expresses the same thought when
he says that Hegel's living God is actually the living man.[15]
Again, though Albrecht Ritschl,[16] rejecting both Hegel's
speculative rationalism and Schleiermacher's subjectivism,
sought to root theology in history, more particularly in the
person of Jesus Christ, he yet conceived the work of Jesus
Christ in history and His person as well as the kingdom of
God in essentially intramundane terms. He failed to see, as
H. R. Mackintosh puts it,[17] that Jesus Christ is indeed *in*
history, but not *of* history. According to Ritschl Jesus Christ,
because of the work He did for men, had for man (merely)
the value of Godhead, and the kingdom of God essentially
served a moral purpose *in* this world. Ritschl's historical
positivism decisively contributed to the fact that in the
second half of the nineteenth century theology became to a

large extent the study of the history of religions including the Christian religion, and his rationalistic moralism, his view of Christianity, as an outlook upon life, as morality, and of reconciliation as the realization (by man) of the ideal of human life[18] prepared the way for that 'Cultural Protestantism' which, adapting the Christian message to the culture of the nineteenth and the beginning of the twentieth century, became one of the main targets of Barth's early theology.

Again, with Harnack, historian rather than theologian,[19] Jesus Christ was not the Son of God who became man, in other words, the incarnate Word of God in the sense of John 1:14, but merely the supreme teacher and revealer of God. In his lectures on *Das Wesen des Christentums* (1900),[20] 'the ablest statement of the Liberal Protestant interpretation of Christianity',[21] the essence of Christianity was seen in the teaching of Jesus, especially in that of the Sermon on the Mount. It accords with this view that according to Harnack it is the Father and not the Son who is part of the Gospel as taught by Jesus. This process of substituting the word of man for the Word of God reached its climax, or rather its rock-bottom, in Troeltsch's theology of scientific religious history,[22] in which Christianity was treated as but one religion among the others and Jesus Christ as a great religious personality. Claiming that theology as such has no special method of its own but simply applies one common to all forms of mental science, Troeltsch employed the idea of a general evolution in religious history 'in such a manner as to make a peculiar or exceptional self-revelation of God . . . wholly inconceivable'.[23]

Contending that 'no religion, even Christianity, is valid universally or for ever, because each faith is but an individual form of the pure spirit of religion and has power and authority only within the concrete and historical conditions under which it first arose',[24] that reduced view of the Christian Faith eventually led him to the conclusion that Christianity could claim validity for the European civilization only, and even that validity was according to his aforesaid proposition only a temporary and a relative one. The cul-de-sac into which theology had thus been led by him, a result which had been made inevitable by his approach to the Christian Faith by means of the history and philosophy of religion, became manifest when in 1914 he finally crossed over from the theological to the philosophical faculty.[25] Even Rudolf Otto's discovery of the category of 'the holy', 'the numinous', was exclusively based on religious–historical and religious–psychological studies.[26]

Closely connected with this development of Protestant theology on predominantly 'religionistic and so anthropocentric and so, in this sense, humanistic'[27] lines and, at least partly, caused by it, there was a third factor which operated as a motive in Barth's theology, namely the failure of the ethics of modern theology in the catastrophe which over-overtook mankind in 1914 at the outbreak of the First World War.[28] Barth recorded his own reaction to the tragic events of that time in these telling words, 'For me personally one day at the beginning of August of that year stamped itself as the *dies ater*. It was that on which 93 German intellectuals came out with a manifesto supporting the war policy of Kaiser William II and his counsellors, and among them I found to my horror the names of nearly all my theological teachers who up to then I had religiously honoured. Disillusioned by their conduct I perceived that I should not be able any longer to accept their ethics and dogmatics, their biblical exegesis, their interpretation of history, that at least for me the theology of the 19th century had no future'.[29] The close and indeed indissoluble relationship between dogmatics and ethics, between faith and obedience, which became a characteristic feature of his *Church Dogmatics*, is already indicated in this early statement of Barth.

3. EARLY DEVELOPMENTS[30]

Applying himself in his search for the Word of God during his ministry to an intensive study of the Bible, in particular of the Pauline writings, Barth discovered (1) that the God of the Bible is entirely different from the God as He had been presented by his theological teachers and the theologians of the past two or three centuries. He then found that the theme of the Bible 'could not possibly be man's religion and religious ethics' but is 'the Godness of God', and by that he means *God's* Godness, in other words, the aseity of the one and only God, His own peculiar nature 'over against not only the natural but also the spiritual cosmos' and further 'God's absolute unique existence, power and initiative above all in His relationship to man'.[31]

He discovered (2) that in the theology of his time as well as in the past two or three centuries man had been magnified at the expense of God and that nothing less than a radical revolution in man's thinking, a turning of the helm through an angle of 180 degrees, was required to re-establish the biblical truth of the supremacy of God and of the transcendent nature of His Word. Since then it became the primary aim of his theological endeavours in the later half of the second decade and the early twenties to demythologize the picture which man had made of himself, man's arrogant idea of being the criterion, the norm, of his and every understanding,[32] and to restore to God and His Word the place in theology and, consequently, in the Church which belongs to them of right according to the witness of the Bible to God's self-revelation in Jesus Christ.

He discovered (3) that man cannot of himself know God and speak of God, that, on the contrary, man in that respect is entirely dependent on God's revelation of Himself in the person and work of His Son Jesus Christ, and that this divine self-revelation is moreover an act of the sovereign and free grace of God. 'Ever since about 1916,' says Barth in his reply, *No*, to Emil Brunner's *Nature and Grace*,[33] 'when I began to recover noticeably from the effects of my theological studies and the influences of the liberal-political pre-war theology, my opinion concerning the task of our theological generation has been this: we must learn again to understand revelation as grace and grace as revelation and therefore turn away from all "true" or "false" *theologia naturalis*'. The meaning of these pregnant words will be made clear in the course of this study. Like an Old Testament prophet Barth then began to pronounce in addresses[34] and in sermons that God is God and man is man, that there is no way from man to God, but only from God to man, in Jesus Christ, that is, and that man is thoroughly mistaken in his assumption that he is able to achieve his salvation by means of his own exertions, namely by means of his morality, his culture, his religion and his piety, which had become his exclusive concern.

In 1919 Barth's famous commentary on *The Epistle to the Romans*[35] appeared in which he worked out his thesis that God is first and foremost the Subject of theology and only secondarily also its object. That commentary, a very hymn in praise of the Godness of God, was the bold attempt not only to reverse the order observed in the past and to make God and not man the starting-point, the centre, and the goal of man's thought, but also to deprive man of all human self-righteousness and self-reliance and of all ideas of self-redemption in order to make room for and to demonstrate the miracle of God's grace in Jesus Christ. Again, it was an uncompromising attack on a theology which had confused theology with psychology (religious experience) and philosophy (speculative rationalism) and faith with piety, and on a Christianity which had exchanged the Gospel of God's sovereign and free gracious dealing with man in Jesus Christ for a religion in which God was treated as a mere object which man imagined he had at his disposal, and which he felt to be beneficial to his moral, cultural and religious life. Only when we recognize the magnitude of the task which Barth had set himself in that writing, shall we be able to do justice to the vehemence and strangeness of the language, style and thought of *Romans*. Again, his severe criticism in *Romans* of man's morality, religion and culture was only intended to demolish man's illusion that his morality, his religion and his culture were sufficient for his salvation. It was not meant to be a rejection or condemnation of morality, religion or culture as such. Writing 'with a joyful sense of discovery'[36] Barth took great pains to work out what he then called, adapting a characteristic concept of Kierkegaard, 'the infinite qualitative distinction between God and man'. In an often quoted passage of his Preface to the second edition of *Romans* (1921), which was a complete re-writing of the first edition, he points out that if he had a system 'it was limited to a recognition of what Kierkegaard called the infinite qualitative distinction between time and eternity. . . . God is in heaven, and thou art on earth. The relation between such a God and such a man, and the relation between such a man and such a God, is for me the theme of the Bible and the essence of philosophy'.[37]

Later on (see below Ch. III, 2) Barth is going to use a rather different language, speaking not only of the majesty of God and of His transcendent nature but also of His 'humanity', for which he had left himself little room in his early theology. To avoid any misunderstanding it is, however, necessary to point out already here that Barth's later emphasis on the humanity of God, that is, God's relationship with man and His turning to man, His desire to be, and the fact that He is, God not otherwise than as man's God, is not to be understood as the abandoning of his former concept of the Godness of God. Rather is it an expansion of the latter. In his address in 1956 on *The Humanity of God*,[38] which does not represent, as may be thought at a first glance, a decisive change in his doctrine of God, he made it abundantly clear that the admittedly one-sided emphasis in his early theology on the Godness of God had been forced upon him by the situation which he had to face during his ministry and in the 'twenties, but that because of Jesus Christ God's Godness, rightly understood, includes His humanity and that for the same reason man's knowledge of God's humanity is based upon and starts from the knowledge of the Godness of God. 'What began to force itself stormily upon us some 40 years ago,' he says in that address, 'was less the humanity than the

Godness of God. . . . What we discovered . . . in those days
was the majesty . . . of the Crucified. . . . The humanity of
God then moved from the centre to the margin.'[39]

On another occasion he went even further and said that
the humanity of God is not the negation but the fulfilment
of the 'wholly other God' of whom he speaks in *Romans*,[40]
meaning that the true Godness of God, without losing its
divine essence, finds its ultimate and supreme expression in
His humanity. That no discontinuity in his theological
thinking is involved at this point, but only a different emphasis in his teaching, is also evident from the fact that in
Romans itself the humanity of God is not entirely neglected;
for He is said to be 'our God' and His 'Yes' to man in Jesus
Christ is said to be greater than His 'No' to man's sinfulness.[41]

To throw into the sharpest possible relief both the Godness
of God and man's utter dependence in everything upon God's
grace in Jesus Christ, Barth employed in *Romans* a graphic–
mathematical–paradoxical language which in part took its
illustrations from the Swiss landscape with its high mountains,
steep abysses, and torrential mountain-rivers, speaking, to
give but a few examples, of God as 'the Wholly Other', of the
Word of God as the *totaliter aliter* breaking in 'vertically from
above', of the 'mathematical point' and the 'tangent' in
which alone God in Jesus Christ and man were supposed to
touch each other, of the 'vacuum' which man must become
to be a fitting object of the divine grace, and of faith as 'a
leap into the abyss'. There is, however, no need here to
study that language, for it has long since been discarded.[42]
For the same reason we do not need to discuss either the
philosophical concepts and ideas of Kant and Plato, which
Barth used in *Romans* to achieve the aforementioned object,[43]
or Kierkegaard's paradoxical and existential way of thinking,
which exerted a strong influence upon the formation of Barth's
early theology and can quite clearly be traced in *Romans*.
In his later theology, especially in his *Church Dogmatics*,
Barth has not only given up this latter mode of thought, but
on many important aspects of his teaching has developed a

view which is fundamentally different from that of Kierkegaard.[44]

We also do not find in his later theology his former thinking in terms of 'crisis', be it the power of God as the crisis of all other power or the *Heilsgeschichte*[45] as the crisis of all history or grace as the crisis from death to life or, above all, the crisis which had been brought on man by Jesus Christ, namely by the judgment whereby God has judged man in and through the death of Jesus Christ on the Cross. This concept of crisis figured so largely in Barth's early theology[46] that the latter was then called 'the theology of crisis'. Finally, in his later theology Barth got beyond another mode of thought which was closely connected with his earlier paradoxical way of thinking and likewise played an important part in *Romans*, namely his dialectical thinking. In the early stage of his theology Barth thought that to bear witness to the truth of God as revealed in His Word he must use the method of statement and counter-statement since only the combination of the two could bring out, as far as humanly possible, the truth of the Gospel. Since in Jesus Christ God has said to man both Yes and No, Barth then felt that, to interpret this Yes and this No and further the No by the Yes, the divine truth, which in itself is not divided, had to be expressed dialectically.[47]

The profound impression created by Barth's uncompromising attack in *Romans* upon Neo-Protestantism in theology and Christianity alike led to his becoming successively professor of theology in Göttingen (1921), Münster (1925) and Bonn (1930). It also contributed to the rise of the so-called *Dialectical Theology*, the rallying-point of which became the journal *Zwischen den Zeiten*,[48] edited by Barth from 1923 till 1933 together with F. Gogarten, E. Thurneysen and G. Merz. In addition to shorter writings[49] he wrote during that period a commentary on *The Epistle to the Philippians* (1928)[50] which, though observing in certain directions a procedure distinctly different from that of *Romans* and using a more restrained language, yet continued the main theological trends of *Romans* in the context of the special theme of *Philippians*. We find here in particular once more the emphasis on the mystery of the majesty and holiness of God, the proposition that there is no bridge from man to God but solely the way from God to man, and the description of Jesus Christ as the end of all religion, including the Christian religion.[51]

In the preceding year (1927) the first volume of *Die Christliche Dogmatik im Entwurf* (Christian Dogmatics in Outline) appeared. It was Barth's first attempt to work out his theology as a whole, and in particular (in that first volume) his doctrine of the Word of God, in opposition to the teaching of modern Protestantism.[52] That attempt proved a failure. Though, in his striving for a theological exegesis of the Bible, he had been able to rid himself gradually of the neo-Kantian concepts of which he had made use in *Romans* and afterwards to depict the Godness of God, he yet still thought that, as far as man is concerned, he could base dogmatics, and in particular his doctrine of the Word of God, on the concepts and ideas of existential philosophy. However, he soon came to realize that he could not proceed in this way without exposing his theology to legitimate criticism, that he had to base the whole of his theology on the Word of God only. Thus, he abandoned his first dogmatic attempt and replaced it by his *Church Dogmatics*, of which the first two half-volumes appeared in 1932 and 1938 respectively. The words he used in the Foreword to 'The Doctrine of the Word of God', developed in these two half-volumes, to make his position clear help to understand the basis of his theology:[53] 'I could and I wanted to say the same thing as before; but now I could no longer say it in the way in which I had said it before. What else was left to me, except to begin at the beginning. . . . I have cut out . . . everything that in the first issue (1927) might give the slightest appearance of giving to theology a basis, support, or even a mere justification in the way of existential philosophy.'

In his efforts to free his theology from any philosophical or anthropological elements which might serve as its basis, be it only a partial one, he was greatly helped by his book, *Fides quaerens intellectum* (1931). Dealing with Anselm's proof of the existence of God, it was written prior to the first half-volume of the *Church Dogmatics*.[54] This book represents a turning-point in Barth's methodological approach to theology; its study is indispensable to anyone who wants to understand the path to knowledge trodden in his theology. For in it he worked out 'his own ideas as to the nature of theology and of the theologian's task',[55] in other words, the epistemology of his theology as embodied, above all, in his *Church Dogmatics*. In the Preface to the Second Edition (1958)[56] he says 'in this book on Anselm I am working with a vital key, if not the key, to an understanding of that whole process of thought that has impressed me more and more in my *Church Dogmatics* as the only one proper to theology'. That key, as we shall see in the next chapter, is the epistemological principle that the knowledge with which the theologian is concerned is faith-knowledge, namely the knowledge that springs from faith in God's revelation in Jesus Christ. God has given Himself, and continually gives Himself, as the object of man's knowledge, and the theologian's task is the exposition of this self-revelation of God in faithful obedience to His Word.[57] 'To give the faithful joy in believing by a demonstration of the *ratio* of their faith'[58] became one of the primary aims of Barth's *Church Dogmatics* as it was that of Anselm of Canterbury.

4. CHURCH DOGMATICS [59]

Though Barth's *Church Dogmatics*, his *opus magnum*, is still awaiting completion, five further volumes being planned in addition to the twelve so far published,[60] it can nevertheless be said without fear of contradiction that it is the most comprehensive dogmatics that has appeared since St. Thomas Aquinas's *Summa Theologica*, surpassing in respect of the range and depth of its thought and the wealth of its material the work of many patristic, mediaeval and reformed theologians. If it were at all possible to sum up its theme in one sentence it might be said, making use of some felicitous words of Hans Urs von Balthasar,[61] that its theme is the joyous message of 'God's eternal Yea and Amen to Himself and His creation' as that message is made known to man, according to the witness of Holy Scripture, in God's revelation in Jesus Christ.

Since in Barth's view (see below, Ch. II, 2) the task of theology is the expository presentation of that revelation on the basis of a theological exegesis of the content of the Bible, his *Church Dogmatics* is distinguished by a thorough concentration on the *Word of God*, and that means, as we shall see (Ch. II, 6), the Word of God as revealed in Jesus Christ, written in Holy Scripture and proclaimed by the Church. It accords with the exegetical and expository character of such a theology that the theological expositions of the *Church Dogmatics* are derived from, and worked out in accordance with, the results of Barth's own interpretation of the content of the Bible. The *Church Dogmatics*, therefore, presents us with these results in the form of exegetical discourses (in small print). Though, as a rule, these discourses have been worked out by Barth before the drafting of the theological expositions which they are meant to justify, they are nevertheless placed in the text after these expositions in order to indicate thereby, on the one hand, that his theological expositions are bound to and determined by the Word of God and, on the other hand, that the theologian, as an autonomous human being, is free to express his own understanding of it.[62] We encounter these exegetical discourses almost everywhere in the *Church Dogmatics*, and many of them are so extensive[63] that offering, as it were, a whole series of commentaries, this Dogmatics is a very mine of sermon material. They are indispensable to a full understanding of the theological expositions preceding them, and anyone who wants to attack the latter will have to examine first whether the biblical exegesis on which they are based is at fault.[64]

Again, the *Church Dogmatics* is wholly *christological* in

the sense that in it, generally speaking, every theological proposition has as its point of departure Jesus Christ, the Son of God and the Son of Man, in the unity of His person and work. This christological concentration of the *Church Dogmatics*, and indeed of Barth's theology as a whole, is 'unparalleled in the history of Christian thought'.[65] It does not contradict the asserted concentration on the Word of God since in Barth's view (see Chs. II, 6, III, 1) Jesus Christ is Himself the Word of God. Again, it does not signify a *Christomonism* in the sense as it was taught and practised, for instance, by Nikolaus von Zinzendorf. In view of Barth's teaching on the Triune God (Ch. II, 7), creation (Ch. III, 3) and the Holy Spirit (Chs. II, 7, III, 6) it may even be doubted whether his theology can be classified as wholly christo-centric, seeing that to both the Father and the Holy Spirit a prominent place is assigned in it.

Again, the *Church Dogmatics*, though written by a Reformed theologian, is marked by an *ecumenical* breadth that is unique in the history of the Christian dogma. Throughout the many volumes of this work, in the course of the development of his own theological propositions, Barth is engaged in a contin-uous critical conversation with past and present theologians of the Roman Catholic, Lutheran and Reformed Churches, and with philosophers from Aristotle and Plato to Martin Heidegger and J. P. Sartre, always clearly indicating both the extent to which he is able to agree and the points at which in faithful obedience to the Word of God there must be a parting of the ways. Thus in these vast tomes we are virtually presented with a compendium, though, of course, a concise one, of the history of the Christian dogma as well as with lengthy treatises on the philosophical systems of many outstanding philosophers. Some of these treatises, such as those on Leibniz (CD, III, 1, pp. 388 ff., 406 ff.; III, 3, pp. 316 ff.), Schopenhauer (CD, III, 1, pp. 334 ff., 337 ff.), Karl Marx (CD, III, 2, pp. 387 ff.), Nietzsche (CD, III, 2, pp. 231 ff.), Martin Heidegger (CD, III, 3, pp. 334 ff., 343 ff., 347 ff.) and J. P. Sartre (CD, III, 3, pp. 334, 338 ff., 346 ff.)

are real masterpieces which also throw an illuminating light on Barth's own theological position with regard to the concepts and ideas of these philosophers.

Again, the *Church Dogmatics* is concerned with the exposition and interpretation of a *story*, the story of God's gracious dealings with mankind in Jesus Christ from eternity. This sublime theme is not only inexhaustible but has many aspects which, though only representing many facets of one and the same truth and, in essence, constituting a unity, can nevertheless be considered only one after the other or side by side. This fact determines Barth's method of exposition. As pointed out elsewhere,[66] the latter, in order to safeguard the dynamic truth of the living Word of God', is 'similar to that of a pointilliste, that is, a painter who obtains his effects of light and atmosphere by small dots or points of pure colour which, viewed at a distance, are blended into a unity by the eye'. The *Church Dogmatics* is therefore like the painting of a vast landscape in which only the sum total of its innumerable details is capable of bringing out its full meaning and of showing how everything hangs together. Hence, if we want to do justice to the one or other aspect of Barth's theology, we shall have to take into account its other aspects as well, seeing the aspect in question in the light of his whole teaching. H. R. Mackintosh's early warning to students of Barth's theology: '*Respice finem*'[67] still holds good. Again, being engaged in the exposition and interpretation of a story, the *Church Dogmatics* uses the style and language of 'direct presentation or even narration'.[68] Barth, as it were, constantly retells and reinterprets the same story, but in conformity with its many aspects does so each time from a different angle and with a view to a correspondingly different theological proposition. Consequently, he uses what has aptly been called 'the spiral method of procedure', relentlessly circling round and round the same point, each time examining a different aspect of it and raising a different set of questions connected therewith.[69] Though this method enables him to bring out, as far as humanly possible, the many-sided truth of the point under investigation, it does not make for easy reading and, to some extent at least, explains why his teaching is so frequently misunderstood.

Finally, the *Church Dogmatics* exhibits a *structure* which is both original and illuminating. In this respect only a few indications can here be given. It may come as a surprise to those who study this structure that Barth regards 'The Doctrine of the Word of God' (CD, I, 1; I, 2), with which his Dogmatics opens, only as 'Prolegomena to Church Dogmatics', though it includes material which forms an essential part of any dogmatics, namely teaching not only on the task of theology in general and of dogmatics in particular (CD, I, 1, par. 1, 2) and on the Word of God, its form, its nature, and its knowability (CD, I, 1, par. 3–7), but also on the Triune God (CD, I, 1, par. 8–12), the Incarnation of the Word of God (CD, I, 2, par. 13–15), the outpouring of the Holy Spirit (CD, I, 2, par. 16–18), Holy Scripture (CD, I, 2, par. 19–21) and the proclamation of the Church (CD, I, 2, par. 22–24). His intention is to make clear thereby that the several subject-matters of the 'Prolegomena to Church Dogmatics' represents in their totality as well as individually the particular path to knowledge trodden in his Dogmatics and thus constitute, as it were, the basis or forecourt of his Dogmatics.[70]

This viewpoint explains the unique place assigned to the doctrine of the Trinity within dogmatics, forming, contrary to tradition, the first part of the doctrine of revelation (CD, I, 1, par. 8–12) and preceding the doctrine of God. For in Barth's view (see below, Ch. II, 7 (2)) the doctrine of the Trinity has its root in the doctrine of revelation, and our knowledge of God as the Triune God is, so to speak, the first fruit of God's self-revelation. Again, it explains why Barth's teaching on the Incarnation of the Word of God and on the out-pouring of the Holy Spirit precedes that on God and on creation. The former teaching constitutes an integral part of revelation as taught by Barth, in other words, of his particular path to knowledge; without the Incarnation of the

Word of God and the outpouring of the Holy Spirit the revelatory process would not be complete (below, Ch. II, 7 (3, 4)).

In his doctrine of God Barth not only deals with the knowledge and the reality of God and what he terms the perfections
of God (CD, II, 1), but also with God's election of grace and
with God's command (CD, II, 2), thus treating God's election
of grace and His command as essential elements in the very
Being of God and, once more contrary to tradition and for
reasons which will become clear in the course of this study,
giving to the doctrine of God's election of grace and to ethics
(general ethics) pre-eminence even above the doctrines of
creation and providence. In his doctrine of creation, dealing
with the work of creation (CD, III, 1), the doctrines of man
(CD, III, 2) and of providence (CD, III, 3) and the command
(special ethics) of God the Creator (CD, III, 4), two features
deserve special interest from the viewpoint of structure and
should be closely studied together, namely the teaching on
'The Yes of God the Creator' (CD, III, 1, par. 42) and on
'God and the Nihil' (CD, III, 3, par. 50).[71] For they not only
render, if viewed synoptically, Barth's view on the theodicy
but are of basic significance to the whole of his theology.
Special reference must also be made to his novel doctrine of
the angels (CD, III, 3, par. 51) which 'is the first large-scale
project of this kind in a very long time'.[72]

Again, the structure of the doctrine of reconciliation exhibits a magnificent symmetry, the profundity of which can
be fully appreciated only if the contents of CD, IV, 1–3 are
placed side by side in columns, each column rendering the
contents of one of the three parts of this doctrine, so that a
synoptic view of them can be obtained. Then the horizontal
and vertical correspondence of the several sections of these
three parts will become recognizable and will make evident
both their mutual parallelism and their uniform irreversible
direction.[73] For Jesus Christ, who has previously been shown
by Barth to be very God, very man and the Godman (CD, I, 2,
par. 15), is in the exposition of His work of reconciliation
correspondingly represented, firstly, in His priestly office (CD,

c

IV, 1) as the Lord (Son of God) who became a servant to accomplish the work of reconciliation, secondly, in His kingly office (CD, IV, 2) as the servant (Son of Man) who became Lord and by His own exaltation exalted man to fellowship with God and, thirdly, in His prophetic office (CD, IV, 3) as the Godman who as the Mediator of man's reconciliation with God is the Guarantor and Witness of that reconciliation. Again, that structure indicates that Jesus Christ's priestly work entails man's justification (CD, IV, 1, par. 61), His kingly work man's sanctification (CD, IV, 2, par. 66), and His prophetic work man's vocation (CD, IV, 3, par. 71). Again, the Holy Spirit, who within the framework of this doctrine of reconciliation is presented as the Spirit of the risen Lord Jesus Christ, is shown to accomplish, in accordance with the threefold work of Jesus Christ and completing it, corporately the gathering (CD, IV, 1, par. 62), upbuilding (CD, IV, 2, par. 67) and mission (CD, IV, 3, par. 72) of the Church and individually the faith (CD, IV, 1, par. 63), love (CD, IV, 2, par. 68) and hope (CD, IV, 3, par. 73) of the Christian. In accordance with Barth's wholly christological epistemology his doctrine of sin, in startling contrast to the structures of other dogmatics, does not precede his doctrine of reconciliation, but for reasons to be discussed later (Ch. III, 6), arises out of the latter or, to put it more concretely, arises out of Jesus Christ's threefold work and actually presupposes it (CD, IV, 1, par. 60; IV, 2, par. 65; IV, 3, par. 70). The last part of the doctrine of reconciliation (CD, IV, 4) will deal with the command (special ethics) of God the Reconciler, and the fifth and last volume of the *Church Dogmatics* is to contain the doctrine of redemption (eschatology).

5. CHARACTERISTIC FEATURES

Any serious student of Barth's theology will be aware of certain particular features of his thinking as a theologian which, continually recurring in his teaching, form an essential part of the latter and must constantly be borne in mind as we study his theology. Two of them are mentioned in the

preceding paragraph, namely his thorough concentration on
the Word of God and the wholly christological character of
his theology. In addition three other particular features
must here be outlined which are of singular importance to a
true understanding of the actual purport and operation of
the basic concepts of his theology, namely (1) the manner in
which his thought moves, (2) the objectivism and historicism
and (3) the actualism of his theology.

Before we turn to these features, it must be pointed out
that Barth's theology, entirely rooted in the Word of God,
does not present us, as philosophical Idealism does, with a
'system' in the sense of 'the interpretation of the whole
through the one which is its ground and its centre, that is, the
thinking ego'.[74] Though 'the thinking ego' and, therefore,
in our context the theologian is obviously the one who has
to work out his theology before he can present it, he is not
wholly independent in his thinking but must 'follow' the
Word of God which determines both the method and the
content of his theology (see below, Ch. II, 2).

Neither does Barth's theology render a system which is
based on the presupposition of a (human) basic view of
things, that is to say, on a preconceived abstract general
idea or, as Paul Tillich does,[75] on a preconceived systematic
principle.[76] Barth's ultimate objection to a system of the
second kind is that in it 'the presupposed basic view acquires
inevitably the position and function which . . . can be
ascribed only to the Word of God'.[77] This applies also to
Tillich's systematic principle according to which in theology, to
put it as simply as possible, philosophy supplies the existential
questions and the Christian message the theological answers
(method of correlation).[78] Since, according to Barth, it is
solely the Word of God which determines the thinking and
speaking of the theologian, and since that Word arises out of
the sovereignty and freedom of God's action and work in the
history of mankind, as that action and work is accomplished
in the revealed Word of God 'as the way which God has taken,
takes and will take with man in the person of Jesus Christ

and through the operation of the Holy Spirit',[79] there is no room in his theology for a system in the aforesaid sense. Starting from the living Word of God as spoken by God Himself in His sovereignty and freedom, in and through the person and work of Jesus Christ, it cannot begin, as a system does, with man-made abstract general principles. The living God is too great to be encased in a system of man's making. In a theology starting in this manner there can be room only for the theological exposition of God's action and work in Jesus Christ, and this theological exposition, on the other hand, based as it is on the exegesis of Holy Scripture, is possible only in faithful obedience to the Word of God and, consequently, is dependent on the free grace of God which reveals that Word to man in the power of the Holy Spirit. As will be shown in the next chapter,[80] it is likewise grace when man hears the Word of God as attested in the Bible and obeys it. Consequently, the theologian must ever again pray for that grace in order that he may be able to expound the Word of God as adequately as is humanly possible.

We shall do well to note already at this point that in Barth's view theology in the last analysis is a question of prayer and the answer to prayer,[81] and it is already for this reason, if not for any other, that theology cannot be presented in the form of a system of man's making, but must always remain open to the guidance of the Holy Spirit; in other words, it will at its best be always 'on the way' and thus will always be *theologia viatorum*.[82] This does not mean that Barth's theology is non-rational in the sense of Rudolf Otto's categories of 'the holy' and 'the numinous'[83] or unscientific. Rather is the opposite true. We must however leave the discussion of this point to the next chapter.

(1) *Movement of Thought.* (*a*) The Word of God is the source, the basis and the criterion of Barth's theology. It constitutes, therefore, on principle the constant point of departure of the movement of his thought. He does not reflect in general and at random. For the Word of God is not an abstract general idea conceived by the human mind

but a particular fact, namely the particular fact of God's
actual revelation of Himself and of His will for man in and
through the concrete person and work of Jesus Christ, who is
Himself the incarnate Word of God, the Lord (Son of God)
who became a servant and the servant (the royal man) who
became Lord. Hence, the Word of God is a particular event,
or rather a series of particular events constituting the
Heilsgeschichte,[84] particular events which not only happened
in the past but continue to happen in this world, in the course
of the history of mankind. Thus Barth's thought constantly
starts from that particular fact, from these particular events,
and this means that his thought continually moves from the
particular to the general. It means that in his theology the
usual movement of thought from the general to the particular
is reversed, and this reversal has far-reaching consequences
for the whole trend of his theology. For it entails that the
basic concepts he employs in his teaching are throughout
derived from that particular event of God's self-revelation
in Jesus Christ; they are not abstract concepts of his con-
triving but are filled with the quite specific and concrete
meaning which they receive from that revelation. In a word,
he never theologizes *in abstracto*, but always *in concreto*.

To put the same thought in a different way, his basic
concepts and their contents are determined and shaped not
by human speculation nor by existential philosophy but by
the *reality* of the self-revelation of the Triune God in Jesus
Christ and through the Holy Spirit and therefore have a
strictly concrete meaning. In his doctrine of the divine
perfections, Barth, showing that all his statements about
God's omnipotence have their final and decisive ground in
the knowledge gained by the divine revelation and work
of reconciliation,[85] says of that (particular) concept of
the divine omnipotence: 'it is not the general' (that is, the
abstract concept of omnipotence) 'which comes first but the
particular. The general does not exist without this particular'
(concept of omnipotence) 'and cannot therefore be prior to
the particular . . . Thus we cannot move from the general to

this particular but only in the opposite direction—from this particular to the general. It is from this particular that we come to this general.'[86] Again, speaking in his doctrine of reconciliation of the obedience of the Son of God who in the very humiliation of His suffering on the Cross for man's sake and in man's place revealed the mystery of His Godhead, Barth states: 'The meaning of His deity—the only true deity in the New Testament sense—cannot be gathered from any notion of supreme, absolute, non-worldly being. It can be learned only from what took place in Jesus Christ.'[87] Again, characterizing both creation and covenant as special acts of God, he says: 'According to Scripture there are no timeless truths, but all truths according to Scripture are specific acts of God in which He unveils Himself, acts which as such have an eternal character, embracing all times, but also a concretely temporal character.'[88]

Thus, as we study his theology, we can constantly see how the meaning and content of general concepts and ideas are determined and shaped by the particular incident to which they apply. Having made the reality of God's revelation in Jesus Christ the basis of his theology, there is therefore no room in it for an abstract idea of God, let alone for Tillich's artificial and, if taken literally, self-contradictory apologetic notion of a 'God above God',[89] nor can or does it start from an abstract idea of revelation. Again, general philosphical concepts such as, for instance, being, time and eternity, as well as the perfections (attributes) of the Triune God, in particular those of His omnipotence, omnipresence and constancy, assume in Barth's teaching a quite specific concrete theological meaning which is wholly and exclusively determined by the particular event of God's revelation in Jesus Christ. This is true even of familar concepts of everyday life such as, for instance, person, personality, father and love, which in Barth's view are exhibited in their original and true meaning in the being of the Triune God only.[90] In this respect—as in so many others—his teaching decisively differs from that of Bultmann who, regarding the communion between God and man as the analogue to the communion between man and man, speaks in this analogical sense, and therefore from the perspective of the human situation, of God's fatherhood, love and care, and even of His grace.[91]

(b) Barth's thought does not move, as logic may seem to require and is the norm in rational enquiries of a general and abstract nature, from possibility to reality but in the opposite direction, that is, from reality to possibility. For instance, he does not enquire, first of all, whether the knowledge of the Word of God and of God and whether revelation, incarnation and faith are possible. On the contrary, he expounds, first of all, the Word of God in its threefold form as the revealed, the written, and the proclaimed Word of God and its nature (CD, I, 1, par. 4, 5) before he goes on to discuss its knowability (CD, I, 2, par. 6). Again, the exposition of the fulfilment of the knowledge of God (CD, II, 1, par. 25) precedes the discussion of the knowability of God (CD, II, 1, par. 26). Again, the objective reality of revelation (Jesus Christ) and the subjective reality of revelation (Holy Spirit) are treated prior to the examination of the question of their possibility (CD, I, 2, par. 13, 16), and the reality of faith is investigated before the possibility of faith (CD, IV, 1, pp. 740 ff.).

This peculiar movement of his thought finds its explanation in the fact, already mentioned above, that his thought, on the basis of faith, takes the Word of God as its permanent starting-point. Consequently, it continually proceeds from the reality of God's revelation in Jesus Christ as attested in Scripture, and the term 'reality', as used in this context, means not only that the revelation of God in Jesus Christ has actually come to pass but is continually taking place and moreover comprises all the data of that revelation. Throughout his entire work Barth takes great pains to impress upon the minds of those who study it the truth that it is only on the ground of the reality of revelation that its possibility too can and must be discussed. And the same applies to the other subject-matters already referred to. It is Barth's contention

that the possibility of these and other subject-matters is to
be derived from and is contained in their reality.[92] With him,
it is always first a question of fact, of reality, on the basis of
faith, and of text (the relevant passages of the Bible), and
only then a question of exegesis and interpretation. Hence,
the whole direction of his theology is determined and pres-
cribed by the *res revelata*, and that means, among other
things, that 'the very definite order of being which Holy
Scripture makes manifest when in its witness to God's revelation it confronts and relates God and man, divine facts
and human attitudes enforces an order of knowing corresponding to it';[93] in short, it means that the exposition of the
reality in question takes precedence over the enquiry into
its possibility.

(*c*) His thought continually moves from thought to action.
This statement must be taken in its strictly literal sense. It
does not mean that this or that theological concept of his
demands a corresponding action as this would not really
involve a movement of thought, but would be action spring-
ing from thought. It means that the very concept itself
comprises both thought and action so that within one and the
same concept a movement of thought is implied from thought
to action and vice versa. In his Gifford Lectures, 1937/38,
which carry the significant title, *The Knowledge of God and the
Service of God*, Barth indicates this movement of thought
by his proposition that the knowledge of God is at once 'in
itself' service of God,[94] again, that the knowledge of God 'is'
obedience to God and therefore is 'itself' already service of
God.[95] Here thought (knowledge) and action (service) are,
so to speak, merged in each other, the thought being expressed by action and the action by thought. There cannot be
the one without the other, and Barth's thought continually
moves from the one to the other. To illustrate this point
further: according to Barth's teaching, especially in his
Church Dogmatics,[96] there cannot be faith, love or hope without or apart from action expressing that faith, love or hope.
The latter are not true faith, love or hope without or apart

from such action. To sum up, the concept itself and as such requires and implies in addition to the thought the corresponding action; in other words, Barth's theological concepts are dynamic.

2. *Objectivism and Historicism.* This feature needs to be stressed and explained right from the outset though, in doing so, much is to be anticipated that will be discussed later on in its proper context. For the knowledge of it is essential to the true understanding of each and every part of Barth's teaching; moreover, no feature of his theology has been more widely misunderstood and criticized than what has been termed his 'objectivism' or 'positivism'.

We just saw that with Barth it is always, first, a question of fact, of reality, on the basis of faith, and that this fact, this reality, is the particular event of God's revelation in Jesus Christ. Consequently, with him it is always, first, a question of an objective happening that has taken place, takes place or will take place *in* the world, and therefore in history. Thus objectivism and historicism are closely correlated in his teaching; in the latter he has fully carried into effect the knowledge that the Christian Faith is based on a historical fact, that is, on Jesus Christ. As pointed out elsewhere,[97] his *Church Dogmatics* is concerned with the exposition and interpretation of a story, the story of God's gracious dealing with mankind in Jesus Christ from eternity.

(*a*) Objectivism in the sense as here understood signifies no less but also no more than Barth's constant reference to, and dependence on, the objective fact of a reality outside of man which is neither of man's making nor at his disposal but, on the other hand, inescapably affects him and determines his destiny. That objective reality is, first and foremost, God Himself, more concretely, the sovereign Lord of man in the reality both of His inner trinitarian life as Father, Son and Holy Spirit and of His revelation to man in Jesus Christ and through the Holy Spirit, further the objective reality of the Godman Jesus Christ, of His incarnation, Cross, resurrection and resurrection-appearances, and the objective reality of His work of reconciliation, including His prophetic work as the risen Lord. Barth never tires of pointing out, and starting from, the objective significance which these (and other) facts (events) have for man, for all men, facts (events) which man is powerless to bring about of his own will, but which, on the other hand, both limit (judge) him and determine his destiny.[98]

In his study of Bultmann's teaching[99] Barth not only insists in opposition to Bultmann's restricted view of the merely kerygmatic significance of Christ that Jesus Christ has in Himself, that is, by virtue of His person as such, objective significance and is Himself the kerygma, but advocates also the objectivity of what has taken place in His life and death on the Cross and in His resurrection. In particular, he emphasizes the primacy of the resurrection of Jesus Christ as such, that is, its significance as an objective event, over against Bultmann's reduced view of the resurrection as a merely inward experience of the Christian believer. Again, in his doctrine of reconciliation Barth clearly distinguishes between the objective and the subjective aspect of man's justification, sanctification and vocation. According to this teaching the justification, sanctification and vocation of all men has already objectively taken place in Jesus Christ, in and through what He has done in His reconciling work for all men and in their place, whereas the individual man's humble and obedient acknowledgement of this work and the appropriation and application of its fruits are required from him—and take place in and through the power of the Holy Spirit—to demonstrate the justification, sanctification and vocation of all men in Jesus Christ also subjectively, that is, in and through the person and witness of individual Christians.[100]

The fact that Barth, in his doctrine of revelation, teaches that God's revelation is achieved objectively in the person and work of Jesus Christ and subjectively in the work of the Holy Spirit in man, and the further fact that, in his doctrine of reconciliation, he acknowledges both an objective and a subjective aspect of man's justification, sanctification and vocation, treating all these objective and subjective realities with equal emphasis and in a balanced manner and regarding each of them to be equally essential to the completion of the work of revelation and the work of reconciliation respectively, should refute the view of a one-sided emphasis by Barth on the objective elements in the Christian Faith,[101] or that with him 'in comparison with revelation, with the objective Word of God, the subjective element, faith, is on a much lower level'.[102] Rejecting in his teaching on 'Man's Vocation' any one-sided emphasis either on the objective or on the subjective elements of the Christian Faith, Barth says: 'The object and theme of theology and the content of the Christian message is neither a subjective nor an objective element in isolation, neither man in isolation, nor God in isolation, but God and man in their encounter and communion, God's dealings with the Christian and the Christian's dealings with God.'[103] The fact that Barth treats the objective elements of the Christian Faith before he deals with its subjective elements, before man's knowledge of God and man's faith, love and hope for instance, ensues from the primacy of the Word of God as the source, basis and criterion of his theology, but does not imply a denial of the intrinsic importance of these and other subjective elements of the Christian Faith. The priority of the Word of God only makes them relative.

Again, Barth's objectivism has to be seen in its true perspective. We must not overlook the fact that in each and every part of his theology it is always God who takes the initiative and acts first and thus is always the primary Subject of the action in question, be it the work of revelation, creation, reconciliation and redemption, or the work of man's justification, sanctification and vocation and the realization of man's faith, love and hope. There would therefore be even more justification for speaking of his subjectivism. In his doctrine of the Trinity, for instance, we are confronted with his basic proposition that God as the Subject of revelation is and remains 'indissolubly Subject' in the sense that we cannot get behind this Subject, making it an object of our human speculation and seeking behind the God who has revealed Himself in Jesus Christ a God of a different kind, a 'God above God' for instance. James Brown, in his penetrating study of Barth's concept of God as the One who is 'indissolubly Subject',[104] has rightly shown that this concept leaves room in Barth's teaching for the other concept of God as 'object', if not 'an object', God being, for instance, the object of His own self-knowledge in the life of the eternal Trinity as well as the object of man's faith-knowledge in revelation. It is, however, important to realize that even where in Barth's theology God is object in this and in other respects, He is yet at the same time, and even primarily, Subject in the most dynamic sense of the word. Throughout the many thousands of pages of the *Church Dogmatics* there constantly blows the revealing, creating, preserving, directing, reconciling and redeeming Spirit of the Living God who allows Himself to become also the object of man's faith-knowledge, love and hope, of man's praise and adoration. In the light of the leading part assigned in Barth's theology to God as the primary Subject of every action discussed therein and in consideration of the active part man, according to Barth's teaching,[105] is destined and called by God in Jesus Christ to play both in the Church and in the world, Barth's objectivism represents itself as a circumscribed, though vitally important, feature of his teaching.

(*b*) Historicism in the sense here understood does not mean that the particular events which form the subject-matter of Barth's theology are treated by him as constituting a part of the history of mankind in the general sense of that term. Speaking of 'history' in the context of his Dogmatics, Barth has not in mind an abstract or general idea of history but assigns to this concept a quite specific and concrete theological meaning. With him history, so to speak, starts in eternity, that is to say, before the creation of the universe. The pure eternal being of God as the being of the Triune God already presents us with a 'history'; in the dynamics of His

inner life as Father, Son and Holy Spirit God is the basic type
and ground of all history.[106]

Again, history in the sense used by Barth was already in
the making when God decided in His eternal decree before
the creation of the world, and therefore in His eternity, to
elect man, all men, in Jesus Christ to be His partner in the
covenant of grace which He then resolved to make with man
in the Godman Jesus Christ.[107] For with Barth the theme of
history is the history of this covenant of grace.[108] That
history, and therefore *Heilsgeschichte*, is for him *the* history,
that is, the true history in and by which all other history is
determined.[109] The latter cannot have 'any independent
theme in relation to this history', that is, to the *Heilsgeschichte*, 'let alone be a general and true history in the context of which the *Heilsgeschichte* can only be one among
others'.[110] This specific theological concept of history as
Heilsgeschichte and thus as the history of the people of God,
to which all other history, so to speak, is but a temporary
appendage, is also clearly expressed in Barth's teaching on
'The Holy Spirit and the Sending of the Christian Community' (CD, IV, 3, par. 72), where he argues that what happens in the world can be viewed and understood only as the
'environment' of the people of God and of the latter's
history.[111]

In the last analysis this theocentric concept of history has
its root, primarily, in Barth's doctrine of God's election of
grace, more specifically in his teaching on God's eternal decree before the creation of the world as the beginning of the
history of God's covenant of grace with man in Jesus Christ
and, secondarily, in his view on the relationship between
revelation and time and between revelation and history. In
respect of these latter aspects of his teaching it must suffice
here to point out[112] that he works with a concept of time that
is derived from and determined by God's revelation in the
event of the presence of Jesus Christ, distinguishing between
the time of Jesus Christ, that is, the time of the years A.D.
1–30, when revelation entered created time and became

history, as true time, fulfilled time, and the time of man, fallen man, as lost time. Just as here God's revelation in Jesus Christ determines the meaning of time, so, and in an inseparable connection therewith, the same revelation determines the meaning of history, making clear that in contrast to all other history the history of the people of God is *the* history, that is, true history in the aforesaid sense. To quote O. Weber's pointed summing up of Barth's position in this matter: 'Revelation is never a predicate of history; on the contrary, history is a predicate of revelation.'[113]

Barth's theocentric concept of history as *Heilsgeschichte* however must not hide from us the fact that the particular events of the *Heilsgeschichte* are nevertheless also historical events in the sense that they take place not only in the midst of the history of mankind but, since *Heilsgeschichte* is history, in and through human beings and events. The whole relationship between God and man is viewed by Barth in this sense as a historical one.[114] Historicism as a characteristic feature of his theology therefore expresses the fact that the particular events which form the subject-matter of his theology have the character of history in this twofold sense; this fact in its turn also helps to explain the feature of peculiarity and concreteness which, as we saw, is characteristic of Barth's theology. Barth's striving for historicity (in the aforesaid twofold sense) can clearly be seen in his persistent endeavour in his doctrine of reconciliation to throw into sharp relief the 'historicity' of the prophetic work of the risen Lord Jesus Christ.[115]

3. *Actualism*. It is hardly possible to exaggerate the importance of this feature which not only dominates every part of Barth's theology and exercises a decisive influence on the subject-matters dealt with therein, but in the last analysis arises out of those leading ideas of his which act as the motive-force of his mode of thought. On the other hand, this feature can easily be misunderstood if it is studied in isolation, that is to say, unless it is viewed in the context of the whole of his teaching. Actualism, as here understood, means that the

essential elements of the Christian Faith such as, for instance, the Word of God, the divine revelation, man's faith, love and hope, the Church and the Christian life are represented as existing only *in actu* and, therefore, as being real and genuine only *in actu*. They exist and are real and genuine only if and when and as long as they owe their existence to an act of God. In other words, they can come into existence, and they can continue to exist and operate, only on the basis of an action of God, an action moreover that has been taken by God in the freedom of His sovereign grace. They must ever again happen in order to be, and thus must ever again possess the character of an event (*actus*).

To put Barth's actualism as pointedly as possible: his theology, generally speaking, does not know of any '*es gibt*' ('there is') nor of any 'having' or 'possessing' that is independent of God's giving, but only a constant 'giving' and 'receiving'. God continually gives and man continually receives. In a word, we are presented in this teaching with a dynamic rather than with a static aspect of the essential elements of the Christian Faith. This kind of actualism has been criticised by H. R. Mackintosh[116] as being 'excessive', neglecting the other aspect of truth that according to the New Testament witness the Christian believers 'are in a certain state or condition'. But before we deal with this criticism, it may be helpful to illustrate first how Barth's actualistic mode of thought operates in his teaching and, further, to consider the leading ideas which motivated it.

The Word of God, Barth teaches, is not a *datum*, something which is given once for all, so that man can take hold of it and possess and control it. Though it is written in Holy Scripture and proclaimed by the Church, it remains the word of man unless God makes it ever again His own Word by His own action. It must ever again become the Word of God in order to be the Word of God. In other words, it becomes God's Word for us whenever it becomes revelation for us through the work of the Holy Spirit in us, and it does so only 'when and where God pleases'.[117] Thus the Word of God is

Animistic

always an act of God, that is, an event, and that act takes place in the freedom of His grace. The Bible and the proclamation of the Church are therefore the Word of God only if and when they *become* the Word of God through God's own action and according to His free and gracious will.[118] 'The Bible is God's Word so far as God lets it be His Word, so far as God speaks through it. By this second equation as little as by our first' (Church proclamation is God's Word) 'can we abstract from God's free act in which and through which here and now He lets it be true in us and for us that man's word in the Bible is His own Word.'[119]

Again, the Christian revelation is treated by Barth as a revelation that continually needs to happen afresh in relation to individual human beings in order to be revelation to them. To use his own words, 'revelation remains revelation and does not become a revealed state'[120] which man can take hold of and manipulate as he thinks fit. Revelation always is and remains an expression of the freedom of God's grace, that is, an event 'in which God, being free, allows this free grace scope to operate'[121] and by which man comes to see and understand and possess knowledge[122] through the direction of Jesus Christ as the exalted Son of Man (CD, IV, 2, par. 64 (4)) and as the Light of life (CD, IV, 3, par. 69 (2)) and in the power of the Holy Spirit working in man. In a telling dictum Barth says: 'the association of the words "there is revelation" is as impossible as the other "there is faith"'.[123]

Again, the being (*Sein*) of the Church, which according to Barth's doctrine of the Church is identical with the being (*Sein*) of Jesus Christ, is characterized by him as *actus purus*, as an activity that is both divine and free.[124] The Church is the true Church of Jesus Christ only if and when and as long as Jesus Christ, the risen Lord, as the Head of His Church is present in the Church in the power of the Holy Spirit, working in and through the members of His Church which is His body. Thus the Church must ever again become the true Church of Jesus Christ in order to be that Church, and this can come to pass only in and through the action of the Holy

Spirit—as the work of the free grace of God in Jesus Christ—which is 'the basis and secret of the existence of the Christian community'.[125] Hence the relationship of the being of Jesus Christ to the being of His Church is wholly dynamic. In virtue of the gracious action of the Holy Spirit it becomes true, and is continually true afresh, 'that the Head does not live without His body nor the body without its Head'.[126] The far-reaching significance of Barth's actualistic concept of man's faith will be discussed in Ch. III, 7, but it may already here be pointed out that the Christian message is conceived by Barth in a wholly actualistic manner: 'the Christian message is such that besides its source and substance, Jesus Christ Himself—in Him it is eternally "actual"—it can and it will become living, practical and effective and therefore "actual" only through its own strength, that is, through the Holy Ghost, only in faith, love and hope'.[127]

In the light of Barth's other teaching this actualism of his does not signify a purely one-sided action on the part of God, depriving man of his freedom and humanity and turning any action of his in relation to God into a purely mechanical event. For in each and every part of his theology Barth makes clear that man is created by God to play an active part in the intercourse between God and man, not only permitting man's free and responsible decision and action but calling for it and even demanding it. The examination of man's role in his relationship with God as viewed by Barth will have to wait for the discussion of his doctrine of man.[128] In order to put his actualistic tendency in its proper perspective, it needs however to be stated by way of anticipation that, while Barth rejects any kind of synergism, he assigns to man a role as God's partner in God's covenant of grace with man according to which man is called to acknowledge and accept by his own free and responsible decision what God has done for him and is continually doing for him and to him in Jesus Christ, and further, to respond to this action of God by free and responsible actions on his part which correspond to God's action and spring from man's obedience to God's holy will

D

and from his gratitude for God's free and gracious gift in Jesus Christ.

Again, Barth's actualism does not mean—in spite of a sometimes unqualified language which may seem to justify the opposite view—that his theology leaves no room for the idea of a 'state' of things. It only denotes that there can be no 'state' which does not arise out of God's constant giving. H. R. Mackintosh overlooks this qualification in his afore-mentioned criticism; moreover, in the light of this qualification his own view does not appear to be very different from that of Barth since he admits that the certain state or con-dition in which the Christian believers are said to be accord-ing to the New Testament witness 'is not self-produced or self-propagated', adding 'God, and God only, sustains them in it'.[129] Further, as far as the work of creation is concerned, Barth, in his doctrine of providence (CD, III, 3), has given up his former notion of a *creatio continua* and now holds that the divine providence takes care of and confirms the work of creation which is said by him to be already accomplished once for all.[130]

The root-cause of Barth's actualism is to be found in his relentless endeavour to safeguard a twofold truth which he continually posits and expounds in his theology, namely the truth of the freedom of God as the sovereign Lord and of His grace in His aseity and in all His works, in revelation as well as in election, creation, reconciliation and redemption, and, therefore, in His whole relationship with man[131] and the further truth of man's constant need of God's initiative and continual action in man's relationship with God and with his fellow-men in face of man's incapability of knowing God, the world and himself and of acting in accordance with that knowledge on the strength of his own faculties. In view of this twofold truth Barth denies that man can either noetically or ontically take hold of God and His works, making them the object of his own independent contemplation and interpreta-tion and possessing, controlling and manipulating them ac-cording to his own intentions and desires. God would no longer be God, revelation would no longer be revelation, and grace would no longer be grace if man were able to do this, and it is precisely because God is God and because man (according to this teaching) does not possess this ability that Barth jealously watches over the independence of God and of His revelation in Jesus Christ from the world and from man and over the freedom of God's grace. It is for the same reasons that he fights a constant battle against all natural theology and against the *analogia entis* in particular.[132]

Does, then, actualism as taught by Barth entail that there is 'act', but not 'being'? In his criticism of Barth's teaching on this point Bonhoeffer claims this to be Barth's position.[133] However, that claim has already been indirectly refuted by the qualification that the idea of a 'state' is excluded only in so far as there can be no state apart from God's constant giving. Act and being are linked up in Barth's theology in such a way that there is no 'being' apart from God's continual action, and this action takes place in the freedom of the divine grace. Man can and does act freely and responsibly and he can and does 'have' and 'possess' provided that his acting, having and possessing is brought about *and* sustained by God's free and gracious action. 'Man "is" and "has" as the living God "is" as such his life-partner and "has" him.'[134]

REFERENCES

[1] *Types of Modern Theology* (1937), p. 181.

[2] Dietrich Bonhoeffer, *Gesammelte Schriften*, edited by E. Bethge, vol. 3 (1960), pp. 110 ff.

[3] The bibliography, compiled by Charlotte von Kirschbaum and published on the occasion of Karl Barth's 70th birthday (10th May, 1956) in the Festschrift *Antwort*, already contains 406 titles of his books, essays, sermons, articles, etc., up to 1955.

[4] *The Word of God and the Task of the Ministry* (1922), published in *The Word of God and the Word of Man*, ET (1928), of *Das Wort Gottes und die Theologie* (1924), pp. 183 ff., 186, 198 f.

[5] Op. cit., pp. 97 ff., 100.

[6] Barth studied theology in Berne, Berlin, Tübingen and Marburg.

[7] See further, E. Caldwell Moore, *An Outline of the History of Christian Thought since Kant* (1912); H. R. Mackintosh, op. cit.; Karl Barth, *From Rousseau to Ritschl*, being the translation (1959) of eleven chapters of *Die Protestantische Theologie im 19. Jahrhundert* (1947).

[8] Karl Barth, op. cit., p. 54.

[9] Op. cit., pp. 14 f.

[10] Op. cit., p. 14.

[11] H. R. Mackintosh, op. cit., p. 64.

[12] Karl Barth, op. cit., pp. 306 f., espec. 334, 344, 353; H. R. Mackintosh, op. cit., pp. 31 ff.

[13] Karl Barth, op. cit., pp. 316, 323.

[14] See further, H. R. Mackintosh, op. cit., pp. 101 ff.; Karl Barth, op. cit., pp. 268 ff.

[15] Op. cit., p. 303.

[16] See further, H. R. Mackintosh, op. cit., pp. 138 ff.; Karl Barth, op. cit., pp. 390 ff.

[17] Op. cit., p. 157.

[18] Karl Barth, op. cit., pp. 393 f.

[19] E. Caldwell Moore, op. cit., pp. 140 ff.

[20] The Essence of Christianity, ET under the title, What is Christianity?

[21] J. K. Mozley, Some Tendencies in British Theology (1951), p. 29.

[22] H. R. Mackintosh, op. cit., pp. 181 ff.

[23] H. R. Mackintosh, op. cit., p. 202.

[24] H. R. Mackintosh, op. cit., pp. 211 f.

[25] Karl Barth, Evangelical Theology in the Nineteenth Century (1957), ET 1959, in SJT, Occasional Papers No. 8, pp. 57 f.; see also CD, IV, 1, p. 387.

[26] The Idea of the Holy (1917), ET 1931 by J. W. Harvey.

[27] Karl Barth, The Humanity of God (1956), ET (1959) in SJT, Occasional Papers No. 8, p. 32.

[28] Karl Barth, op. cit., pp. 33, 34.

[29] Evangelical Theology in the 19th Century, loc. cit., p. 58. See also Barth's brief theological autobiography in CD, II, 1, pp. 634 ff.

[30] Karl Barth, On Systematic Theology, SJT, vol. 14, No. 3 (1961), pp. 225 ff.; Prof. T. F. Torrance, Introduction (1962) to Karl Barth, Theology and Church, Shorter Writings 1920–28, ET (1962), pp. 10 ff.; the same, Karl Barth, An Introduction to His Early Theology, 1910–1931 (1962).

[31] The Humanity of God, loc. cit., p. 34.

[32] Bultmann, p. 127.

[33] Both these essays were written in 1934; ET under the title Natural Theology (1946), p. 71.

[34] The Word of God and the Word of Man, passim.

[35] ET of the sixth edition, 1933.

[36] Preface to the first edition, see op. cit. (note 35), p. 2.

[37] Op. cit., p. 2, 10.

[38] Loc. cit., pp. 31 f., 40 ff.

[39] Op. cit., p. 31.

[40] Georges Casalis, Karl Barth. Person und Werk (1960), p. 56.

[41] Romans, loc. cit., pp. 38, 40 ff., 327 and passim.

[42] The Humanity of God, loc. cit., p. 35.

[43] Karl Barth, Credo, ET (1936), p. 185.

[44] A study of these differences, for which there is no space here, would be a fascinating subject.

[45] This untranslatable German technical term is rendered 'history of salvation' in the authorized ET of Church Dogmatics; it embraces, however, God's entire gracious dealing with man from eternity to eternity, whereas the phrase 'history of salvation' has a much more restricted meaning.

[46] See Romans, loc. cit., pp. 36, 57, 69, 91 ff., 225 and passim.

[47] H. R. Mackintosh, op. cit., pp. 266 f.; T. F. Torrance, Introduction to Theology and Church, p. 22; the same, Karl Barth, An Introduction to His Early Theology, pp. 48 ff.

[48] 'Between the Times', that is, the interval between the time of the resurrection of Jesus Christ and the time of His final revelation.

[49] Published partly in the *Word of God and the Word of Man* (see above, note 4) and partly in *Theology and Church* (see above, note 30).

[50] ET 1962.

[51] Ibid., pp. 12, 100, 105; as to Barth's concept of religion see below, Ch. II, 8.

[52] Preface to *Die Christliche Dogmatik im Entwurf*, p. vii.

[53] CD, vol. I, part I, ET by Prof. G. T. Thomson (1936), pp. vii, ix.

[54] ET 1960 under the title *Anselm: Fides quaerens intellectum*.

[55] J. W. Leitch, SJT, vol. 14, no. 3 (1961), p. 298.

[56] *Anselm*, p. 11.

[57] Op. cit., pp. 16 ff., 21, 28, 39, 151, 171.

[58] Op. cit., p. 15.

[59] Apart from vol. I, part 1 (see note 53), the existent volumes of the *Church Dogmatics* have been translated by a group of scholars under the joint editorship of Dr. G. W. Bromiley and Prof. T. F. Torrance (see Short Bibliography, p. 192).

[60] G. Casalis, op. cit., p. 25.

[61] *Karl Barth, Darstellung und Deutung seiner Theologie*, second edition (1952), p. 36, quoted in H. Gollwitzer, *Karl Barth's Church Dogmatics, a Selection with Introduction* (1957), ET 1961, pp. 1 f.

[62] H. Gollwitzer, op. cit., p. 5.

[63] Comp., e.g., the exegetical discourses on Rom. chs. 9–11 in CD II, 2, pp. 202 ff., 213 ff., 240 ff., 267 ff. (80 pages) and those on Gen. chs. 1 and 2 in CD, III, 1, covering the greater part of that volume.

[64] It is at this point that many of Barth's critics fail.

[65] H. Gollwitzer, op. cit., pp. 19 f.

[66] *The Teaching of Karl Barth on the Doctrine of the Imago Dei*, The Presbyther, vol. 5, No. 4 (1947), p. 13.

[67] Op. cit., p. 314.

[68] H. Gollwitzer, op. cit., p. 11.

[69] Editors' Preface to CD, 1, 2, pp. vii f., rendering an admirable account of Barth's method of exposition.

[70] CD, I, 1, pp. 26 ff.

[71] As to the meaning of the term, 'the Nihil', see Ch. III, 3.

[72] O. Weber, *Karl Barth's Church Dogmatics* (1950), ET 1953, p. 195.

[73] G. Gloege, *Theologische Literaturzeitung*, 1960, No. 3, p. 163.

[74] Dietrich Bonhoeffer, op. cit., p. 120.

[75] *Systematic Theology*, vol. I (1953), Preface p. ix f. and pp. 8, 11 ff.

[76] CD, I, 2, pp. 861 ff.; TT, pp. 23 f.

[77] CD, I, 2, p. 862.

[78] *Systematic Theology*, vol. I, pp. 8, 67 ff.

[79] CD, I, 2, pp. 856 f.

[80] Ch. II, 2.

[81] *Anselm*, pp. 35 ff., espec. 39; *Gifford*, pp. 243 ff.; CD, I, 1, p. 25; I, 2, pp. 776, 840, 843; TT, p. 95.

[82] *The Word of God and the Word of Man*, p. 99; CD, II, 1, p. 209; Gollwitzer, op. cit., p. 4.

[83] *The Idea of the Holy, passim*.

[84] See above, note 45.

[85] CD, II, 1, pp. 599 ff.

[86] CD, II, 1, p. 602.

[87] CD, IV, 1, p. 177.

[88] CD, III, 1, p. 60.

[89] *The Courage to Be* (1952), pp. 182 ff.; *Systematic Theology*, vol. II (1957), pp. 13 ff.; see also Daniel Jenkins, *Beyond Religion* (1962), pp. 10 ff., 50 ff.

[90] See below, Chs. II, 7, III, 2, 6.

[91] *Jesus Christ and Mythology* (1960), pp. 68 f.

[92] Comp., e.g,. CD, II, 1, pp. 63 ff.

[93] CD, I, 2, p. 5.

[94] *Gifford*, p. 103.

[95] Ibid., p. 104; see also CD, II, 1, p. 26.

[96] See below, Ch. III, 6.

[97] Above, par. 4.

[98] Comp., e.g., *The Christian Understanding of Revelation* (1948) in Karl Barth's *Against the Stream*, pp. 207 f., 235 ff.; CD, I, 2, pp. 1 ff.; IV, 1, pp. 514 ff.; IV, 2, pp. 264 ff.; IV, 3, pp. 6 ff., 572 ff.

[99] *Bultmann*, pp. 95 ff., 100 ff., 109 ff.; also CD, III, 2, pp. 443 ff., 451 ff.

[100] See below, Ch. III, 6.

[101] P. Tillich, *Systematic Theology*, vol. I, pp. 4 ff.; as to Dietrich Bonhoeffer's criticism of what he terms Barth's *Offenbarungspositivismus* (the positivistic character of his teaching on revelation), see below, Ch. II, 7.

[102] E. Brunner, *Dogmatics*, vol. I, pp. 349 f.

[103] CD, IV, 3, p. 498.

[104] *Subject and Object in Modern Theology* (1955), pp. 140 ff., espec. 141.

[105] Below, Ch. III, 5.

[106] CD, III, 1, pp. 66 ff.

[107] Below, Ch. III, 2.

[108] Below, Ch. III, 3.

[109] CD, III, 1, pp. 59 ff.

[110] Ibid., p. 60.

[111] CD, IV, 3, p. 685.

[112] See further, CD, I, 2, pp. 45 ff.

[113] O. Weber, op. cit., p. 58.

[114] CD, III, 1, p. 66.

[115] Below, Ch. III, 6.

[116] Op. cit., pp. 314 ff.; see also Gwilym O. Griffith, *Interpreters of Man* (1943), pp. 212, 219.

[117] CD, I, 1, p. 79.

[118] CD, I, 1, pp. 99 ff., 122 ff.

[119] CD, I, 1, p. 123.

[120] CD, I, 2, p. 118.

[121] CD, I, 1, p. 132.

[122] CD, IV, 2, p. 313; see also Gollwitzer, op. cit., p. 9.

[123] CD, I, 1, p. 44.

[124] Ibid., pp. 3, 44.

[125] CD, IV, 2, pp. 614 ff.; IV, 3, pp. 756 ff., espec. 760; see also *Gifford*, pp. 160, 169 ff.

[126] CD, IV, 3, p. 762.

[127] *Against the Stream*, p. 190.

[128] Ch. III, 5.

[129] Op. cit., p. 316; this also answers Bonhoeffer's criticism of Barth's actualism, see E. Bethge, *The Challenge of Dietrich Bonhoeffer's Life and Theology*, Alden-Tuthill Lectures 1961, The Chicago Theological Seminary Register, vol. LI, No. 2, pp. 8 f.

[130] Comp. CD, III, 3, pp. 6, 68 ff. with CD, I, 2, pp. 688 f.; III, 1, p. 60.

[131] Bonhoeffer, *Akt und Sein* (1931), ET *Act and Being* (1962) by B. Noble, p. 11, makes the same point.

[132] See below, Ch. II, 3.

[133] Op. cit., pp. 80 ff.; see also E. Bethge, op. cit., pp. 9 f.

[134] CD, III, 4, p. 663.

II.—THE WORD OF GOD AS THE SOURCE
AND CRITERION OF THEOLOGY

1. The Church as the Sphere of Theology

THEOLOGY and Church are closely bound up with each other in Barth's teaching. For to him theology is not merely what it literally means, the science namely of God but, as Christian theology, it is 'theanthropology', the science of God as the God of man and of man as the man of God.[1] The Church, on the other hand, as the living community of the living Lord Jesus Christ, is the being of Jesus Christ or, more particularly, the earthly-historical form of existence of Jesus Christ Himself, His body, created by Him and continually renewed by the power of the Holy Spirit, the Spirit of the risen Lord Jesus Christ Himself.[2] 'Because He is and in that He is, the Church is'[3] or, more concretely, because He is the risen Lord and in that as such He lives and reigns in His Church which is His body and of which He is the Head, the Church exists. According to Barth's actualistic concept of the Church[4] the latter is primarily not an institution rooted in this world but an event, a continually fresh encounter, in the power of the Holy Spirit, between God and man in Jesus Christ as the Word of God proclaimed by His Church and received, believed and obeyed by the members of His Church.[5] It is this preaching and hearing by the Church of Jesus Christ as the Word of God in and through the power of the Holy Spirit whereby the Church continually becomes afresh the true Church of Jesus Christ. Thus theology and Church have this in common that both of them are concerned with the mutual relationship, intercourse and communion between God and man in Jesus Christ. However, whereas it is the foremost task

41

of the Church to proclaim the Word of God and therefore
Jesus Christ as God's Word to man, the Church has the further
task of making sure, as far as is humanly possible, that the
Word of God it proclaims and hears is truly the Word of God,
and it is theology which renders this service.

The Church examines, criticizes and revises its language
about God, the universe and man by the theological propositions which theology works out on the basis of the revelation of God in Jesus Christ. In this way theology, as dogmatics, serves the proclamation of the Christian Gospel by
the Church. Again, theology thereby proves itself, firstly, to
be possible only within the Church and, secondly, to be a
function of the Church, expounding and interpreting the
Word of God which is to be proclaimed by the Church and in
the Church on the basis of faith and in obedience to the Word
of God as attested in Holy Scripture. This is why Barth
gives to his dogmatics the title *Church Dogmatics*. There
would be no theology if there should not exist a Church ob-
liged to witness to the Word of God. On the other hand, 'in
theology the Church gives a critical account, both to itself
and to the world, of the appropriateness or otherwise of its
praise of God, its preaching, its instruction, its evangelistic
and missionary work'.[6]

2. *Fides quaerens intellectum*

'Any sound theology must have an epistemological foundation.'[7] When Barth, in his *Church Dogmatics*, abandoned
his previous attempt to use the existential–philosophical approach to theology as a partial epistemological basis of *Die
Christliche Dogmatik im Entwurf*[8] and instead made the
Word of God the sole source and basis of his theology, he did
so because he had come to realize that the knowledge of the
absolute truth about God, the universe and man can be obtained only from God Himself. For God, who is the Truth
and the source of every other truth, has Himself revealed that
truth to man in the Word He has spoken to man in His Son
Jesus Christ, and as the living God He continues to do so

through the prophetic office of the risen Lord Jesus Christ. In that revelation God has given Himself, and continually gives Himself, as the object of man's knowledge, and it is He who also illumines man's mind through the work of the Holy Spirit in man so that man may know God, the world and himself.[9]

Since God Himself has spoken, and continues to speak, in Jesus Christ and through the Holy Spirit, it would be presumptuous on man's part to speak his own word as regards the things that pertain to God, that is, to speculate about them. Man can only listen to God's Word as the one and only truth from which all other truth is to be derived. Barth holds that the vicarious sacrificial death of Jesus Christ on the Cross has revealed to man, when seen in the light of His resurrection, that man is incapable of knowing by means of his innate capacities and endowments God, the world and man as they *really* are, that, on the contrary, God Himself had to come into this world in the person of the Godman Jesus Christ and had to live and die as a man for the sake of His fellow-men to enable man (among other things) to acquire that knowledge. G. Wingren, in his criticism of the Word of God as the sole basis of Barth's theology,[10] fails to realize that the latter's path to knowledge in theology is not determined by any preconceived negative concept of man, in particular a presupposed incapacity of man to know God and His will apart from Scripture, but by his theological interpretation, based on the exegesis of the Bible itself, of what, in the light of the resurrection, has taken place at the crucifixion of Jesus Christ. It is precisely as a result of this theological-biblical interpretation that Barth refuses to obtain the Christian truth from anywhere else than from the Christian truth itself as it is revealed by God in Jesus Christ and attested in Holy Scripture. Consequently, anything which has its origin in man, for instance in his structure as a human being (anthropology), in his thinking (philosophy), in his experience (man's religion and culture), is excluded as a source and basis of Barth's theology.

Since man, in order to know the truth about God, the world and man, needs to be illumined by the Holy Spirit, he requires faith in order to know or, to express the same thought differently, he can obtain the knowledge of that truth only by believing in it, that is, only by faith. Consequently, faith is the presupposition of that knowledge and this entails that the knowledge in question is always faith-knowledge, that is, knowledge that springs from faith in the revelation of God in Jesus Christ.[11] Faith, therefore, constitutes the starting-point of all theological thinking; the latter can be and is only a repetition and exposition of the contents of that faith. Thus man's faith and his knowledge are not antitheses, as Kant thought,[12] but, on the contrary, the very nature of faith requires knowledge: 'just because we possess the certainty of faith, we must hunger after the *fidei ratio*'.[13] In Barth's theology, as in that of Anselm of Canterbury, faith (*credere*) precedes knowledge (*intelligere*) and, on the other hand, knowledge, of necessity, follows faith (*fides quaerens intellectum*). This is the epistemological principle underlying his theology, the special path to knowledge trodden in his *Church Dogmatics*. That knowledge, as faith-knowledge, is a special kind of knowledge. It differs from everything else which man calls knowledge not only in its content, its mode of origin and form but, above all, by the fact that it is unconditionally bound to its object, to the truth of the revelation of God in Jesus Christ.[14] It is the history in which man by his encounter with the living Lord Jesus Christ in the power of the Holy Spirit becomes aware of another history that is binding upon him, the history namely of the Godman Jesus Christ.[15]

Again, this faith-knowledge is not only bound to the truth of the revelation of God in Jesus Christ, but that truth, as the truth of faith, cannot be argued. In that God, who is the Truth, Himself reveals that truth to men in His Word, that is, in Jesus Christ and by the power of the Holy Spirit, that truth cannot be questioned as to whether it is true and why it is what it is.[16] Thus, for instance, it cannot be argued whether God *is* and why He is what He is. Barth's statement as to the meaning of Anselm's 'proofs'[17] applies, generally speaking, also to his own epistemological position: 'the *ratio veritatis* inherent in the Articles of the Christian *Credo* is itself at no point the subject of discussion but on the contrary it forms the self-evident basis of discussion'. Consequently, he always starts from the revelation of God in Jesus Christ as his God-given basis without arguing the truth of that revelation. Confining himself to the recounting and expounding of that revelation, he asserts the inner consistency of the *intellectus fidei* and maintains that the intellectual exploration of the contents of the Christian Faith is self-convincing and self-proving.[18]

In his view there is therefore no need for a special apologetics.[19] Whereas E. Brunner[20] holds that the ideologies of the present day which are opposed to the Christian message demand an intellectual discussion of the Christian Faith in the light of these ideologies and thus necessitate an apologetic (defensive) or rather eristic (offensive) theology, and whereas P. Tillich's[21] systematic theology is entirely written from an apologetic standpoint, answering the questions implied in the temporal 'situation' in the light of the Christian Gospel, Barth claims that 'the Gospel is generally intelligible and explicable as surely as its content is rational'.[22] 'Even in respect of the most obstinate unbeliever,' he says, 'it can be accomplished that the inner consistency and to that extent the meaning of the Gospel-message is intelligible to him.'[23] He insists therefore that 'a proper dogmatics is at all times the best apologetics and basically the only possible dogmatics'.[24] Hence you will not find in his theology any of the many arguments for the existence of God in which mediaeval and modern theologians alike indulge. God has proved Himself by speaking to man in His Son Jesus Christ, and thus there is no need for these arguments which in Barth's view in any case can never reach the reality of God. Since the unbeliever is lacking the very presupposition of the true knowledge of God, that is, faith, one may wonder whether apologetics is really so superfluous as Barth thinks it is. However, at the bottom of his negative attitude to apologetics there seems to be the conviction that where God's own revelation of His truth fails to convert the unbeliever, there man's apologetics cannot succeed either. For 'everyone comes to have faith, can have faith and has faith who does not try to evade the action of God in His revelation in Jesus Christ'.[25]

Since in Barth's doctrine of the Word of God faith and reason are related to each other in such a way that by virtue of man's faith his reason is unconditionally bound to its object, this entails that this unique object, the revelation of God in Jesus Christ, determines both the content of man's thought (knowledge) and the specific mode of the operation of his reason (the path to knowledge). For man's faith, in one sense, is his reason focused on the knowledge of God and His truth; man's reason, therefore, is determined, both as regards the content of its knowledge and the mode of its operation, by the object of his faith. Thus faith is a rational event. Though its cognitive element, according to Barth's teaching, by no means exhausts the meaning of faith, it yet constitutes an integral part of faith.

In his *Church Dogmatics* as well as in other writings[26] Barth repeatedly emphasizes that no *sacrificium intellectus* is required from him who believes. Man's faith is indeed said by Barth to be the work of the Holy Spirit in man, God's free and gracious gift to man in Jesus Christ, yet he firmly states that it is man and not, as Bonhoeffer[27] erroneously assumes to be Barth's teaching on this matter, 'a heavenly *alter ego*' (the Holy Spirit taking man's place in the act of believing) who thinks, wills and makes a decision in that he believes. Faith, as a human activity, is man's active decision for the object of his faith, his acceptance of that object and his active participation in it.[28] Again, the intellectual investigation of the contents of the Christian revelation and, therefore, dogmatics is a rational enterprise, not only because man's faith enquiring into its object is itself a rational activity but, first and foremost, because the object of man's faith, the revelation of God in Jesus Christ, is a rational event. For in

His revelation God imparts to man His Word and that Word, as the Logos and thus as the Truth of God, is the source and fountain of all rationality. Hence, as T. F. Torrance, in his interpretation of Barth's teaching on revelation, rightly points out,[29] 'in revelation theology is concerned with a depth in objective rationality that transcends that of any other kind of knowledge and of every other kind of science'. Faith-knowledge, based on revelation, is intrinsically rational as it flows from the Word of God the very nature of which is rational.

Thus Barth's theology, and in particular his *Church Dogmatics*, is a sustained scientific and critical examination and exposition of the object of faith which constitutes its God-given and therefore indisputable point of departure as well as its basis. He is, however, careful to point out that, though theology, as dogmatics, is a 'science', it must remain true to its own peculiar task and, consequently, cannot be measured by the standards valid for other sciences nor has anything to learn in their school as regards its own method.[30] Discussing the role of (in this sense only) systematic theology, he says:[31] it 'cannot wish to prove the truth of the Word of God either directly or indirectly. The victory and triumph of this truth *intra et extra muros ecclesiae* cannot be its work. Since it actually relies upon this truth, it can only attest it in its own particular manner. It can only trust that the truth will prove itself. This trust is its ('apologetic') strength in relation to the whole cumulation of Christian and non-Christian thought-forms, ideologies, myths, world-views and religions. . . . In this trust it endeavours, wherever possible, to do both pure and thorough intellectual work, faithful in the midst of the other sciences to its own law.'

Finally, faith-knowledge is indirect knowledge in that it is mediated by the Word of God and, consequently, in a certain sense is limited knowledge because the human element enters both the communication (in Jesus Christ) and the transmission (through Holy Scripture and the proclamation of the Church) of that Word. The discussion of these aspects of faith-knowledge as well as the exposition of faith-knowledge as God's gift, obtainable only by His free grace, must however wait until we come to consider both the nature of the Word of God and the mystery of revelation (below, par. 6, 7).

3. Natural Theology

By 'natural theology' Barth understands that form of teaching which declares that man in himself and as such, and therefore by nature and not by grace, possesses the capacity and power to inform himself about God, the world, and man. Being 'an avowed opponent of all natural theology,'[32] Barth wages throughout his theological work a relentless war on it, prominently in his noted controversy with E. Brunner on 'nature and grace',[33] fundamentally, though briefly, in his Gifford Lectures,[34] and in detail and penetratingly in his *Church Dogmatics*.[35] For it is his firm conviction that natural theology owes its existence to a radical error on the part of man.

He categorically denies that man can know God, the world and man *as they really are* apart from God's particular and concrete revelation in Jesus Christ, no matter whether man assumes that he can achieve this knowledge by means of his innate capacities and endowments or whether he thinks that he can gain it on the ground of a general revelation in creation or history. The opposite view of natural theology, Barth holds, is an illusion. From his own standpoint natural theology, as far as it is actually practised, exists in direct opposition to a theology based on the Word of God, leading to a 'knowledge' of God, the world and man which is different from what, according to God's own revelation in Jesus Christ, they really are, and thus to error and falsehood. It cannot, therefore, be a preparation for or, as in Roman Catholicism, a substructure of a theology based on revelation; in a word, it can in no wise be a legitimate part of theology. E. Brunner[36] now admits that natural theology is not a reliable basis for Christian theology, but, on his assumption of a general revelation in creation, holds that 'it is still a very important

part of Christian theology, especially in the doctrine of man'.[37]
It is however this very assumption of his which, as we shall
see, Barth regards as unfounded. On the other hand, P.
Tillich's view[38] that Barth's uncompromising rejection of any
kind of natural theology 'in the last analysis is a self-deception as the use of human language in speaking of revelation
shows' ignores the fact that from Barth's standpoint that
human language is itself the result of God's revelation in
Jesus Christ. Man could not speak of revelation as he does
unless it first happened to him.

What is behind Barth's statement that 'every' natural theology is 'incontrovertibly impossible'?[39] Though we cannot
describe all the ramifications of his closely argued case against
natural theology in general and against the doctrine of the
analogia entis as the inner core of natural theology in particular, three basic thoughts of his may briefly be outlined to
indicate the general trend of his reasoning.

Firstly, it is only by the self-revelation of God in Jesus
Christ and through the power of the Holy Spirit and, therefore, only by an act of God's free grace and by faith that man
can know God as He Himself has actually shown Himself to
be according to the witness of Holy Scripture. That God, for
instance, is the Triune God in His three modes of being as
Father, Son, and Holy Spirit, and that He is really (and not
merely on the basis of human speculation, in particular on the
basis of an analogy) the Lord over all things and in His one
undivided Being at once the Creator as well as the Reconciler
and Redeemer, again, that He is absolutely unique, not only
in His aseity, divinity, sovereignty and freedom but also in
His incomparable love, which led Him to be not only the God
who is 'for us' but also the God who in Jesus Christ is 'with
us' and in Him assumed our human nature—all this man could
not possibly know apart from that revelation. Claiming that
the 'uniqueness' of God can be known only by His revelation,
Barth says: 'In the face of the Cross of Christ it is monstrous
to describe the uniqueness of God as an object of natural
theology. In the face of the Cross of Christ we are bound to

say that knowledge of the one and only God is gained only
by the begetting of men anew by the Holy Spirit.'[40] Again,
Barth holds that the *analogia entis*, starting from the presupposition of a 'being' common to man and God, assumes
that the being of God is similar to the being of man and that,
consequently, man, at least in general, can gain a knowledge
of God apart from His revelation.[41] It is one of Barth's main
objections to it that it splits up the thought of God, that is,
His unity, separating His being from His acting, that is, from
His real work and action in Jesus Christ and contemplating
not only God the Creator apart from God the Reconciler and
from God the Redeemer but a (neutral) being of God in general and *in abstracto*. For we know God exclusively as the
One who acts upon us as the Triune God.[42] He *is* who He is
in His *acting*. His acting expresses His being, and His being
is revealed in His acting. Since He is the Living God, it is not
possible to abstract His real work and action in favour of a
being of God in general. Holy Scripture does not allow us
'this splitting up of the concept of God', this contemplating
of one aspect of God in separation from His other aspects.[43]

Secondly, the possibility of natural theology is excluded
by the work of reconciliation as an act of divine sovereignty
and of the free grace of God in Jesus Christ. In the preceding
section (par. 2) reference has already been made to the crucial
importance of Barth's theological–biblical interpretation of
Jesus Christ's vicarious sacrificial death upon the Cross and
of His subsequent resurrection for the question of man's
knowledge of God, the world and himself. In his doctrine of
reconciliation his position in this respect, and in particular
with regard to natural theology, is made evident by his
statement that God's gracious work of reconciliation 'is the
place and the only place from which as Christians we can
think forwards and backwards, from which a Christian knowledge of both God and man is possible' and that 'it is here that
all natural theology perishes even before it has drawn its first
breath'.[44] For this work of reconciliation is 'the Word in
which God Himself has set the beginning of knowledge in the

vacuum where there is no beginning for man as estranged
from God and himself'.[45] It reveals that fallen man, because
of his sinfulness, is estranged from God and, consequently, is
no longer open and ready for Him and for that very reason
needs faith and thus grace in order to know God, the world
and man as they really are. For, according to Barth's doctrine of sin,[46] man's sin is man's enmity towards the grace of
God. Sinful man does not want to live by the grace of God
and in everything be dependent on it because in his sinfulness,
and therefore in his enmity towards the grace of God, he is
no longer open and ready for God's grace. Hence he is unable and even refuses to receive his knowledge of God, the
world and himself from that grace, that is to say, through
God's revelation in Jesus Christ and by faith, but makes the
(futile) attempt to acquire that knowledge by his own efforts.
Natural theology, Barth claims,[47] is 'the unavoidable theological expression of the fact that in the reality and possibility of man as such an openness for the grace of God and
therefore a readiness for the knowability of God in His revelation is not at all evident'.

The work of reconciliation demonstrates the impossibility
of natural theology also in another direction. When God
assumed human nature in Jesus Christ, the Son of Man who
is also and primarily the Son of God, 'He ceased to all eternity
to be God only, assuming and having and maintaining to all
eternity human nature as well'.[48] Since then He, the risen
Lord, the Living Christ, is, as Barth puts it rather boldly
'God in the flesh'.[49] Since then God is God in this association
with the human nature of Jesus Christ. To know God in this
form is however impossible for any natural theology.[50]

Thirdly, natural theology is incompatible with the free and
sovereign grace of God in Jesus Christ. In Barth's theology
the Reformation truth of *sola gratia* has found its most comprehensive expression. In later chapters (Chs. III, 2, V.) it
will be shown that with Barth God's grace in Jesus Christ is
the beginning of all the works of God *ad extra*, including even
the creation of the universe and of man, and that man, as

E

God's creature and reconciled with God in Jesus Christ, is represented by him as being in everything dependent on that grace, including his knowledge of God, the world and himself. If, however, the sovereign and free grace of God is thought of as operating alongside nature, however high above it it may be put, it is no longer the grace of God but grace which man himself ascribes to himself.[51] Again, if God's revelation in Jesus Christ and, therefore, His free and gracious action in His revelation is used as a source of knowledge alongside a knowledge of God proper to man as such, it is no longer the free and gracious revelation of God.[52] To grasp the full meaning of these uncompromising propositions, we must remind ourselves [53] that Barth uses the terms 'nature', 'grace' and 'revelation' neither in an abstract or general sense nor as indicating or expressing an objective state of affairs but in the light of his theological exegesis of the Bible and therefore as concepts with a quite specific concrete meaning and a distinctly actualistic quality. 'Nature' and 'grace' in particular denote specific personal activities: whatsoever man does is 'nature', and whatsoever God does is 'grace'. For what Barth is fundamentally concerned with in his theology is God and man in their mutual relationship. Since Barth rejects any kind of synergism, holding that man is incapable of co-operating with God in any way except in the power of the Holy Spirit and thus in faith and therefore by grace, this means that nature cannot operate alongside grace without depriving the sovereign and free grace of God of its true character as grace; this applies also to natural theology as a human activity.

Whenever Barth uses the terms 'nature' and 'grace' in one and the same passage and relates them to each other, he uses them in a strictly antithetical sense, that is to say, in the sense of 'not nature but grace'. This formula, which is a far cry from Thomas Aquinas' famous proposition: *'gratia non tollit naturam sed perficit'*,[54] runs like an unbroken thread through the whole of Barth's theology; it can almost be described both as the hall-mark and the alarm-signal of his

theology and is based on his view that in the mutual relationship between God and man it is God and not man who
takes the initiative and does the work. However, no depre-
ciation of either nature or man is implied in this view since
according to Barth's doctrine of creation both the world and
man are the 'good' creation of God;[55] nor does that view
exclude man's free and responsible action in response to God's
action. Though nature is only the scene and the instrument
of the operation of God's sovereign and free grace, the latter
operates through nature, that is to say, the gracious God
acts in and through the free and responsible acting and working of man; man is no mere channel through which God's
grace operates.[56]

Finally, Barth argues in detail that natural theology is both
under an illusion and, in the light of the theology of the
Word of God, superfluous as far as it maintains man's independent existence as such and on that account tries to
justify the self-explanation of man as such and thereby itself.
This section of his teaching deserves careful study, but cannot
be discussed here. It is summed up in his proposition that
there is only the man for whom Jesus Christ has died and
risen again and whose affairs He has taken in His own
hands, no matter whether man accepts this position of his in
faith or refuses to do so.[57]

4. THEOLOGY AND PHILOSOPHY [58]

In his later theology, especially in his *Church Dogmatics*,
Barth has carried out a clear division between theological and
philosophical thought and has done so with a determination
and consistency as perhaps no other theologian before him.
Having bound his theology exclusively to the Word of God,
to the concrete event of the revelation of God in Jesus Christ,
he not only discarded philosophy as a basis, even if it be only
a partial one, of theology,[59] but in his entire theological work
endeavoured to ensure that his own thinking as a theologian
is constantly determined by the Word of God and not by the
word of man, in other words, that it is constantly governed

and directed by the living reality and truth of God's concrete revelation in Jesus Christ and not by any abstract and general concepts or ideas, especially not by any particular philosophy. In this respect his theology differs decisively from the theological work of Thomas Aquinas and Schleiermacher before him and of Bultmann and Tillich in his own time, who have either bound their theology to a particular philosophy of their age or at least combined it with such a philosophy. In the last analysis Barth's rejection of Bultmann's theology rests upon the argument that the latter has bound his theology to the existentialist philosophy of Martin Heidegger.[60]

Since in Barth's view the concrete message of the Bible as analysed by biblical–exegetical theology is both the real and the epistemological ground of theology, that message as the Word of God, continually given afresh by God in His free and sovereign grace, cannot be anticipated with, nor can it be explained on the basis of, any presupposed general metaphysics, theory of cognition, ontology, anthropology or even philosophy of religion.[61] This basic view of his, however, does not imply a complete ban on philosophy within the realm of theology. He not only acknowledges philosophy's right to exist within its own limits, but, firmly relating it to theology in Jesus Christ as God's Word to man and, therefore, as God's wisdom for man,[62] claims that the 'right' philosophy of the created universe and of human life is given us by God's own Word and therefore by Jesus Christ who 'is made not only our justification, sanctification and redemption but also our wisdom'.[63] He also emphasizes the duty of theology constantly to keep in view the thinking of the surrounding world, not in order to derive its standards (criterions) from it or to come to terms with it and compromise but in order to present the *fides* in the form of the *intellectus fidei* in the inner consistency of the latter.[64]

Again, Barth does not object to the use of a specifically philosophical terminology in theology, which he admits can hardly be avoided as after all every reader of the Bible, consciously or unconsciously, brings with him some sort of

philosophy, that is, a personal view of the fundamental nature and relationship of things.[65] But, in accordance with the
fundamental principle that the living reality and truth of the
Word of God, of God's revelation in Jesus Christ, must be
the master of our thinking and therefore must not be do-
minated by our thinking, he insists that any philosophical
concepts we may employ in theology must be subordinated
to the witness of revelation supplied to us in Scripture. In
other words, they must serve and not master the exposition
of that reality and truth and, therefore, can only be used for
the purpose of elucidating and illustrating that reality and
truth.[66]

Consequently, wherever he employs philosophical concepts
in his theology, he does not use them in the abstract and
general (neutral) sense which is normally ascribed to them
in philosophy but invests them with the specific meaning and
content which they take from the Word of God, from God's
revelation in Jesus Christ. An interesting example of this
kind is the fact that, in order to arrive at a true classification
of the divine attributes, he rejects the thomistic *via triplex*,
that is, the *via negationis, eminentiae* and *causalitatis*, precisely because this method or rather its results do not agree
with what is communicated to us in revelation and replaces
it by a doctrine of the divine perfections which, though making use of philosophical concepts, fills these concepts with the
specific concrete meaning they assume in the light of God's
revelation in Jesus Christ.[67] In this respect as well as in the
context of other aspects of his theology he warns against a
twofold danger that may arise out of the use of philosophical
concepts in theology, namely the danger of tumbling back
again out of the concrete into the abstract, out of the living
reality and truth of God's concrete revelation in Jesus Christ
into the realm of abstract ideas, and the further danger of
letting theological thought be influenced by the content which
these concepts normally have in philosophy. If that content
is a definitive one and as such is at variance with the Word
of God as the only object and criterion of the theologian,

then a philosophical concept with such a fixed content should not be used by him.[68]

A brief word must be added on the use of the concept of analogy in Barth's theology. Though, as we saw,[69] he rejects the *analogia entis*, once described by him 'as the invention of Antichrist',[70] he uses the concept of analogy and does so, first and foremost, in order to qualify man's knowledge of the Word of God and of God Himself.[71] Thus, the conformity of man's knowledge of God to the living reality and truth of God and the conformity of the Word of God as preached by the Church to the Word of God in itself and as such, a conformity accomplished only in faith and thus only by grace, is characterized by Barth as *analogia fidei*, that is, as 'the correspondence' (in faith) 'of the thing known with the knowing, of the object with the thought, of the Word of God with the word of man in thought and in speech'.[72] Brunner's view[73] that Barth's use of the *analogia fidei* presupposes the *analogia entis* fails to see that Barth's concept of the *analogia fidei*, like all his theological concepts,[74] is actualistic in essence in that the reality described by the analogy of faith both originates and remains grounded in the sovereign and free grace of God and, consequently, neither starts from nor leads to an objective state of affairs, an order of being that, as Brunner seems to assume, is independent of that grace. Again, Barth uses the concept of *analogia relationis* to describe the correspondence or, more precisely, the similarity in spite of all dissimilarity of the relationship between God and man and between man and his fellow-men to the relationship between the Father and the Son within the innertrinitarian life of God. This anology plays an important part in Barth's doctrine of creation, in particular in his teaching on the image of God in man.[75]

5. THEOLOGY AND SCIENCE [76]

In a theology as thoroughly christological as that of Barth a final conflict between theology and science is not to be expected; on the contrary, it entails and actually envisages a fruitful co-operation between these two activities of the human mind. In such a theology there is therefore no danger that its teaching will be at variance with the results of scientific discoveries; it has nothing to fear from them. For in Jesus Christ, who according to Barth's teaching on creation [77] is the centre and meaning of the cosmos, of history and of man's existence,[78] God and man, God the Creator and His creature, and thereby God and the world, have met once for all and are for ever united in one and the same person. The divine and the human, the supernatural and the natural, are thus shown to exist not in a permanent separation and aloofness from each other but in the unity of both of them. Hence there is no unbridgeable gulf between the two but rather a close association between God's divinity and man's humanity, between the kingdom of God and the world of man.

Moreover, in Jesus Christ, in His person and work, there has taken place the fulfilment of God's covenant of grace with man which from eternity has been the purpose for which this universe and in it man has been created by God. Creation, reconciliation and redemption form an inseparable unity in Barth's theology. Each of them being the work of God and originating and remaining grounded in His free and sovereign grace, they serve, individually and jointly, one undivided divine purpose, the fulfilment of that covenant of grace which God in His eternal decree before the creation of the world [79] decided to accomplish in His Son Jesus Christ. As the Son of God who, to achieve this purpose, assumed human nature in the man Jesus of Nazareth, Jesus Christ is both the Lord of heaven and earth and the Lord of all living things, and thus He is also the Lord and Author of every law that governs the universe and human life. Hence, these laws cannot be at variance with His truth which is the truth of God (Jn. 14:6); theology and science cannot ultimately contradict each other.

Again, theology and empirical (exact) sciences differ from each other in respect of the source of their knowledge and

the nature of their object.[80] Whereas in Barth's theology the
Word of God, God's revelation in Jesus Christ, is both the
source of its knowledge and the object of its investigation,
empirical (exact) sciences draw their knowledge from the
phenomena and concrete objectivities of the universe, both in
nature and in history, which they explore as their proper
object and the laws of which they try to discover. Because
of the Incarnation of the Word of God that took place on this
earth and in the midst of the history of mankind, and because
of the revelation accomplished thereby as well as by the life,
death and resurrection of Jesus Christ in the time of Pontius
Pilate, governor of Judea (Lk. 3:1), theology cannot disregard these phenomena and concrete objectivities of the
universe. It studies them, however, not for their own sake
but because of their relatedness to God as their Creator, Reconciler and Redeemer, and it is this relationship which
theology tries to expound on the basis of God's revelation in
Jesus Christ. In the sphere of creation, in particular, theology,
in accordance with its special source of knowledge and the
peculiar nature of its object, can and must move freely where
natural science, because of its incapability of reaching beyond
the limits of human thinking, has its appointed boundary.
On the other hand, there is free scope for natural science beyond what theology describes as the work of the Creator.[81]

Though theology and empirical (exact) sciences pursue to
that extent different tasks, there is however, at least in a certain sense, a close affinity between theology and science as
regards the nature of the method employed by both of them.
In another context (above, par. 2) Barth's theology has already been described as a sustained scientific and critical
examination and exposition of the object of faith and to that
extent as a science beside other sciences. Though, as we then
saw, it cannot be measured by the standards valid for the
other sciences and, on account of the particular task it has to
accomplish, must remain faithful to its own law, yet, like
science, it investigates and explains its special object in a
thoroughly scientific manner in that, like science, it allows

its object, that is, God's revelation in Jesus Christ, to determine both the scope and content of its knowledge and the method whereby this knowledge is to be achieved. Moreover, as far as the exegesis of Holy Scripture is concerned, Barth in no wise objects to the critical investigation of the biblical texts with the help of the methods of the modern science of history, including those of Form-criticism. The only reservation he makes in that respect is that they must not claim to be the one and only method for true exegesis.[82] For it is the *Word* which is to be exposed in the words of the Bible[83] and, therefore, Jesus Christ, very God and very man, as God's Word to man.

6. THE WORD OF GOD

Theology is *ministerium verbi divini*;[84] it serves the Word of God, which is its object, by making sure, as far as is possible for man and therefore on the basis of faith and thus by grace, that this Word is proclaimed by the Church (see above, par. 1). To render this service, it uses the Word of God as the *source* from which it derives its knowledge, as the *basis* on which it establishes its propositions, and as the *criterion* by which it measures the correctness of these propositions. As previously pointed out, it does so because absolute truth about God, the world and man is to be found only in the Word of God, and because that absolute truth has been made known to man, and will continue to be made known to him afresh, by virtue of the sovereign and free grace of God who Himself has revealed that truth to man in the Word He has spoken to him in the person and work of His Son Jesus Christ and continues to do so throughout the ages by means of the prophetic office of the risen and living Christ.

Passing on from this to the question of what Barth has in mind when he speaks of the Word of God, we find that his theology does not and, from its standpoint, cannot give us a simple and straightforward answer to this question.[85] He does not and from his viewpoint cannot provide us with a precise definition of the Word of God that is valid once for all.

The reason for this restraint is not so much that in his teaching the Word of God appears in three different forms and has many aspects, but that an actualistic quality is peculiar to it [86] according to which the Word of God is never a *datum*, something static which man can handle, scrutinize, define and classify like an object that is at his disposal but is always a concrete act of God, an event, a miracle, the materialization of which in each individual case is entirely dependent on the sovereign and free grace of God and, consequently, cannot be anticipated by any definition of man's making. In accordance with the movement of Barth's thought from the particular to the general [87] the Word of God is not an abstract idea or concept nor a general truth but a particular act (event) in that God speaks His Word now to this and now to that individual through the word of the Bible and through the proclamation of His Word by the Church in word and sacrament. And this Word of His is not merely divine speech imparting knowledge but speech which as such is at once action, decision, electing, creating, changing, judging, reconciling, forgiving and calling. It is the Word of the Lord and, therefore, it is a word of power, a dynamic word that challenges, rules and demands obedience. Again, contrary to Rudolf Otto's assumption, it is a rational and not an irrational event as the very nature of the Word of God is rational (above, par. 2).

In the last analysis the Word of God, with Barth, is the living Lord Jesus Christ Himself, [88] speaking to man, to particular men, through the witness which both Holy Scripture and, on the basis of Holy Scripture, the Church bear to Him and revealing to them the truth of God as embodied in the unity of His person and work. According to the First Article of the famous 'Theological Declaration' in 1934 of the Synod of the Confessing Church of Germany at Barmen, which essentially was Barth's work, 'Jesus Christ, as He is attested to us in Holy Scripture, is the one Word of God which we have to hear and which we have to trust and obey in life and in death.' The importance attributed to this state-

ment by Barth within his own theology can be gathered from
the fact that in his *Church Dogmatics* he not only devotes to it
a special commentary at the close of the section on 'The
Knowability of God'[89] but uses it also as his thesis for the
section on 'The Glory of the Mediator' which opens his teaching on Jesus Christ as the true Witness.[90] The significance
of this controversial statement and the arguments advanced
in its favour will be discussed in the next chapter.[91] In the
present context it may suffice to say that Barth does not
deny that God in His freedom may speak His Word to us
also in other ways, 'through Russian Communism or a flute
concerto, a blossoming shrub or a dead dog' for instance.[92]
But he contends that we, that is to say, the Church and the
individual Christian, being neither prophets nor apostles, are
not commissioned by Jesus Christ as our Lord and as the
Head of His Church to spread what we so hear as an independent proclamation of the Word of God. Consequently,
theology as a function of the Church has to concentrate on
that Word of God which it is the Church's special commission
to proclaim in word and sacrament, the Word of God namely
to which witness is borne in Holy Scripture.[93] Behind this
at a first glance arbitrary restriction of the scope of the
Word of God there is Barth's firm conviction, based on the
authority of Holy Scripture itself, that in the revelation of
God in Jesus Christ as attested in Holy Scripture the Church
has received the essential truth which God desires His
Church to hear and pass on to those inside and outside the
Church and of which man, every man, is in need.

According to Barth's doctrine of the Word of God the latter exhibits two main aspects. Primarily and originally it is
'the Word which God speaks by and to Himself in eternal
hiddenness',[94] the Word namely which according to Barth's
teaching on the Trinity (below par. 7) God the Father speaks
to His Son in the eternal mystery of His innertrinitarian life
and which, as we shall see,[95] has a special and concrete significance in the context of Barth's teaching on God's election
of grace. Secondarily and subsequently it is the Word

addressed by God to man in Jesus Christ. From these two main aspects of the Word of God Barth draws the conclusion that God could have confined Himself to speak His Word to Himself, to His Son, in His eternity, and that it is therefore an act of grace that He speaks His Word also to man. G. Wingren, in his criticism of this teaching,[96] overlooks the first main aspect of the Word of God when he assumes that Barth's desire to maintain God's freedom and his alleged negative concept of man induce him to deny the necessity of God's Word being addressed to man. Any spoken word, by its very nature, requires someone to whom it is addressed. But this requirement is fulfilled when God speaks His Word to His Son and thus to Himself.

In its second main aspect the Word of God appears in three forms,[97] as the Word of God namely that is revealed, written and proclaimed. As the revealed Word of God it is spoken by God to prophets and apostles in Jesus Christ;[98] as the written Word of God it is attested in Holy Scripture; as the proclaimed Word of God it is conveyed by the Church in its preaching and in its sacraments. It would, however, be a serious mistake to conclude from these propositions that Barth identifies the words of the Bible or the Church's proclamation with the Word of God. He makes perfectly clear that both the Bible and the proclamation of the Church are but the result of human activities and on that account are in themselves merely the word of man and not the Word of God, being afflicted with all the limitations and weaknesses which are inevitably bound up with anything human. He claims, however, that by the grace of God and in the power of the Holy Spirit they can *become* and in that case *are* the Word of God when and where God pleases.[99] The Bible as well as the proclamation of the Church become the Word of God whenever God speaks His Word through them, in other words, they are but the channel through which God's Word is made known to man. It is in this event that they become and in so far are the Word of God. In respect of the Bible in particular Barth says that 'it is to its being in this becoming that the tiny word "is" relates in the statement that the Bible is God's Word'.[100] Again, 'it is the miracle of revelation and of faith' when in the proclamation of the Church 'man's language about God . . . is primarily and decisively God's own language'.[101]

The existence of three forms of God's Word to man does not mean that we are confronted with three several Words of God. It is one and the same Word of God, God speaking to man in Jesus Christ, which is realized in these three forms. It is true, the first form, the revealed Word of God, establishes the two other forms in that both Holy Scripture and the Church's proclamation, based on Holy Scripture, bear witness to the revealed Word of God. However, the latter, as we have just seen, become themselves the Word of God whenever God speaks His Word through them. Moreover, the revealed Word of God never meets us anywhere in abstract form; our knowledge of it is but indirectly, arising out of the witness of the Bible and the Church's proclamation to it.[102] In a significant passage Barth describes the mutual relationship between the three forms of God's Word to man as follows: 'The *revealed* Word of God we know only from the Scripture adopted by Church proclamation or from Church proclamation based on Scripture. The *written* Word of God we know only through the revelation which makes proclamation possible or through the proclamation made possible by revelation. The *proclaimed* Word of God we know only by knowing the revelation attested through Scripture or by knowing the Scripture which attests revelation.'[103]

How do we come to know the Word of God if neither the words of the Bible nor the words used by the Church in its proclamation of the Word of God are in themselves the Word of God and if we also do not know the revealed Word of God apart from the witness which both Holy Scripture and the Church's proclamation bear to it? A conclusive answer to this question cannot be given until we have reached Barth's teaching on the subjective aspect of revelation (par. 7). At this point it can however already be stated that the Word of God, like God Himself, can be known only indirectly, that is to say, it must always come to us clothed 'in the garments of creaturely reality' [104] in order that we may be able to apprehend it, be it that it meets us in the humanity of Jesus Christ Himself, in the earthly vessels of Holy Scripture and of the proclamation of the Church or in the creaturely symbols of bread and wine at Holy Communion.[105] In Barth's own words, 'we do not possess the Word of God otherwise than in the mystery of its worldly form';[106] it must be veiled in order to unveil.

God's veiling of His Word and, consequently, of Himself in order to unveil His Word and Himself plays a decisive part in Barth's doctrine of the Word of God, in particular in his teaching on revelation; this aspect of his theology, therefore, deserves careful study.[107] In it the self-veiling and the self-unveiling of God and of His Word—it is God who effects both —are so closely interwoven with each other that the one cannot be understood apart from the other. In that God veils Himself and His Word He unveils, and in that He unveils Himself and His Word He veils. The worldly form of the Word of God without the divine content imparted to it by the Word of God, that is, by Jesus Christ, is not the Word of God, and the divine content without the worldly form is also not the Word of God. The worldly form and the divine content have to be grasped in their togetherness in order to be comprehended and known as the Word of God; but this knowledge, as Barth constantly emphasizes,[108] takes place only in faith and thus only by grace. For the worldly form of the Word of God does not only mean that the latter meets us in the garments of creaturely reality but has the further significance that the Word of God meets us in the creaturely reality of fallen man. The indirectness of our knowledge of the Word of God is thus a twofold one. The latter is concealed from us not only by the creaturely reality in which it is clothed but also by man's sinfulness which prevents him from recognizing and accepting it as God's Word. The Word of God in its worldly form is therefore not in itself transparent.

It needs man's faith and, consequently, the work of the Holy
Spirit in man creating that faith and thus God's grace that it
may be recognized and accepted as God's Word. Here too
we must refer to Barth's basic view,[109] founded on his interpretation of the revelation that has taken place in the resurrection of the crucified Jesus Christ from the dead, that man,
fallen man, is incapable of truly knowing God, the world
and man by means of his innate capacities and endowments
and therefore needs God's gracious help and thus faith in
order that he may be led to the Word of God by the Spirit
of the living Lord Jesus Christ Himself, now through the
worldly form of the Word of God to its divine content and
now through that content to its worldly form.

Thus the Lord who gives the Word is also the Lord who
gives faith. It is He who through the work of the Holy
Spirit in man makes man open and ready for His Word (see
below, par. 7). Hence Barth's final answer to the epistemological problem of the knowability of the Word of God is
is that the Word of God becomes knowable by making itself
knowable through the gracious work of the Holy Spirit in
man.[110] 'The possibility of knowing the Word of God is God's
miracle on and in us just as much as are the Word itself and
the utterance of it.'[111] In this connection too it needs to be
pointed out that no disparagement of human nature, in particular no denial of man's freedom, ability and obligation to
take responsible decisions is implied in this teaching. For
Barth argues in detail that man's faith, though evoked by the
work of the Holy Spirit in man, is a thoroughly human experience, that it is really *his* faith: 'in faith he is by no
means a block of wood or a stone'.[112] In that man believes,
he really acts in that he acknowledges the *Word* of God as the
Word of *God* and accepts it by his own free will and in
obedience to God's will as a Word from God that is addressed
to him and concerns him intimately and decisively. But the
fact *that* he believes by acting in this manner is the work of the
Holy Spirit.[113] In that man determines himself in the aforesaid manner, his self-determination is 'subordinated' to his

determination by God. His self-determination only 'follows' God's determination. It does not take the latter's place
as the Pelagians hold; again, it does not co-operate with
God's determination as the Semipelagians assume nor does
it exist simultaneously with God's determination in a unity
of tension as Augustine teaches.[114] The emphasis is on the
words 'subordinated' and 'follow' which clearly indicate
Barth's own standpoint in this matter.

Again, the knowledge of the Word of God and therewith
the possibility of knowing it, which the objective reality of
that knowledge entails,[115] must continually be given afresh
to man by the free grace of God. Man cannot work with the
Word of God and with that faith whereby and wherein the
Word of God is known as with a capital sum that is at his
disposal. This applies also to the religious man, even the
Christian, as Barth argues at length.[116] It follows from the
actualistic quality of the Word of God and of man's faith and
further from the fact that man, even Christian man, is and
remains a sinner (*homo simul iustus et peccator*) who precisely because of this is incapable of knowing the Word of God,
that is, of acknowledging, accepting and obeying it in word
and deed, apart from the experience of faith which must continually be granted to him afresh in that the Word of God
comes to him ever anew in the power of the Holy Spirit and
by that power illuminates his mind and sanctifies and
directs his will. The Word of God is the Word of grace precisely because it speaks to us, and can speak to us, only in
and through its worldly form, and because we are and remain
sinners. It 'ceases to be grace or grace itself ceases to be grace
when we ascribe to man a disposition towards this Word, a
possibility of knowledge independent of it and peculiar in
itself over against this Word'.[117]

Finally, the norm of the knowledge of the Word of God,
the criterion of theology (dogmatics), is to be found neither
in a universal human possibility, as modernism suggests, nor
in an ecclesiastical factor, the teaching-office of the Church
for instance, as Roman Catholicism claims, but solely in the

Word of God itself as the absolute truth of God. For the Church ventures to speak about God and to regard its own word as the Word of God, but is able and empowered to do so only if and when God Himself has first spoken about Himself to the Church in His Word and continues to do so in and through the word of the Church. Thus only the Word of God itself can be the criterion of whether or not the Church's proclamation is in agreement with God's own Word, and whether or not the teaching of theology (dogmatics), which has to safeguard the rightness of the Church's proclamation, renders the true exposition and interpretation of the Word of God.[118]

7. REVELATION

(1) *The Concept.* There exist perhaps as many different concepts of revelation as there are different theologies. Each of these theologies ascribes a different meaning to revelation with the result that widely differing conclusions are drawn from these different concepts as to the nature, form, content, sphere and scope of revelation.[119] Barth does not deny that there are many revelations. As a Christian theologian he is however concerned only with the Christian understanding of revelation and holds that the Christian revelation is a unique revelation that cannot be compared with anything else that is called revelation.

As the Word of God is the source, the basis and the criterion of his theology, the Word of God also determines his concept of the Christian revelation. The latter is based upon, flows from and is actually identical with the revealed Word of God.[120] The Word of God as addressed to man is the Living God Himself in His revelation, and revelation is the coming of the Word of God, of God Himself in His Word, to man, a divine action initiated, executed and consummated by the sovereign and free grace of God. The Christian revelation is therefore a specific 'reality' of its own. Hence, Barth does not derive his concept of revelation from any general idea of revelation. He does not enquire into the meaning of revelation

F

in general, as Tillich does in the course of his pheno-
menological approach to the basic concepts of theology,[121]
and, consequently, refuses to take his concept of revelation
from either philosophy or the universal history of religion.

In accordance with the movement of his thought from the
particular to the general he obtains his concept of revelation
from that particular event in which the Word came, and
continually comes again, to man, the revelation, that is, of
God in Jesus Christ.[122] For him the Christian revelation is
a particular, a concrete and a rational event: 'the Word became flesh and dwelt among us' (Jn. 1:14),[123] and this concept, contrary to G. Wingren's entirely mistaken interpretation of Barth's position in this matter,[124] is by no means
confined to the fact of the birth of Jesus, that is, to the
Incarnation of the Word of God, but includes His life, His
teaching, His passion, His death and, above all, and from the
standpoint of revelation even primarily, His resurrection as
well. Hence, it is the revelation of the Triune God, of the
God, that is, who, according to the witness of Holy Scripture
and the Church's proclamation based upon that witness, 'is
the Father of Jesus Christ, is Jesus Christ Himself, is the
Spirit of this Father and of this Son'.[125] Barth conceives of
this specific divine act of revelation in this way that the
Triune God Himself is 'in unimpaired unity yet also in unimpaired difference' Revealer, Revelation and Revealedness.[126]
He means thereby that it is God the Father who in His
eternity before the creation of the world decided to reveal
Himself to man in His Son Jesus Christ[127]; that it is God
the Son who in obedience to this eternal decree of His Father
executes and objectifies this revelation in His own person and
work in that He assumed human nature in the man Jesus of
Nazareth and, living and dying as a man among His fellow-
men and for their salvation, accomplished the work of reconciliation which according to Barth's teaching has also and
primarily a distinctly revelatory character; and that it is
God the Holy Spirit who consummates this revelation by
making man open and ready for it so that man is capable of

receiving it and actually receives it.[128] Thus God is throughout the Subject of revelation. The latter is and remains His act, His work, in all ages and in relation to all men, to individual men.

It is important to note that Barth's concept of revelation requires as an integral part of it that the revelation as understood by him 'gets through' to man. With him this revelation is revelation only if it is recognized, acknowledged and accepted by man. Whereas Jesus Christ in the unity of His person and work represents the objective aspect of revelation, the work of the Holy Spirit in man whereby man is enabled to receive this (objective) revelation in faith represents the subjective aspect of revelation. It is only when we realize the decisive significance of the latter aspect for Barth's concept of revelation that we shall be able to understand both his concentration on God's revelation in Jesus Christ as the one and only revelation of basic importance for theology (dogmatics) and his rejection of a general revelation in nature or in history as a second source of revelation besides that of God's revelation in Jesus Christ.

Dietrich Bonhoeffer fails to do justice to this aspect of Barth's concept of revelation in his criticism of what he terms Barth's 'positivism of revelation'.[129] Sharply distinguishing between the objective and the subjective aspect of revelation Barth does not dispute that God, and that means the Triune God, can and does reveal Himself also in nature and in history but contends that this objective revelation does not and cannot get through to man, to fallen man, and therefore is not revelation as understood by him. This is one of his main reasons why, in opposition to E. Brunner,[130] he rejects the proposition of a general revelation in creation for which, as he claims on the basis of a detailed exegesis of the relevant Scripture-passages, support cannot be found in the Bible.[131] Moreover—and this is perhaps his most decisive argument against the hypothesis of a general revelation in creation— the latter does not and cannot reveal God, the world and man as they really are because it needs the knowledge of God's work of reconciliation in Jesus Christ and thus the knowledge of Jesus Christ Himself, of His person and work, to attain to that true knowledge.[132] In Barth's view true knowledge of God, the world and man is not possible apart from the knowledge of God's work of reconciliation in Jesus Christ because it is only in and through that work and thus in and through Jesus Christ that we come to know who and what God and man really are and that the world has been created by God and for what purpose. This is why his theology leaves no room for a revelation or for revelations prior to that one which has taken place in Jesus Christ, and why such concepts as original, partial and progressive revelation are debarred from it.

The controversy raging round this teaching appears to be obscured by the fact that those who are engaged in it use different concepts of revelation. Since Barth's exclusive concern is with that revelation which exhibits the true being and nature of God, the world and man, and since he can find that revelation only in the person and work of Jesus Christ, all the other so-called revelations are not regarded by him as revelation in the proper sense of the word. The latter, in his view, do not and cannot exhibit the truth that is revealed in the person and work of Jesus Christ and therefore can only lead to the knowledge of 'idols'. For the same reasons Jesus Christ is for Barth neither 'the final revelation', as R. Niebuhr holds,[133] nor 'the crown of the revelation', as W. Temple claims,[134] but *the* revelation. This revelation, which happened once for all in the fulness of time, does and must indeed continually 'happen' afresh (see above, Ch. I, 5 (2)) to individual men by means of the prophetic office of the risen Christ and in the power of the Holy Spirit. It is however always the same revelation: Jesus Christ the same yesterday and today and for ever (Heb. 13:8).

Since the Christian revelation is a specific and concrete operation of the Triune God in the aforesaid sense, neither the Bible not the proclamation of the Church are in themselves and as such revelation; they bear witness to it.[135]

Revelation, that is, God Himself in His revelation, gave rise to Holy Scripture attesting this revelation, and the Church's proclamation is based on the witness of Holy Scripture. The Bible and the Church's proclamation can indeed become the Word of God by the free grace of God and in the power of the Holy Spirit (above, par. 6) and in that case become identical with revelation. But even then they are only derivately and mediately what revelation is originally and directly, namely the Word of God that the Living God Himself has spoken and continues to speak in and through the crucified and risen Christ.[136] Again, the doctrinal propositions which the Church professes (dogmas) are not revelation either. As the work of man they are only a human attempt to formulate the content of the divine revelation and thus are always only on the way to the truth of revelation. In revelation God reveals and communicates neither general truths nor doctrines but Himself, His work and His will for the world and for man.[137]

Again, tradition is not revelation. Rejecting the Roman Catholic Church's recognition of tradition as a source of revelation, Barth claims that the Church is exclusively under the authority of Holy Scripture, that is to say, under the authority of the prophetic-apostolic witness of the Bible to Jesus Christ as the Lord and as the Head of His Church. As God's Word to man He, and He alone, is the source of all knowledge and truth in His Church.[138]

As the self-revelation of the Triune God the Christian revelation is a personal revelation from subject to subject, from God to man, and thus represents itself as an I-Thou relationship, the Spirit of God communicating with man's spirit. Since it is the Lord who communicates in this manner with His creature, there is no getting behind or beyond that revelation; the latter sets the boundary of the theologian's thinking; he can always only make God's revelation in Jesus Christ the starting-point of his thinking.[139] Again, there cannot be any abstraction between revelation and its content. As God reveals Himself to man in Jesus Christ and through the Holy Spirit, so He is in Himself, in His eternal reality. Otherwise revelation would not be revelation. Barth strongly repudiates the idea that God in Himself could in any way be different from what He shows Himself to be in His revelation in Jesus Christ.[140] The fact that Barth speaks of God also as the hidden God does not imply a contradiction. He means thereby that precisely because God in His revelation in Jesus Christ makes Himself known to us as the Lord and further as the Father, Son and Holy Spirit, He meets us as the hidden God. For man would not know God as *this* God but for the fact that God Himself reveals Himself as such to man.

Man's finite mind and even more his sinfulness prevent him from ever attaining to a truly adequate knowledge of God as the Lord, of God's incomparable majesty and freedom and of His triune being except in faith and thus by grace.[141] In this connection special attention should be given to the distinction between the primary and the secondary objectivity of God which Barth draws in so far as God is the object of man's knowledge.[142] Since God, like His Word, can be known by man only indirectly through the mediation of the worldly forms in which His Word is clothed (above, par. 6), He is directly known, that is, He is primarily and immediately objective, only to Himself within His innertrinitarian life, whereas man can know Him only in secondary or mediate objectivity, only in His self-revelation 'through objects which we can see, hear or handle, through objects appropriate to our comprehension'.[143] In so far revelation is at once an unveiling and a veiling (above, par. 6). More will be said about this in the discussion of what Barth terms 'the mystery of revelation'. But the aforesaid distinction between the primary (God as He is in Himself) and the secondary (God as known by man) objectivity of God already makes clear that and why in this life we cannot see but only believe and that and why we now know only 'in part' (1 Cor. 13:12). On the other hand, Barth leaves us in no doubt that what we can and do know by the grace of God and in faith is true knowledge. 'His (God's) secondary objectivity is fully true, for it has its correspondence and basis in His primary objectivity'.[144]

(2) *The Triune God.* Barth's doctrine of the Trinity (CD, I, 1, pp. 339–560), 'undoubtedly the greatest treatise on the Trinity since the Reformation',[145] not only constitutes an integral part of his doctrine of the Word of God but is also the first part of his doctrine of revelation (above, Ch. I, par. 4). For it has its exclusive root in the Christian concept of revelation, in God's self-revelation in Jesus Christ. Just as Jesus Christ is *the* revelation, so He holds the key-position in the formulation of the doctrine of the Trinity. According to the witness of Holy Scripture He reveals Himself not only as the incarnate Word of God and thus as very God as well as very man but also as the Son of His Father, and He does so moreover in the power of the Holy Spirit who according to the same witness is once more no other than God Himself.

Since the Word of God and, consequently, God's self-revelation in His Word, in Jesus Christ, is the starting-point of Barth's theology, the question of who this self-revealing God is precedes the other question of whether He exists and what He is. The former question is answered in God's self-revelation in Jesus Christ in this way that He is the Triune God 'who reveals Himself in a like manner as the Father in His self-veiling and holiness, as He does as the Son in His self-unveiling and mercy, and as the Holy Spirit in His self-impartation and love'.[146] Thus the doctrine of the Trinity not only arises out of the biblically attested revelation but analyses and concretely and conclusively explains the content of revelation. Moreover, it demonstrates that and why revelation is possible. Again, it fundamentally distinguishes the Christian doctrine of God (the Triune God) as Christian and thus marks off the Christian concept of revelation as Christian in face of all other possible doctrines of God and concepts of revelation.[147] It is for this reason that in Barth's *Church Dogmatics* it precedes the doctrine of God, forming an essential part of the doctrine of the Word of God as the particular path to knowledge trodden therein, and constitutes the first part of the doctrine of revelation. It is for the same reason that it occupies a dominant position in Barth's theology as a whole, determining everything else in it. With Barth everything starts with the God who has revealed Himself in His Word, in Jesus Christ, as the Triune God.

Again, he insists that the doctrine of the Trinity can proceed from nowhere else than from the Christian (biblical) concept of revelation. He rejects in particular the *vestigia trinitatis*, that is, the analogues to the Trinity to be found in phenomena taken from nature, culture, history, religion or man's soul-life, as a second source of the doctrine of the Trinity, arguing that they are but an expression of the (in his view) indefensible *analogia entis* and, even if used only as illustration, may lead to the concept of a God who is different from the God of revelation. In his opinion the real *vestigia trinitatis* are to be found in the worldly forms of the revealed, written and proclaimed Word of God and thus in the creaturely forms which God Himself has assumed in His revelation.[148]

The wealth of Barth's thought on the Trinity cannot be presented here even in outline; a few salient features of his teaching on this subject-matter may however be briefly adumbrated.

His view of the innertrinitarian life of God is similar in character to that of N. Berdyaev. Like this Russian thinker,[149] whose mystical speculation is otherwise so alien to Barth's scientific frame of mind, he stresses the basic dynamism of the divine life. In the Triune God the Father and the Son are united with one another through the Holy Spirit in a living communion of mutual love, and the eternal will of the Father is accepted, obeyed and executed by the Son in the power of the Holy Spirit. In the Trinity the dynamic freedom of God, of His divine life, is powerfully expressed in that, without ceasing to be free as the Father, He is able, as the Son of God, to be free for man in Jesus Christ and, as the Holy Spirit, to be free in man. God cannot only come to man in His Son Jesus Christ, He can also be in man through the Holy

Spirit. In other words, He is free to be not only God in Himself, in His eternity, that is, to be transcendent, but to be both God for us and with us in Jesus Christ and God in us in the Holy Spirit,[150] that is, to be immanent. Again, the dynamic life of the Triune God is unfolded in three sections, dealing with God the Father, God the Son, and God the Holy Spirit respectively.[151] Based on a thorough theological exegesis of the Bible, these sections endeavour above all to show that what God is to us in His revelation He is originally and primarily in Himself. Thus, for instance, He is our Father because He is, first of all, in Himself the Father of His Son. He is the Son come to us, or the Word of God spoken to us, because He is so antecedently in Himself as the Son or Word of God the Father. By receiving Him in the Holy Spirit and thus by faith and in love we become the children of God because, as the Spirit of the love that unites God the Father with His Son, God is antecedently the Spirit of love in Himself.

Though Barth occasionally uses language verging on Tritheism, he strongly emphasizes the oneness of God in His threeness. He even contends that the doctrine of the three-in-oneness of God means the final and decisive confirmation of the insight that God is one. In a striking fashion he argues that the anti-Trinitarians, who regard themselves as the real champions of Christian monotheism, are bound to deny either the revelation of God or His oneness in that Jesus Christ, if He is not Himself God, could not reveal God as He is in Himself because of the absence of the real presence of God in His person and, if, on the other hand, He owns this power of revelation, must be a more or less deified creature, 'an hypostasis not divine but half-divine', and in that case would break up the unity of God.[152] To avoid any suspicion of Tritheism Barth refrains from speaking of three 'persons' in the one and only God and instead speaks of God's revelation in three 'modes of being'. This latter term is meant to express that God as Father, Son and Holy Spirit respectively is three times the one God 'in a special way', in a threefold 'repetition' grounded in His Godhead.[153] No Sabellianism is implied in this teaching since no change or transformation in God is assumed in His revelation as Father, Son and Holy Spirit respectively. God is always and everywhere the one Lord, the one personal God, the 'I' that meets the 'Thou', in His three modes of being, both in His eternity and in His revelation. His three modes of being are always present in unity. There is no act of God, no perfection of His, which would not in like manner be the act, the perfection, of the Father, of the Son and of the Holy Spirit.

On the other hand, Barth designates God the Father primarily as God the Creator, God the Son primarily as God the Reconciler and God the Holy Spirit primarily as God the Redeemer, insisting at the same time that in creation as well as in reconciliation and redemption God is always at work in the unity of His three modes of being. Here he seems to be involved in logical contradictions but argues that he is only following the witness of Holy Scripture and that it only signifies an 'appropriation' when by isolation he regards, for instance, God the Father as the Creator though the Son and the Holy Spirit are said to be that with Him. Moreover, he points out that in respect of the distinction of the three modes of being in God the *mysterium trinitatis* in the last analysis remains a mystery that cannot be solved by any kind of rationalizing; as far as possible the truth can only be established by expounding the biblically attested revelation.[154].

Again, he understands the distinguishable form of the three modes of being of God in terms of their individual relations, above all their individual genetic relations, to one another, the Son being begotten of the Father and the Holy Spirit proceeding from both the Father and the Son.[155] Barth's vigorous defence of the *filioque* of the Nicaeno–Constantinopolitan Creed in the face of the teaching of the Eastern Churches that in the eternal innertrinitarian being of God the Holy Spirit proceeds from the Father and only in revelation is actually given by the Son is of special import-

ance in view of future talks on Church unity.[156] Apart from
the diverse genetic relations in which Father, Son and Holy
Spirit are said to stand to one another Barth rejects any
kind of teaching which would imply inequality in their
essence or dignity, in particular any kind of Subordina-
tionist Christology which in his view would in the last resort
mean the denial of revelation itself.[157]

(3) *Objective Revelation*. Though Barth for didactic reasons
deals separately with the objective and the subjective aspect
of revelation, he regards them as a unity, the form and the
content of revelation, as here understood, being inseparable
from each other. For the Christian revelation always simultaneously involves the act of revealing and the impartation
of revelation to individual men. In the unity of the person
and work of Jesus Christ it attains its objective reality and,
in consequence of Barth's arguing from reality to possibility
(above, Ch. I, 5 (1b)), thereby proves also its objective possibility. In Jesus Christ as the objective reality of the divine
revelation there is presupposed and grounded and brought to
our knowledge also its objective possibility.[158] In Him God's
freedom for man has found its manifest expression in that it
is God Himself who directly speaks to us in the person and
work of Jesus Christ. The revelatory character of the person
and work of Jesus Christ, as previously pointed out, is to be
found not only in His incarnation but in His entire life and
work and in His passion and death as well as in His resurrection and ascension. Barth attributes great importance to the
revelatory aspect of Jesus Christ's person and work to which
he constantly refers in his *Church Dogmatics*. If he sometimes
seems to emphasize this aspect more than Jesus Christ's
threefold work of justification, sanctification and vocation,
he does so because without this revelatory work reconciliation, and that means justification as well as sanctification and
vocation, could not effectively be achieved. In fact, with
Barth revelation itself is already part of the reconciling work
of Jesus Christ since it means the restoration of the communion of sinful man with God.[159]

In his teaching on revelation Barth deals with the doctrine of the person and work of Jesus Christ only in a preparatory fashion, developing it only in so far as it demonstrates that God has actually revealed Himself objectively in the person, and work of Jesus Christ and why He is able to do so (CD, I 2, pp. 1–202). That doctrine is then more fully worked out in his doctrine of God's election of grace (CD, II, 2) and in his teaching on reconciliation (CD, IV, 1–3) so that the synopsis of these three aspects of his theology is required to achieve a comprehensive understanding of his views on this subject-matter.

For Barth as the theologian of the Word of God it is impossible to begin, as Schleiermacher and Ritschl did before him, with the historical Jesus and then to argue that God was in Christ. Nor can he with Tillich[160] speak of 'Jesus as the Christ' in whom the 'New Being' is said to have appeared. His starting-point is the primary fact—the fact that is revealed to the eyes of faith in the name of Jesus Christ as attested in Holy Scripture and therefore cannot be argued but can only be accepted and interpreted—of Jesus Christ as the incarnate Word of God in the strict sense of John 1:14 (forty pages are devoted to the theological exegesis of this text[161]), in other words, the primary fact of Jesus Christ as very God and very man, the Son of God (= God the Son) become man in the man Jesus of Nazareth.[162] Following in this respect in general the teaching of the Ancient Church, he strongly emphasizes that Jesus Christ is eternally the Son of God who assumed human nature and existence in the man Jesus of Nazareth, again, that He is the eternal thought of God who precisely as the Godman Jesus Christ was eternally in the mind of God (below, Ch. III, 1, 2) though he did not appear in the flesh until the birth of Jesus.

Hence with Barth all reflections about Jesus Christ begin and end with the fact that He is the Son of God.[163] This fact dominates his entire thought about the person and work of Jesus Christ. It determines in particular his thought about Jesus Christ Himself. The Son of God is the Subject of His person whereas His manhood is but the predicate of His Godhead. It is the Son of God who as man wills and acts in Jesus Christ; it is in the Son of God that Jesus Christ has His exclusive existence as man. To Barth this is the central mystery of the Incarnation, revealed in the resurrection of Jesus Christ, as it means that in Jesus Christ not only God and man, divine nature and human nature, became one in an inconceivable manner but that in Him the Creator has become Himself a creature.[164] This mystery is neither solved nor meant to be solved by the Chalcedon formula (A.D. 451) on the two natures of Jesus Christ, which Barth too only adopts in order to explain, as far as possible, how the divine and the human are related to each other in the person of Jesus Christ.[165] The human nature of Jesus Christ has no independent existence (doctrine of the *anhypostasis*) but acquires and has existence exclusively in the Son of God who assumed human nature and existence in Him (doctrine of the *enhypostasis*). In other words, as far as Jesus Christ's person is concerned, it is not a question of the adoption by the Son of God of an already existing human being or of idealizing or deifying a particular man.[166] On the other hand, Barth points out that this teaching does not mean a denial of the humanity of Jesus Christ who is said to lack not humanity but human existence or being of its own.[167] It is difficult to see how Jesus Christ can be said to enjoy full humanity if the Son of God is the Subject of His being and acting, but Barth would refer us in this respect to the witness of Holy Scripture and regard this difficulty as part of the mystery of the Incarnation.

His notable defence of the Virgin Birth, of the conception of Jesus Christ by the Holy Spirit and birth of the Virgin Mary, described by him as 'the miracle of Christmas', should be carefully studied.[168] For Barth the Virgin Birth has not ontic but noetic significance. It is a necessary sign which accompanies and indicates the mystery of the revelation of God in Jesus Christ, of the Son of God come in the flesh, and for that reason is essential to the true understanding of the

Christian revelation. It makes evident (*a*) that the *vere Deus vere homo* cannot be understood intellectually but only spiritually and (*b*) that God alone is the Author of the 'new creation' of the Godman Jesus Christ. Again, it excludes any kind of synergism in that it excludes man, sinful man, as God's fellow-worker in the birth of Jesus Christ. Even the Virgin Mary merely accepts in obedience what God has willed for her and creates in her by the power of the Holy Spirit.[169] Hence, the Virgin Birth is in Barth's view also a sign of God's judgment upon man and of His free and sovereign grace towards him.[170]

Since the human nature and existence of Jesus Christ cannot be separated from the divine mode of being and existence of the Son of God as the Subject of His person, Barth is not interested in the so-called 'historical Jesus', if considered in isolation, and rejects both the 'Life of Jesus movement' and the Jesus-worship, in particular the Roman Catholic 'heart of Jesus' cult. In his view all endeavours to deal with the man Jesus as if he existed independently from the Son of God contradict the truth of revelation. Jesus Christ is and remains the mystery of revelation in that in Him God, without ceasing to be God, exists as man, as a particular man, in a particular place, and at a particular time. In this mystery Christology has its limit since man cannot go behind the mystery involved in the unity of the two natures of Jesus Christ.[171]

One of the striking features of Barth's Christology is the way in which he argues that in Jesus Christ, in His person and work, no reduction takes place either of His deity or of His humanity, but that on the contrary both His deity and His humanity find their fullest expression and even reach their climax in the unity of His person and work. The majesty of God is so great and His freedom is so incomparable that He is not prevented either by His deity or by our humanity and sinfulness from being our God in Jesus Christ and from having intercourse with us in Him as with His own, and that even in His condescension to His creature and in the lowli-

ness of His existence as the man Jesus of Nazareth He can
still remain the Lord and show forth His majesty. The omnipotence of God, His love and His glory, reach their climax
in the very fact that He can so utterly humble Himself in
Jesus Christ by becoming in Him what we are, that is flesh,
and by suffering and dying as a man in our place and for our
salvation and at the same time can exalt man so highly that
the man Jesus of Nazareth was no less than God Himself.[172]
To Barth the mystery of the deity of Christ consists in this
that God as God is able and willing to condescend and humble
Himself in this way. For the meaning of Christ's deity, he
holds, cannot be gathered from any abstract notion of supreme, absolute, non-worldly being, but can be learned only
from what took place in Him.[173]

In opposition to many modern Kenotic theories of the
person of Jesus Christ the self-emptying of Jesus Christ (Phil.
2:7)—the *Kenosis*[174]—is understood by Barth not as a temporary diminution, let alone cessation, of His divine attributes
but as the renunciation or self-deprivation of His being in the
form of God *alone*, assuming the form of a servant without
detracting from His being in the form of God. Claiming that
his interpretation of the *Kenosis* is that of Augustine (*Sermo*,
183, 4 f.), Barth contends that Jesus Christ in His self-emptying did in no respect cease as man to be who He is, that is,
the Son of God, but took it upon Himself to be the Son of
God 'in a way quite other than that which corresponds and
belongs to His form as God', that is, to be the Son of God in
the form of a servant, thereby concealing His divine glory
from the world until it was revealed in His resurrection.[175]

On the other hand, Jesus Christ, in that the Word of God
became flesh, was real man, the Son of God assuming our
human nature with all its limitations and weaknesses, including its sinfulness. However, though His humanity was
our own familiar humanity, He did not and, being the Son of
God, He could not sin; for He could not be in enmity towards Himself.[176] In assuming sinful human nature He
sanctified it so that sin was excluded.[176] In becoming the

same as we are, the Son of God was the same in quite a different way: what we do is omitted, and what we omit is done. Here the ultimate meaning of the Incarnation, as far as the humanity of Jesus Christ is concerned, is indicated in that now in the flesh that is not done what all flesh does. We are shown the real man as God meant him to be in creating him. Barth contends that the sinlessness of Jesus is not to be understood as a superhuman quality in Him since the commission of sin is not an attribute of true human existence. It only means that Jesus unlike all other men did not want to be like God but accepted that He is 'flesh' and therefore stood under the judgment of God and could live only by the grace of God. This contention does not answer the question whether Jesus could have behaved as He did if He would not have been the Son of God. However, Barth himself concedes that he cannot, and will not try to, solve the mystery to which the questions involved in the sinlessness of Jesus point. He therefore refrains from expressing a final opinion on the so-called monothelite controversy—the question of whether or not Jesus Christ had true human will, different from the will of God though not independent of it—but acknowledges the legitimacy of its concern.[177]

It is precisely because Jesus Christ is Himself true God and true man that He reveals to us and can reveal to us who God is and what He is and who we are and what we are. As the Son of God He represents God to us, and as the Son of Man he represents us to God. In this way He is God's revelation to us and our reconciliation with God.[178] In Him 'God is not just a word or a systematic principle but the reality and *prima veritas* which of itself sets itself at the head of all other thoughts and gives them a specific direction and content'.[179] Only through Him do we know that God is the Triune God who as the Father is hidden from our eyes and as the Son is manifest to us in Jesus Christ by the power of the Holy Spirit, that God is our Father and therefore our Creator. With Barth the objective revelation in Jesus Christ, the reality of Jesus Christ itself, has in particular critical significance in that it reveals to man that 'in the cosmos God is hidden and man blind' and that in consequence of that the revelation of God in Jesus Christ is needed to change this situation and in fact has done so.[180] In bringing God and man together in Jesus Christ, it reveals God as the Lord of eternity, as the Creator, Reconciler and Redeemer and exhibits man as a creature, a sinner, one who as God's enemy is doomed to death but is saved in Jesus Christ by the sovereign and free grace of God.[181]

(4) *Subjective Revelation.* It is the work of the Son or Word of God that God can speak to us; it is the work of the Holy Spirit that we hear the Word of God.[182] The decisive significance of the subjective aspect for Barth's concept of revelation has been pointed out (above, par. 1). The unity of the objective and subjective aspect of revelation has been stressed (above, par. 3). This unity also entails that the subjective revelation cannot be treated as an independent theme as in Barth's view has been done in Pietism and by the Oxford Group Movement. It is not the addition of a second revelation to objective revelation. Its exclusive task is to get the latter across to man, that is, God's revelation in Jesus Christ and thus Jesus Christ Himself. This, and this alone, is what the Holy Spirit does in revelation; on the other hand, that this takes place, is the work of the Holy Spirit.[183] He is the subjective reality of revelation and, consequently, the subjective possibility of revelation.[184] Here we are once more confronted with Barth's method of arguing from reality to possibility (above, Ch. I, 5 (1b)).

Having demonstrated that God is free for man in Jesus Christ, Barth goes on to show that man is free for God in the Holy Spirit. Contrary to tradition he designates the Holy Spirit as the Redeemer, the Lord, that is, who makes us free for God.[185] It has already been pointed out that the Holy Spirit as the eternal Spirit of love is the common factor uniting the Father and the Son in a communion of mutual love within the inner life of the Triune God and as the same Spirit is at work in the birth of Jesus by the Virgin Mary so that by

G

His creative power the new creation of the Godman Jesus
Christ came into being. In a similar way it is the same Spirit
who makes men, individual men, open and ready for God,
for His Word, for Jesus Christ, creating in them that faith
whereby they come to believe in Jesus Christ as the Son of
God and as their Lord and Master whom He, the Holy Spirit,
Himself reveals to them as such and thereby bringing about
that they too become a new creation, namely children of
God who know and love and praise God in His revelation.[186]

Thus revelation implies the creation by the Holy Spirit of
the 'new man' who is *capax Dei*. Consequently, in its objective aspect it can be received by man only in faith and therefore only by grace; again, in its subjective aspect it is on the
human side an event of faith. For in accordance with his
basic view that man, fallen man, is incapable of knowing God,
the world and man as they really are by his innate capacities and endowments Barth contends that there is no point
of contact for the Word of God in man as such but that this
point of contact has to be created by the work of the Holy
Spirit in man or rather is actually created thereby according
to the witness of Holy Scripture. Consequently, it is a theological point of contact and not an anthropological one. He
justifies this view by arguing that in the subjective revelation
of the objective revelation, that is, of the reality of Jesus
Christ, of His person and work, we are shown by the Holy
Spirit that without the latter's work in man we are not free
for God. The Holy Spirit shows us that we are sinners and
thus enemies of God's grace, and therefore cannot hear the
Word of God, that is to say, perceive, accept and obey it as a
Word from God unless the Holy Spirit, 'the Teacher of the
Word', enlightens us about it, instructs us in it, and persuades us that it concerns us directly and presently.[187] 'In
the Holy Spirit,' Barth says, 'we know that we cannot ascribe
to man any freedom of his own for God, any possibility of
his own to become the recipient of revelation.'[188] It is God
Himself who opens our eyes and ears for Himself and, in so
doing, He tells us that we cannot do it of ourselves, that of

ourselves we are blind and deaf. In his doctrine of man,[189] it
it true, Barth speaks of the unity of man in his creaturely
structure as the soul of his body as 'one of the natural points
of contact', and indeed the basic one, for the covenant of
grace made by God with man in Jesus Christ; he speaks there
also of man's capability of apprehending the God who meets
him and reveals Himself to him and of desiring, willing and
acting in response to that revelation. This teaching of his,
however, is not at variance with that on subjective revelation since, what Barth has in mind, is that man in his
creaturely structure is capable of responding to the creative
work of the Holy Spirit in him in a manner which has still to
be explained. As so often, Barth's proposition that there is
no point of contact in man as such has to be understood in a
qualified sense.[190]

Barth does not tell us how it comes to pass that there are
men who believe.[191] Arguing once more from reality to possibility he declares that we cannot account for the mode of
the Holy Spirit's working, which he describes as a mystery
and as a miracle of God's grace, but can only accept its result,
that is, man's faith, as a fact and for that reason as a possibility as well. We face, as he terms it, 'a necessary leap in
thought'[192] where the subjective reality of revelation in the
strict sense of the concept is already behind the man who believes. That leap in thought, he points out, is however not a
salto mortale since the leap from God to man has already taken
place in the outpouring of the Holy Spirit. Nor does it involve a theological irrationalism in view of the rational
character of the revealed Word of God.

Again, though the subjective reality of revelation is characterized by him as the work of the Holy Spirit, this does not
mean that man has no active part to play in it but that man's
active participation in it is merely the result of the prior
work of the Holy Spirit in man.[193] Man's participation in
the event of faith 'has nothing whatsoever to do with a
magical invasion of the interrelated totality of our physico–
psychical human nature by supernatural factors and forces'

but is achieved 'in man's own experience and activity, in that act of self-determination which we call our human existence'.[194] Though man is indeed confronted by something outside of himself and over against himself whereby his whole existence is determined, God does not quench man's ability, will and accomplishment; He only subordinates it to His own. The Holy Spirit only persuades and convinces man that the objective revelation, Jesus Christ, concerns him directly and presently and exists precisely for him, and man on his part apprehends this truth in the Holy Spirit by virtue of his own reasoning and, on the strength of his own decision, accepts it as true and valid for himself.[195] On the other hand, it is God's prior action in revelation, the reality of Jesus Christ and the revelation of that reality in the hearts of men by the work of the Holy Spirit in man, which both enables and determines man to take this decision and, consequently, to follow his Master and to obey and serve Him.[196]

The work of the Holy Spirit to which this result is due is characterized by Barth as man's liberation from blindness and bondage to sin. It consists in the creation of man's 'freedom' which is very different from what man regards as his freedom. This concept of man's freedom, which with Barth is once more a theological and not a philosophical one, plays a vital part in many aspects of his theology, especially in his ethics (below, Ch. IV). It is man's freedom *for* God, that is, his freedom to turn to God, to believe in Him and to obey, love and praise Him, in short, his freedom to be a child of God, a dimension which man, sinful man, does not possess of himself but which is created by the work of the Holy Spirit in man, enabling him to receive God's revelation in Jesus Christ in faith and to live by that faith.[197]

Here the question arises of why some believe and others refuse to believe though faith is said to be the work and gift of the Holy Spirit. Barth has no final answer to this question. In his view man's resistance to the work of the Holy Spirit in him belongs to what is described by him as the impossible and inexplicable, though very real, conduct of man; in other words, it belongs to the realm of the Nihil (see Ch. III, 4), whereas man's positive response is said to be the result of the work of the Holy Spirit. We shall see later on (Ch. VI) that Barth is here really begging the question. His important discussion of the Church as the 'area' in which the subjective revelation occurs can here only be referred to.[198] In it the life of the children of God for Jesus Christ's sake is described as being from the human viewpoint the reality of both the Church and the subjective revelation. Again, the unity of the objective and subjective revelation is safeguarded also by Barth's proposition that the Holy Spirit who creates the reality of subjective revelation is no other than the Spirit of the risen Christ.[199]

8. RELIGION

In his teaching on this subject-matter Barth sharply distinguishes between religion as a human activity and faith as that event in the life of man which is the work of the Holy Spirit in man and as such God's gift to man (above, par. 2). His criticism of religion, highly praised by Dietrich Bonhoeffer,[200] has been widely understood as the rejection of all human religion.[201] This, however, was never his view. Already in *Romans*,[202] for all its fierce onslaught on man's religion, he says, with true religion in mind, that religion is the unavoidable reflection in man's soul, in his experience, of the miracle of faith which has taken place in his soul. In the two sections of his *Church Dogmatics* (CD, I, 2, par. 17. 2, 3) on 'Religion as Unbelief' and on 'True Religion' he has made clear that two kinds of human religion exist of which he rejects the one, but not the other.[203]

The aforesaid misunderstanding is due partly to his unguarded language on religion in *Romans* and to his peculiar method of stating, for the sake of emphasis, a recognized truth first in unqualified form and of qualifying it afterwards, and partly to a misinterpretation of the ambiguous German term *Aufhebung* as used in the title of the section on religion in KD, I, 2, par. 17. This term has a twofold meaning, a negative one: 'abolition' and a positive one: 'exaltation',[204] and Barth uses it in both these connotations so that the title of CD, I, 2, par. 17, which at present reads 'The Revelation of God as the Abolition of Religion',[205] should have been rendered 'The Revelation of God as the Abolition *and* Exaltation of Religion'.[206] For, to put Barth's position as succinctly as possible, he is fighting against man-made and man-owned religion, which God's revelation in Jesus Christ has unmasked, and thereby abolished, as unbelief, and he is advocating the truth of the justification and sanctification of the religion of sinful man as manifested by that same revelation, in other words, the truth of the exaltation by that same revelation of religion to true religion as man's faithful and obedient response in thought (true religious knowledge), word (true worship) and deed (true Christian witness) to the objective reality of Jesus Christ, revealed to man in the subjective revelation of the Holy Spirit. Just as sinful human flesh was justified and sanctified and thus exalted by its assumption by the Son of God in His incarnation, so the religion of sinful man is justified and sanctified and thereby exalted by its enlightenment and direction through God's revelation in Jesus Christ. 'It is because we remember and apply the christological doctrine of the *assumptio carnis* that we can speak of the *Aufhebung* (= exaltation) of religion.'[207]

Because of man's sinfulness no human religion, not even the Christian religion, can be in itself and as such true religion; it can however become true religion, Christian religion can become true religion, from without, namely as a work of faith in and obedience to the divine revelation in Jesus Christ, and thus only by grace.[208] True religion, according to Barth, like justified man is 'a creature of grace'.[209] Here we encounter once more his actualistic mode of thought (above, Ch. I, 5 (3)), which makes it impossible for him to identify the Christian religion or Christianity with the Gospel.

Barth's deliberately provocative statement: 'religion is unbelief',[210] if considered in the light of what he says about true religion, attacks the man, the religious man, who imagines that he can reach out to God, that is, can know Him and can justify and sanctify himself by means of his own religious efforts (man-made religion), thus confusing his religion, his piety, with faith. Again, it attacks the man, the religious man, who imagines that he can transform God's revelation in Jesus Christ into religion and, therefore, into something which he can master so that he is able to handle that revelation as if he possessed and owned it (man-owned religion). Here man identifies revelation with religion, making it inoffensive and a means of his self-justification and self-sanctification. In both cases man, religious man, refuses to live by and from the grace of God which has been revealed to him in Jesus Christ through the power of the Holy Spirit and is continually granted to him afresh by God. Relying upon his own strength, he refuses to depend on that grace as the source, the basis and the meaning of his life in all its aspects including the religious one, and it is precisely this rebellion of man, of religious man, against God's grace in Jesus Christ which Barth characterizes as unbelief. For man shows by this behaviour that he believes in himself rather than in God.

Barth's intention here is not to pass a negative value-judgment. He claims that he is merely repeating God's judgment upon all man-made and man-owned religion as that judgment has been expressed in God's revelation in Jesus Christ.[211] The latter has critical significance also in so far as it tells man by the very fact of its occurrence that his attempt to know God and to justify and sanctify himself by his own religious efforts is futile; that God's revelation in Jesus Christ had to take place in order that there may be true religion and that, though revelation as a divine event, to be effective, must issue in religion as a human event, the latter, to be true religion, must ever again become true religion through God's constantly renewed revelation of His grace in Jesus Christ. For man, even Christian man, is and remains a sinner. To put the difference between religion as unbelief and true religion, as seen by Barth, in a nutshell: in the former man does the talking and thus shows that he does not believe; in the latter man listens to God's Word and thus shows that he believes; again, in the former man tries to live a religious life by his own resources, rejecting God's grace; in the latter he lives by faith and thus by and from grace; again, in the former the Christian revelation is explained in terms of religion, making it one of the world's religions; in the latter religion is explained in the light of the Christian revelation with the result that the Christian religion is marked off as the one and only true religion in so far as it lives by and from the grace of God in Jesus Christ.[212]

Barth's objection to the religionism of Neo-Protestantism from the eighteenth to the twentieth century is precisely this that it understood the Christian revelation in terms of religion and thus as one of many religions, though perhaps as relatively the best of all religions, thereby losing sight of the uniqueness of the Christian revelation and of its superiority over human religion, a superiority 'which does not allow us even to consider religion except in the light of revelation'.[213] To the extent that the Christian Church, confronted with the revelation and grace of God in Jesus Christ, recognizes and accepts the truth that its religion, because of the sinfulness of those who practise it, is in need of justification (forgiveness of sins) and sanctification and, consequently, lives by and from that grace in the power of the Holy Spirit, it is the place of true religion. For then, and only then, its religion is, or rather becomes, a work of faith in and obedience to God's revelation in Jesus Christ and thus true religion. The free grace of God in Jesus Christ is the ground and mystery of the truth of the Christian religion since that truth is enclosed in the one name of Jesus Christ as the very heart of the divine reality of revelation which alone constitutes the truth of the Christian religion.[214] The relationship between the name of Jesus Christ and the Christian religion in the sense of true religion is explained by Barth as the continual creation, election, justification and sanctification of the Christian religion by the free grace of God as that grace is continually revealed and granted afresh in and through the person and work of the crucified and risen Lord Jesus Christ.[215]

REFERENCES

[1] *Evangelical Theology in the 19th Century*, p. 55; IET, p. 12.

[2] CD, IV, 1, pp. 660 f.

[3] Ibid., p. 661.

[4] See above, Ch. I, 5 (3).

[5] CD, I, 1, p. 299.

[6] CD, IV, 3, p. 879; IET, pp. 37 ff.

[7] N. Micklem, *The Abyss of Truth* (1956), p. 5.

[8] See above, Ch. I, 3.

[9] *Anselm*, p. 171; CD, I, 1, pp. 11 ff.; IV, 3, pp. 183 ff.

[10] *Theology in Conflict* (1958), pp. ix, xxii and pp. 23 ff., 108 ff., 159.

[11] *Anselm*, pp. 15 ff., 28, 39; CD, I, 1, pp. 12, 17 ff., 314; IV, 3, pp. 846 ff.

[12] John Baillie, *The Sense of the Presence of God* (1962), p. 4.

[13] *Anselm*, p. 21.

[14] *Gifford*, pp. 25 f.

[15] CD, IV, 3, pp. 183 ff.

[16] *Romans*, pp. 287 f.; *Anselm*, p. 60; CD, I, 1, p. 31; IV, 3, pp. 847 ff.

[17] *Anselm*, 60.

[18] CD, IV, 3, pp. 846 ff., espec. 882.

[19] Ibid., p. 882; TT, pp. 62 f.

[20] *Dogmatics*, vol. I, pp. 3, 98 ff.

[21] *Systematic Theology*, vol. I, pp. ix f., 5 ff.

[22] CD, IV, 3, p. 849.

[23] Ibid., p. 848.

[24] Ibid., p. 882; TT, pp. 62 f.

[25] *Gifford*, p. 107; compare with this John Baillie's view (op. cit., p. 84), that it is not possible to argue with a total agnostic, and Alasdair Macintyre's statement in *Metaphysical Beliefs* (1957), p. 211: 'Belief cannot argue with unbelief; it can only preach to it.'

[26] E.g. *Gifford*, pp. 107 ff.; CD, IV, 1, pp. 740 ff.; IV, 3, p. 848.

[27] *Act and Being*, p. 102.

[28] CD, IV, 1, p. 742; L. Malevez, *The Christian Message and Myth* (ET 1958), p. 206, in his polemics against Barth's teaching on revelation, overlooks this point which establishes a definite relation between the Word of God and human reason.

[29] T. F. Torrance, Introduction to *Theology and Church*, p. 27; as to the epistemological status of faith compare also John Baillie, op. cit., pp. 60 ff.

[30] CD, I, 1, pp. 3 ff., 315 ff.

[31] *On Systematic Theology*, loc. cit., pp. 225 ff., espec. 228.

[32] *Gifford*, p. 6.

[33] *Natural Theology*, pp. 67 ff.

[34] *Gifford*, pp. 3 ff.

[35] CD, I, 1, pp. 147 f., 219, 448, 540; I, 2, pp. 123, 263 ff.; II, 1, pp. 76 ff., 85 ff., 162 ff., 215 ff., 453; IV, 1, pp. 79 ff.; IV, 2, pp. 100 ff.

[36] *Dogmatics*, vol. I, pp. 32 ff., 133 ff.; vol. II, pp. 21 ff., 26 ff.

[37] Ibid., vol. II, p. 23.

[38] *Systematic Theology*, vol. II, p. 16.

[39] CD, II, 1, p. 85.

[40] Ibid., p. 453.

[41] See further, G. C. Berkouwer, *The Triumph of Grace in the Theology of Karl Barth*, ET 1956, pp. 179 ff.

[42] CD, II, 1, pp. 79 ff.

[43] Ibid., p. 84; see also TT, 30.

[44] CD, IV, 1, p. 81.

[45] Ibid.

[46] See Ch. III, 6.

[47] CD, II, 1, p. 135.

[48] CD, IV, 2, p. 100.

[49] Ibid., p. 101.

[50] CD, IV, 2, pp. 100 ff.

[51] CD, IV, 1, p. 139.

[52] Ibid.

[53] See Ch. I, 5 (1, 3).

[54] Summa theol. I a qu. I art. 8 ad. 2.

[55] See Ch. III, 3.

[56] See Ch. III, 5.

[57] CD, II, 1, pp. 128 ff., espec. 161 ff.

[58] See further, T. F. Torrance, Introduction to Theology and Church, pp. 31 ff.; the same, Karl Barth, An Introduction to his Early Theology, 1910–1931, pp. 148 ff.; L. Malevez, The Christian Message and Myth, pp. 191 ff.

[59] See above, Ch. I, 3.

[60] Bultmann, pp. 120 f.

[61] On Systematic Theology, p. 226; CD, I, 1, p. 325; I, 2, p. 483; IV, 3, p. 849; TT, pp. 19 f.

[62] Dogmatics in Outline, pp. 65 f.; CD, II, 1, pp. 406 ff., espec. 432 ff.

[63] CD, II, 1, pp. 432, 439.

[64] CD, IV, 3, p. 882.

[65] CD, I, 1, p. 141; I, 2, pp. 715 ff., 727 ff.; Bultmann, p. 45; TT, p. 98.

[66] CD, I, 2, pp. 483, 715 f., 727 ff., 732, 735.

[67] CD, II, 1, pp. 322 ff., espec. 346 ff.

[68] Dogmatics in Outline, pp. 39, 47; Credo, pp. 183 ff.

[69] Above, par. 3.

[70] CD, I, 1, p. x.

[71] CD, I, 1, pp. 11 f., 279 f.; I, 2, pp. 270, 297, 471; II, 1, pp. 223 ff., 243; TT, p. 66; see also A. B. Come, An Introduction to Barth's Dogmatics for Preachers (1963), pp. 142 ff.

[72] CD, I, 1, p. 279.

[73] Dogmatics, vol. II, p. 24.

[74] See above, Ch. I, 5 (3).

[75] See below, Ch. III, par. 3, 5.

[76] See further, T. F. Torrance, Introduction to Theology and Church, pp. 8 f., 38 ff.; the same, Karl Barth, An Introduction to His Early Theology, 1910–1931, passim; Errol E. Harris, Revelation through Reason (1959), pp. 13 ff.

[77] See below, Ch. III, 3.

[78] CD, III, 4, p. 577.

[79] See below, Ch. III, 2.

[80] T. F. Torrance, Introduction to Theology and Church, pp. 39 f.

[81] CD, III, 1, pp. ix f.; see also below, Ch. III, 3.

[82] Credo, pp. 186 ff.; CD, I, 2, pp. 492 ff.; Barth is certainly not a fundamentalist, see next paragraph and TT, pp. 26 f., 41.

[83] Romans, pp. 6 ff.

[84] Ibid., p. x; CD, I, 1, pp. 284 ff.; IET, pp. 15 ff.

[85] Comp. CD, I, 1, pp. 98 ff.

[86] See above, Ch. I, 5 (3).

[87] Ch. I, 5 (1a).

[88] Dogmatics in Outline, pp. 17 f.; CD, I, 2, pp. 1 ff.; IET, pp. 22 f.

[89] CD, II, 1, pp. 172 ff.

[90] CD, IV, 3, p. 3.

[91] See below, Ch. III, 1.

[92] CD, I, 1, p. 60.

[93] Ibid., pp. 60 ff.

[94] CD, I, 1, p. 218.

[95] See below, Ch. III, 2.

[96] Op. cit., p. 119.

[97] CD, I, 1, pp. 98 ff.

[98] It may come as a shock to some of our readers that Jesus Christ is assumed by Barth to have spoken also to the prophets, but see below, Ch. III, 1.

[99] See above, Ch. I, 5 (3); Gifford, pp. 177 f.; CD, I, 1, pp. 79 ff., 98 ff., 122 ff., 284 ff.

[100] CD, I, 1, p. 124.

[101] Ibid., p. 104.

[102] Ibid., p. 136.

[103] Ibid.

[104] CD, I, 1, p. 189.

[105] CD, I, 1, pp. 184 ff.; II, 1, pp. 50 ff., 179 ff.

[106] CD, I, 1, p. 188; The German term Welthaftigkeit, here translated 'worldly form', means literally 'being fixed to the world'.

[107] CD, I, 1, pp. 184 ff.; I, 2, pp. 122 ff.

[108] CD, I, 1, pp. 198 ff.; see also above, par. 2.

[109] See above, par. 2.

[110] CD, I, 1, pp. 213 ff.

[111] Ibid., p. 282.

[112] Ibid., p. 280.

[113] Ibid., pp. 226 ff., 260 ff.

[114] Ibid., pp. 227 f.

[115] Ch. I, 5 (1b).

[116] Ch, I, 1, pp. 239 ff., espec. 252, 256 f.

[117] Ibid., I, 1, pp. 221, also 17 ff., 193, 259, 468; II, 1, pp. 21, 69 ff.; TT, p. 26.

[118] Ibid., I, 1, pp. 45 ff.

[119] Compare the surveys in Karl Barth, *Against the Stream*, pp. 205 ff.; John Baillie, *The Idea of Revelation in Recent Thought* (1956), pp. 3 ff.; N. Micklem, *The Abyss of Truth*, pp. 61 ff.

[120] CD, I, 1, pp. 124 ff., 333 ff.; I, 2, pp. 1 ff.

[121] *Systematic Theology*, vol. I, pp. 118 ff.

[122] *Against the Stream*, pp. 208, 211; CD, I, 1, pp. 127, 333 f.; I, 2, pp. 1 ff.

[123] *Against the Stream*, p. 211; CD, I, 1, p. 134.

[124] *Theology in Conflict*, pp. 112, 122.

[125] CD, I, 1, p. 334.

[126] CD, I, 1, p. 339.

[127] See below, Ch. III, 2.

[128] CD, I, 1, pp. 339 ff.; I, 2, pp. 1 ff., 203 ff.

[129] *Letters and Papers from Prison* (Second edition 1956), pp. 123, 126, 148 f.; see also E. Bethge, op. cit., p. 37; John D. Godsey, *The Theology of Dietrich Bonhoeffer* (1960), pp. 253, 276 ff.; Regin Prenter, *Dietrich Bonhoeffer und Karl Barths Offenbarungspositivismus* in *Die Mündige Welt*, vol. III (1960), pp. 11 ff.

[130] *Dogmatics*, vol. I, pp. 21,134; vol. II, pp. 22, 26 ff.

[131] CD, I, 2, pp. 304 ff.; II, 1, pp. 97 ff.

[132] *Credo*, p. 25; CD, I, 1, pp. 457 ff., 469 ff.

[133] *The Nature and Destiny of Man*, vol. I, pp. 142, 153.

[134] *The Universality of Christ* (1921) in *About Christ* (1962), p. 20.

[135] *Against the Stream*, pp. 217 ff.; CD, I, 1, pp. 124 ff.; I, 2, pp. 457 ff., 743 ff.

[136] CD, I, 1, p. 131.

[137] Ibid., pp. 16, 304 ff.

[138] *Credo*, pp. 179 f.; CD, I, 2, pp. 538 ff.

[139] Anselm, p. 152; CD, I, 2, p. 6.

[140] CD, I, 1, pp. 533 ff.; II, 1, pp. 51 ff.

[141] *Gifford*, pp. 27 ff.; CD, II, 1, pp. 3 ff.

[142] CD, II, 1, pp. 15 ff., 50 ff.; J. Brown, op. cit., pp. 150 ff.; T. F. Torrance, Introduction to *Theology and Church*, pp. 45 f.

[143] J. Brown, op. cit., p. 152.

[144] CD, II, 1, p. 16; see also CD, I, 1, pp. 12 f.

[145] Prof. G. T. Thomson in his Translator's Note to CD, I, 1, p. v; H. R. Mackintosh, op. cit., p. 300, concurs with this view, whereas R. S. Frank's brief and in part inaccurate outline of Barth's teaching on the Trinity (*The Doctrine of the Trinity* (1953), pp. 177 ff.) fails to do justice to the originality of that teaching.

[146] CD, I, 1, p. 438.

[147] Ibid., p. 346.

[148] Ibid., pp. 383 ff.

[149] N. Berdyaev, *The Destiny of Man* (1937), pp. 31 ff., 37 ff.; Gwilym O. Griffith, *Interpreters of Man*, p. 199.

[150] CD, I, 1, pp. 381, 516.

[151] Ibid., pp. 441 ff., 457 ff., 513 ff.

[152] Ibid., pp. 403 ff.

[153] Ibid., pp. 406 ff.

[154] CD, I, I, pp. 421 f., 452 f.; see also TT, pp. 47 f., 58 f.

[155] CD, I, 1, pp. 416 ff.

[156] Ibid., pp. 541 ff.

[157] Ibid., pp. 405, 416, 437 f.

[158] CD, I, 2, p. 25.

[159] CD, I, 1, p. 468.

[160] *Systematic Theology*, vol. I, pp. 53 ff.; vol. II, pp. 102 ff.

[161] CD, I, 2, pp. 132 ff.

[162] Ibid., pp. 10 ff.; see further, T. H. L. Parker, 'Karl Barth and the Fourth Gospel', in *Studies in the Fourth Gospel*, edited by F. L. Cross (1957), pp. 52 ff.

[163] CD, I, 1, p. 475.

[164] *Credo*, pp. 38, 63 ff.; CD, I, 2, pp. 10 ff.; II, 1, pp. 661 ff.; IV, 1, pp. 157 ff.; IV, 2, pp. 154 ff.

[165] CD, I, 2, pp. 122 ff.; IV, 1, pp. 132 ff.; IV, 2, pp. 51, 59 ff., 72 ff.

[166] CD, I, 2, pp. 20 f., 147 ff.

[167] Ibid., pp. 164 f.

[168] *Credo*, pp. 63, 68 ff.; CD, I, 2, pp. 172 ff.; IV, 1, pp. 207 ff. As to Barth's critical discussion of Mariology see CD, I, 2, pp. 138 ff.

[169] CD, I, 2, pp. 185 ff.

[170] Ibid., pp. 187 ff.

[171] Ibid., pp. 124 f.; see also IET, p. 29.

[172] *Gifford*, pp. 64 f.; CD, I, 2, pp. 2, 31 ff.; II, 1, pp. 517 f., 662 f.; IV, 1, pp. 134, 175 ff.

[173] CD, IV, 1, p. 177.

[174] Compare with this the critique of all Kenotic theories of the person of Jesus Christ by D. M. Baillie, *God Was In Christ* (1948), pp. 32, 94 ff. and John A. T. Robinson's concept of the Kenosis in *Honest to God* (1963), pp. 74 f. as Jesus' utter self-emptying of His own self as *man* (!).

[175] CD, I, 2, pp. 36 ff.; II, 1, pp. 516 f.; IV, 1, p. 180; TT, p. 64.

[176] CD, I, 2, pp. 40 ff., 147 ff.; TT, p. 68.

[177] CD, I, 2, pp. 155 ff.

[178] Ibid., p. 151.

[179] CD, III, 2, p. 552.

[180] CD, I, 2, pp. 28 ff.

[181] CD, I, 1, pp. 466 f.; I, 2, pp. 40 ff.

[182] CD, I, 1, p. 468.

[183] CD, I, 2, pp. 238 ff.

[184] Ibid., pp. 203 ff., 242 ff.

[185] *Credo*, p. 130; CD, I, 1, pp. 207 f., 513 ff.; I, 2, pp. 203 ff.

[186] CD, I, 1, pp. 513 ff., 556; I, 2, pp. 203 ff., 362 ff.

[187] CD, I, 1, pp. 271 ff., 516; I, 2, pp. 242 ff., 263 ff.

[188] CD, I, 2, p. 246.

[189] CD, III, 2, pp. 366 ff., 399 ff.

[190] L. Malevez, *The Christian Message and Myth*, pp. 122 f., overlooks this point in his criticism of Barth's denial of a point of contact.

[191] CD, I, 2, pp. 233 ff., 266 ff.

[192] Ibid., p. 234.

[193] Here attention must be drawn to a serious mistranslation in CD, I, 1, p. 518, the last but one line, where 'on our behalf' should read 'for our benefit', that is, being meant for us (comp. KD, I, 1, p. 475: *'für uns'*); otherwise, how could Barth speak of man's participation in revelation?

[194] CD, I, 2, p. 266; see also TT, p. 92.

[195] See above, Ch. II, 2; *Gifford*, pp. 108 f.; CD, I, 1, pp. 513 ff.; I, 2, pp. 236 ff., 257 ff., 265 ff.; J. Brown, op. cit., pp. 142, 145, 159 ff.

[196] CD, I, 1, pp. 535 f.

[197] CD, I, 1, pp. 513 ff., espec. 522 ff.; I, 2, pp. 203 ff.; J. Brown, op. cit., 164.

[198] CD, I, 2, pp. 210 ff., espec. 221 ff.

[199] Below, Ch. III, 1 and CD, I, 1, p. 518; IV, 2, pp. 319 ff.

[200] *Letters and Papers from Prison*, pp. 123, 126.

[201] N. Micklem, *The Abyss of Truth*, pp. 113 ff.; see also John

Baillie, *The Sense of the Presence of God*, pp. 177 ff., 189; might not Bonhoeffer's concept of a 'religionless Christianity' rest upon the same misunderstanding?

[202] Loc. cit., p. 129.

[203] Likewise Daniel Jenkins, *Beyond Religion*, p. 29.

[204] The German verb *aufheben* means both to abolish or annul and to raise or lift up, elevate, exalt; about the use of this term by Dietrich Bonhoeffer in its latter sense see John D. Godsey, *The Theology of Dietrich Bonhoeffer*, p. 57, note 29.

[205] CD, I, 2, p. 280.

[206] In that case John Baillie (op. cit., p. 180) might have been less surprised by Barth's teaching on 'true religion' in the final subsection of CD, I, 2, par. 17.

[207] CD, I, 2, p. 297.

[208] Ibid., pp. 325 ff.

[209] Ibid., p. 326.

[210] See further, Daniel Jenkins, op. cit., pp. 26 ff.

[211] *Gifford*, p. 106; CD, I, 2, pp. 297 ff., 337; see also II, 1, pp. 128 ff.

[212] CD, I, 2, pp. 326, 344 ff.

[213] Ibid., pp. 283 ff., 294 ff., espec. 295.

[214] Ibid., pp. 338 ff.; John Baillie's account of this teaching (op. cit., pp. 189 ff.) is not entirely accurate and the conclusions drawn therefrom cannot be accepted since Barth, in speaking of the name of Jesus Christ, thereby means the whole reality implied in that name, that is, the person and work of Jesus Christ.

[215] CD, I, 2, pp. 346 f.

III.—JESUS CHRIST, THE KEY TO THE UNDERSTANDING OF GOD, THE UNIVERSE AND MAN

1. THE PLACE OF JESUS CHRIST IN THEOLOGY

THE heading of this chapter, if considered by itself, may seem to advance an excessive claim. However, it describes accurately Barth's position in this matter. In fact, he has defined it thus himself[1] and, as will be indicated in the course of this chapter, has implemented this fundamental principle in his theology with a consistency and thoroughness unsurpassed in the history of Christian dogmatics. With him Jesus Christ is the bridge between God and the world, between God and man, in literally every respect, not only intellectually, that is, from the perspective of revelation, but also from the standpoint of election, creation, reconciliation and redemption. In contrast to Tillich's restricted view of Christology as a function of soteriology, Jesus Christ being confined to the role of the Bringer to mankind of the 'New Being' whereby man is saved from the old being,[2] Barth's theology, as already pointed out,[3] is wholly christological in that in it, generally speaking, Jesus Christ is made the point of departure of every theological proposition. Emphasizing the necessity of connecting all theological statements with that of Jn 1:14, Barth says: 'a church dogmatics must be christologically determined as a whole and in all its parts as surely as the revealed Word of God, attested in Holy Scripture and proclaimed by the Church, is its one and only criterion and as surely as this revealed Word of God is identical with Christ'.[4]

To Barth, as he argues in that part of his teaching on 'The Glory of the Mediator' (CD, IV, 3, par. 69) which is entitled

'The Light of Life',[5] Jesus Christ is the one great truth that
embraces every other truth. How did he arrive at this proposition which reflects Jesus's own saying in Jn 14:6? On
what grounds does he justify this tremendous concentration
on Jesus Christ as the one Word of God (above, Ch. II, 6),
as *the* revelation (ibid., 7), that reveals to man the whole
truth about God, the universe and man, a concept which
many of his critics[6] from their standpoint regard as too nar-
row since in their opinion God can and does reveal His truth
also in other ways? As so often, this divergence of views is
due, partly, to a different interpretation of the terminology in
question and, partly, to a different kind of approach to the
problem under discussion. To Barth, Jesus Christ and the
Gospel He proclaims mean something much more comprehensive than what his critics understand thereby; moreover,
his approach is theocentric and theological while theirs is
anthropocentric and historical. Whereas his critics, following
the traditional view, regard the Incarnation of the Word of
God as the beginning of the story of Jesus Christ and of the
Gospel, Barth's concept of that story and of the Gospel, in a
radical reversion of the traditional view, starts in eternity.
With him Jesus Christ and the Gospel originate with the
eternal decree (below, par. 2) of God before the creation of
the world to be not only man's God but to become Himself
man in the Godman Jesus Christ. For him that pre-temporal
divine decree is already in itself and as such an integral part
of the Good News which Jesus Christ proclaims to all men.
Thus his view on the significance of Jesus Christ for the
world as well as for mankind and on the meaning of the
Gospel He proclaims is quite different from that of his critics.
G. Wingren's ultimate objection,[7] endorsed by John Baillie,[7]
that Barth's teaching on Jesus Christ as the exclusive source
of man's knowledge of God is 'entirely unbiblical' is begging
the question since the latter too bases his teaching on a
thorough theological exegesis of the Bible.

To explain Barth's train of thought on this crucial point a
parable may be helpful which arises out of a survey of his

theological work as a whole and is supported by several of his own statements. His theology is like a vision dating from what may be termed the resurrection-period. It is as if he had walked with Jesus and His disciples during the forty days between Jesus Christ's resurrection from the dead and His ascension when Jesus no longer appeared to His disciples only as the man Jesus of Nazareth whom they had known in the flesh but, as the crucified and risen Lord Jesus Christ, was now truly revealed to them in the full majesty and glory of His Godhead. Then Barth had come to see as in a vision, a vision however based upon and corroborated by Holy Scripture and thus no mere speculation, that the thought of man, the thought of the Godman Jesus Christ and of His fellowship with men, had been with God from eternity. That experience, as if by means of a powerful searchlight, illuminated to Barth everything, not only retrospectively beyond the Incarnation right back to the innertrinitarian life of God and His eternal decree before time but also prospectively right to the end of time and beyond it. For it was then revealed to him that Jesus Christ is not only the eternal Son of God in His union with humanity but also the Lord of heaven and earth who in anticipation of what will take place in His eternal Kingdom at the final revelation of Him as the Lord of the cosmos and of all men has already now communion with individual men, with His disciples, and, further, that all this had been planned by God before time, in His eternity. It is for this reason that Barth stresses the decisive importance of the Easter event and of the forty days afterwards for our knowledge of God, the world and man.[8] In this connection we shall do well to remind ourselves of his teaching on the resurrection of Jesus Christ and His resurrection-appearances as objective events (above, Ch. I, 5 (2)), events that took place not merely in the faith of His disciples, as Bultmann maintains,[9] but outside of them and in conflict with their lack of faith.[10]

To the objections raised against the proposition that Jesus Christ is the one and only Word of God, the one and only

Light of life, objections with which he deals in detail,[11]
Barth's answer is that we have no option in this matter in
view of the person and work of Jesus Christ as attested in
Holy Scripture. In other words, the proposition that Jesus
Christ is the one Word of God is a christological one.[12] In
this connection the numeral adjective 'one' needs to be
qualified since Barth uses it in a specific sense. In speaking
of Jesus Christ as the one Word of God, he means thereby (a)
that the one comprehensive truth of God in its perfect unity
and wholeness is to be found only in Jesus Christ since He is
the one, the only Word of *God* which God Himself *directly*
speaks to man in and through His person; (b) that the various
truths to be found in the creaturely world do not express a
truth of their own but only witness to the truth of the one
Word of God; (c) that God's self-manifestation in Jesus Christ
is the one true Light of the one Truth whereas the lights of the
creaturely world are but refractions of this one true Light and
manifestations of the one Truth.[13] Hence, whenever Barth
speaks of Jesus Christ as the one and only Word of God or the
one and only Light of life, the words 'one and only' have to be
understood with this qualification in mind; on the other
hand, the other (partial) truths are made relative by and
subordinated to the one great truth in Jesus Christ as the one
Word of God.

In his teaching on the glory of God (CD, II, 1, par. 31. 3)
Barth sees the δόξα τοῦ θεοῦ expressed in the fact that God
'can and will not only exist but co-exist'.[14] To him all the
works of God are therefore works of this divine glory, and it
is Jesus Christ, the Son of God and the Son of Man, who for
him is the beginning of all the works of the divine glory as
He is their centre and their goal. For prior to all God's
action *ad extra* the self-declaration of God (to someone else)
as His glory has its true and original place in the eternal co-
existence of the Father and the Son by the Holy Spirit. The
Son in His relation to His Father is the eternal archetype and
prototype of God's glory in His outward manifestation, in
God's co-existence with another, with man, in the Godman

H

Jesus Christ and through Him with all men.[15] The striking feature of this teaching, in our present context, is that Barth is able to speak already at this point not only of the Son of God but of Jesus Christ. However, we must not forget that with Him the eternal Son of God is the Subject of the God-man Jesus Christ (above, Ch. II, 7 (3)). Moreover, he claims that Jesus Christ—and that includes His humanity—and in Jesus Christ man himself was with God from eternity, namely in God's thought and will.[16]

For a fuller explanation of this contention we shall have to await the discussion of Barth's doctrine of God's election of grace (below, par. 2). According to that doctrine the eternal decree of God before the creation of the world, already refer-red to in various contexts, constitutes the basis of all reality outside the being of the Triune God. Consequently, Jesus Christ as the Elect of God, in whom all men are elected to fellowship with God, and thus (in and with Jesus Christ) man himself have in this decree their basic reality.[17] It is in this sense and for this reason that Barth regards Jesus Christ as the very beginning of all the ways and works of God *ad extra* and of His glory, describing Him as the first thought and will of God, the first and eternal Word of God, and characterizing Him as the content and form of the (first) divine thought of grace, will of grace, and decree of grace before the creation of the world.[18] Again, it is in this sense and for this reason that, for instance, he can say that Jesus Christ has called the Old and the New Testaments into exist-ence which witness to the expectation and recollection respec-tively of the revelation, that is, of Jesus Christ.[19] Paradoxical as this statement may appear, seeing that the Godman Jesus Christ did not come into being until the birth of Jesus of Nazareth, it makes sense if we take into account Barth's teaching that in the eternal election of God before time Jesus Christ, and in and with Him man, is the first, that is, the primary object and content of the principal and basic will of God, and that the Old and the New Testaments testify to this Jesus Christ either in expectation or in recollection.[20]

2. The Electing God

In accordance with the special path to knowledge trodden in his theology (above, Ch. II, 2) Barth rejects as inadmissible the question of whether there is a God and even denies the need of proving that there is one. 'God is known through God and through God alone.' [21] He Himself has revealed Himself to man in His Word, in Jesus Christ. Hence Barth also refuses to enquire whether God is actually known and whether He can be known. His starting-point is the fulfilment of the knowledge of God in Jesus Christ. Consequently, he states that God *is* and that He is actually known to us in and through the person and work of Jesus Christ and therefore, according to the argument from reality to possibility (above, Ch. I, 5 (1b)), can be known by us. [22]

This knowledge is knowledge of faith (above, Ch. II, 2), demanding man's love, trust, obedience and service (above, Ch. I, 5 (1c)), and, as the work of the Holy Spirit in man, is born of grace (above, Ch. II, 7 (4)). Again, it is not only subjective (man's) knowledge but is also objective knowledge: because the Triune God knows Himself directly in primary objectivity in that the Father knows the Son and the Son the Father in the unity of the Holy Spirit, He is and can be indirectly known as such by man in secondary objectivity (as a separate object) in and through the person and work of His Son Jesus Christ. [23]

Again, it is concrete knowledge, knowledge of the Triune God (above, Ch. II, 7 (2)), and even more concretely knowledge of God in His union with man in Jesus Christ and therefore knowledge of God both in His Godness, that is, in His divine majesty and freedom as the Lord, and in His humanity, that is, in His turning to man in the Godman Jesus Christ. Thus it is the knowledge of God's capacity to be in His one Person both transcendent and immanent, both the Lord (Son of God) who in the man Jesus of Nazareth became a servant and the servant who as the true, the royal, man was exalted to the right hand of His Father in His resurrection

and ascension and thus became the Lord in that from then
onwards God, the Triune God, is eternally God in this
association of His divine nature with the human nature of
the crucified and risen Jesus Christ.[24] This concreteness of
Barth's concept of God is of fundamental importance for his
theology as a whole; it dominates every aspect of it, in particular his teaching on the Reality (CD, II, 1, pp. 257 ff.) and
Perfections (CD, II, 1, pp. 322 ff.) of God. At the root of it is
his proposition that God's being cannot be separated from
His acting since God as the object of our knowledge of God
creates His own precedence by His self-revelation in Jesus
Christ. The latter determines not only who He is and what
He is but also how we must think of Him. We know about
God exclusively as the One who acts upon us. He is who He
is in the act of His revelation, the personal, the living God
who does not want to be without man and in and through
Jesus Christ is not without man; the God who in the freedom
of the Lord and thus of His own free will and by His free
grace seeks and creates fellowship between Himself and us in
Jesus Christ and thus loves us because from eternity He is in
Himself, that is, without us, the loving God in the mutual
love of the Father and of the Son in the unity of the Holy
Spirit.[25] Hence Barth rejects any abstract idea of God, any
idea of God as the impersonal Absolute, the Supreme Good
(*summum bonum*), the World-Spirit or the World-Cause for
instance, and also refuses any contemplation of God's being
in abstraction from His real work and action. It is chiefly,
though not exclusively, for this reason that he is utterly
opposed to the doctrine of the *analogia entis* (above, Ch. II, 3)
which in his view, in complete disregard of the reality of
God as the latter is actually revealed to us in the person and
work of Jesus Christ, splits up God's one undivided Person
in a being of God in general and in His attributes and actions
in particular.[26] It is for the same reason that he prefers to
speak of the 'reality' of God, a concept that holds together
God's being and His act.[27]

Since in Jesus Christ it is once for all established that God is not without man, God's Godness, rightly understood, includes His humanity.[28] In Barth's mature theology, in contrast to *Romans* (above, Ch. I, 3), the humanity of God, the fact that He is a God who is not only for us but in Jesus Christ is also with us, is thrown into sharp relief, both for its own sake and in order to explain the true character of the Godness of God, of His divine nature. For the latter has found its supreme expression in what took place in the birth, life, death and resurrection of His Son Jesus Christ. 'God could not be more glorious as God,' says Barth, 'than in this inconceivable humiliation of Himself to man and the no less inconceivable exaltation of man to Himself.'[29] Again, speaking of Jesus Christ as very God, he says: 'It is in the light of the fact of His humiliation that on this first aspect [as very God] all the predicates of His Godhead, which is the true Godhead, must be filled out and interpreted.'[30] In his address (1949) on 'The Christian Message and the New Humanism',[31] Barth even speaks of the humanism of God, of His lovingkindness towards man in Jesus Christ, and characterizes it as the essence of the Christian message.

Nevertheless, God's Godness is with him still the first and fundamental thing to be said of God since it is God Himself in the second mode of His being as the Son of God who in Jesus Christ is the Subject, speaking and acting with the authority of the sovereign Lord. Hence, though in Barth's present doctrine of God, God in view of the Godman Jesus Christ is no longer exclusively 'the Wholly Other', thereby answering past criticisms that according to that teaching God has nothing in common with man, God is for him still 'the Wholly Other' in the twofold sense that as the eternal Lord and Creator of the universe He is essentially different from mortal man as His creature and that, though He is the Lord, He is at once the Suffering Servant.[32] In that He has this latter form, Barth argues, God is for us the Wholly Other, the strange God; for that strange form contradicts man's natural feelings and thoughts concerning God.[33]

As Barth's concrete concept of God is the starting-point of

his teaching on the reality and the perfections[34] of God, that teaching exhibits a thoroughly graphic character. Unlike the teaching of the scholastics it is neither shackled by the definitions of abstract philosophical concepts nor is it compelled to employ Procrustean methods to adapt it to these definitions. On the contrary, the latter, as previously pointed out (above, Chs. 1, 5 (1a); II, 4) receive their meaning and content from Barth's concrete concept of God, based on God's self-revelation in Jesus Christ, and thereby, at least some of them, in a startling fashion assume a new meaning and content. Thus the teaching in question manifests both a freedom of style and a closeness to the biblical picture of God which impart to it a grandeur and beauty of its own.

We can here only refer to this teaching in which God's being is defined (1) as His being as the One who loves and (2) as His being in freedom.[35] This twofold definition of the one and undivided nature of God subsequently determines the whole structure of Barth's doctrine of God's perfections in that the latter are said to be either those of the divine loving or those of the divine freedom, God, the Triune God in His three modes of being as Father, Son and Holy Spirit, being Himself in His one undivided nature all these perfections and being each of them wholly so that in each of these several perfections the others are manifested as well.[36] In other words, He is (perfections of the divine loving) wholly gracious and holy, merciful and righteous, patient and wise; again, He is (perfections of the divine freedom) wholly one and omnipresent, constant and omnipotent, eternal and glorious.

With this teaching we have not yet reached the end of Barth's doctrine of God. To be truly Christian, the latter, in his view, has to include another aspect of the reality of God. That aspect is manifested in the fact, revealed in Jesus Christ, that God stands in a definite relationship *ad extra* to another.[37] This relationship is viewed by Barth as belonging to the Person of God as such, that is, to His reality, and therefore to the doctrine of God in the narrower sense of

this concept, in as much as it rests upon a distinct attitude
of God which, inherent in the very nature of God as the One
who loves in freedom, is expressed in His free and gracious
decision before the creation of the world and of man to unite
Himself in the person of His eternal Son with man in the
man Jesus of Nazareth and in Him and through Him with
the people represented by Him and, consequently, to determine Himself, that is, to elect Himself to fellowship with man
and man to fellowship with Himself, and to do so quite concretely in the person of Jesus Christ.

Here we have arrived at Barth's doctrine of God's election
of grace (CD, II, 2, par. 32–35), the doctrine of God as the
One who from and to all eternity is the Electing God in the
aforesaid concrete sense. According to this teaching the
Christian God is this God or He is not God at all. It is no
exaggeration to say that the heart of Barth's theology beats
in this doctrine in which he radically departs from all past
and present teaching on predestination, above all from
Calvin's doctrine of predestination. Contrary to everything
which has been taught about this subject-matter so far,
Barth describes this doctrine as the sum of the Gospel 'because of all words that can be said or heard it is the best'.[38]

Again, he assigns to it a pre-eminent place in his *Church
Dogmatics* in that, as God's predestination not merely of man
but, originally and primarily, of Himself, he makes it an
integral part of his doctrine of God,[39] thus giving it precedence
over the doctrine of providence and even over the doctrine
of creation, which in their turn are bound to be decisively
influenced by this sequence. In the opinion of other theologians it belongs either to the doctrine of providence (Thomas
Aquinas) or to the doctrine of creation (Calvin).[40] Breaking
new ground in obedience to what he had discovered in his
meditation upon the witness of the Bible to Jesus Christ,[41]
his theological exegesis of that witness leads him to transfer
the crucial point of the *Heilsgeschichte* from the Incarnation
of the Word of God to eternity and to find it in an eternal
decree of God before time.[42] This eternal decree, in other

words, God's eternal election of grace which is ultimately grounded in God's innertrinitarian love (above, Ch. II, 7 (2)) and as God's free grace in Jesus Christ represents itself as an overflowing of that love, is for Barth the eternal beginning and the eternal basis of all the ways and works of God *ad extra* and therefore, as will subsequently be shown, in Jesus Christ. At the same time it is for him an expression of God's eternal, free and unchanging grace towards man. For its precise meaning is that in it God resolved once for all to determine Himself in Jesus Christ for *sinful* man and *sinful* man for Himself and therefore to take upon Himself in Jesus Christ the rejection with all its consequences which sinful man deserves, while man, sinful man, is elected by Him in Jesus Christ to participation in His own glory.[43]

This decree, or rather the doctrine of God's election of grace as a whole, is thus glad tidings, pure Gospel, and not, as in Luther's and Calvin's teaching on double predestination, a mixed message of joy and terror, of salvation and damnation. It does not confront us, as in the teaching of the latter, with a *decretum absolutum*, whereby according to the inscrutable will of an absolute God, a *Deus nudus absconditus*, mankind either before the Fall (Supralapsarians) or after the Fall (Infralapsarians) is divided into those who are elected for salvation and those who are rejected and, consequently, are destined to eternal damnation. On the contrary, it presents us with a *decretum concretum*, revealed to us and therefore known to us in the person and work of Jesus Christ, whereby God in the overflow of His love and in the freedom of His grace determined within Himself in His eternity before time and space, as we know them, that in His Son He would be gracious towards man even though man would rebel against Him and, therefore, in Jesus Christ would submit in man's place and for man's salvation to the punishment of suffering and death which sinful man deserves.[44]

Barth's ultimate objection to the concept of a *decretum absolutum*, in particular to Calvin's teaching on double predestination, is that in the last analysis and contrary to God's self-revelation in Jesus Christ it tears God and Jesus Christ asunder and thereby loses sight both of the true nature of God as a loving God and of the election which has actually taken place in Jesus Christ.[45] He also regards it as a serious mistake on the part of the Reformers that in their teaching on predestination they have made the election of individuals their first and ultimately exclusive concern whereas in his view the original and primary object of God's election of grace is Jesus Christ. The people who, called by Jesus Christ, believe in Him, in other words, His Church which is His body, are elected in Him and through Him. Finally, there are also individuals who through the witness of the Church to Jesus Christ are brought to faith in Him. Hence with Barth the order of predestination is an entirely different one. The election of individuals is for him only the last problem of the doctrine of predestination, namely the *telos* of the election of the community of God (Israel and the Church), whereas the election of Jesus Christ is its first problem.[46]

What is Barth's argument in favour of this order of predestination? How does he justify his proposition that Jesus Christ is the basis of the doctrine of election?[47] Above all, where does he find the eternal decree of God which for him is the beginning of all the ways and works of God *ad extra*? His starting-point is once more the Word of God, and the Word of God as addressed to man is Jesus Christ (above, Ch. II, 6). In Jesus Christ, above all in His divine-human nature, the meaning of God's election is revealed. For that which has taken place at the very centre of the divine self-revelation, that is, in Jesus Christ, in His person and work, is, seen in the light of His resurrection, God's election. As the eternal Son of God who became man in the man Jesus of Nazareth, suffered and died on the Cross that sinful man may forever have fellowship with God, Jesus Christ is Himself the eternal decree or rather the realization of that resolve of God within Himself in His eternity before the creation of the world which is termed the eternal decree of God. It is only in Jesus Christ and through Him that God could carry out and has carried out His eternal plan with man, His eternal election of Himself to fellowship with man and of man to fellowship with Himself, and it is for this reason that Jesus Christ is the original and primary object of God's election, God's first and eternal thought and will in His election.[48]

The main arguments advanced in support of this proposition can be summarized as follows:[49] (1) from eternity God not only willed to co-exist with man but in His humility, and because He is merciful, also willed to become Himself man in the man Jesus of Nazareth; (2) it is only by becoming Himself man and thus being the God who is not only for us but in Jesus Christ is with us that God could give concrete reality and effectiveness to His promise 'I will be your God' and to His command 'Ye shall be my people'; (3) only Jesus Christ as the true man, who was without sin and rendered perfect obedience, was and is God's faithful partner in God's covenant of grace with man, the fulfilment of which is the eternal purpose of creation (below, par. 3); (4) only in Jesus Christ, in His person and work, God's covenant of grace with man, broken by the sin of man, could be and is restored for the eternal benefit of all men; (5) only Jesus Christ, His person and His work of reconciliation, could be and is God's perfect answer to human sin, safeguarding God's faithfulness both to Himself and to man (below, par. 6). Barth contends that these thoughts and intentions had been with God from eternity, that from the very beginning they had constituted an integral part of God's eternal plan with man.[50] This shows that with him Jesus Christ is neither an afterthought of God, some sort of emergency solution in the face of man's actual sinfulness, nor merely God's retort to human sin. On the contrary, he claims that God willed and created the world primarily for the sake of Jesus Christ, in whose person and work God's positive will in His relationship with man, namely His fellowship with man as God's faithful covenant-partner, would find and has found its perfect fulfilment, whereas all other men, because of sin, could have and actually have fellowship with God only in Jesus Christ and through Him.[51]

To Brunner's anthropocentric-historical objection [52] that it is inconceivable that all men, 'even those who lived thousands of years before Jesus', should have their being in the history of Jesus, that the history of human existence should derive from that of the man Jesus, Barth gives the theocentric-theological answer, with God's eternal decree in mind, that in the history of Jesus we have to do with the reality which underlies and precedes all other reality as the first and eternal Word of God.[53] Again, contrary to the traditional teaching of the Christian Church, Barth claims, as indicated in the afore-mentioned arguments and expounded in his doctrine of reconciliation (CD, IV, 1, pp. 46 ff.), that the thought of sinful man's reconciliation with God in Jesus Christ and of God's fellowship with sinful man, thereby made possible for Him and for man, was in the mind of God before the world and man were created and thus even before sin became a reality. The unparalleled precedence thereby given to the idea of reconciliation over creation and sin has to be seen in the light of Barth's teaching on creation (below, par. 3), the Nihil (below, par. 4) and reconciliation (below, par. 6) before its true meaning can be grasped.

Jesus Christ is both the Electing God and the elected man.[54] He is the Electing God as the eternal Son of God who in obedience to God's eternal decree before time, namely in obedience to the Word spoken to Him by His Father within the innertrinitarian life of God and accepted by Him as the Son in the mutual love of the Holy Spirit which unites Him with His Father, elected Himself to become the Son of Man in the man Jesus of Nazareth and to take upon Himself by His passion and death on the Cross the rejection which should have been the lot of sinful man. He is the Electing God also because those who are represented by Him are elected in Him and through Him.

At the same time he is the elected man in that as the man Jesus of Nazareth he lives the perfect life of the true man which God has willed for man as His covenant-partner, in everything depending upon the grace of His heavenly Father and rendering to Him that perfect obedience which is supremely expressed in Jesus' prayer at Gethsemane (Mk. 14:36). Because He, and He only, is this man, He is not only the first of the elect, let alone one of the elect, but *the* Elect and as such is exalted to eternal union with His Father in heaven, whereas all other men are elected in Him and through Him since it is He, and He alone, who enables them to stand before God as those who, though they are still sinners, yet are justified by faith in Him and as such are represented by Him.

Barth too teaches a double predestination which however is quite different from the one taught by the Reformers. He finds it in the twofold aspect which the election of Jesus Christ presents. In Jesus Christ, as revealed in His person and work, God elected Himself for rejection, damnation and death, but sinful man for election, blessedness and eternal life. In other words, the predestination that has taken place in Jesus Christ has the twofold content that God willed to lose in order that man may gain.[55] In the freedom of His grace God elected in Jesus Christ the lost man, the sinner, who is pardoned because God willed to suffer and die in his place. Hence in this double predestination God's Yes and God's No is expressed. But whereas His Yes is intended for man, whom according to His eternal plan with man He has graciously elected for fellowship with Himself in spite of man's sinfulness, He has chosen the No, the rejection, for Himself. There is, Barth teaches,[56] but one who is rejected by God and that is Jesus Christ who in His twofold capacity as the Son of God and as the Son of Man submitted to this rejection of His own free will and in obedience to God's eternal decree by sacrificing Himself on the Cross for the salvation of all men. Thus Jesus Christ is both the Elect of God and the only rejected.

Logically, this latter position would entail the doctrine of the *apokatastasis*, the teaching of universal salvation. However, believing in a higher divine logic which surpasses the logic of finite human mind, Barth maintains in view of the freedom of the divine grace and on scriptural grounds that the question of whether or not ultimately all men will be saved must remain an open one.[57] If this is true, one might wonder why in that case he feels justified to speak of Jesus Christ as the only rejected, and one might ask whether we have here another example of his peculiar method first to make an unqualified statement and to qualify it afterwards. However, as his teaching on 'The Determination of the Rejected' [58] and on 'The Perdition of Man' [59] shows, the meaning of the proposition of Jesus Christ as the only rejected is the limited one that Jesus Christ is the only one who from eternity was intended to suffer the penalty of death, whereas by his vicarious sacrificial death the way to eternal salvation would be, and actually has been, opened to all men; in other words, the sins of the latter, because of the forgiveness of sin offered in Jesus Christ, no longer necessarily and un-unavoidably result in rejection. Thus, from eternity, God's will in Jesus Christ is directed towards the salvation of all men 'in intention';[60] rejection cannot again become the portion of those who, having heard the call of Jesus Christ, believe in Him and thus, through faith in Him, become the children of God.

Of those who do not believe in Him no more can be said in Barth's view than that they too are determined to hear the Gospel of Jesus Christ and with it the promise of their election and thereby to come to faith in Him, which is the goal of man's election in Jesus Christ.[61] The Christian community can only testify to this promise, and this is the service to which it is constantly called in respect of every human being.[62] For all men are elected in Jesus Christ, and the difference between the elect and other men merely consists in the fact that the former, by the grace of God and in the power of the Holy Spirit, actually live the life of the elect; in other words, their life as the elect is only the fulfilment of their election.[63] As to Barth's actualistic teaching on the divine predestination as a living act, an event, an eternal occurrence, and his uncompromising rejection of any idea of synergism in the doctrine of God's election of grace see CD, II, 2, pp. 180 ff.

3. COVENANT AND CREATION

In view of the source and criterion of Barth's theology we shall not expect him to base his doctrine of creation on either natural science or philosophy. The origin and the purpose of creation are not legitimate objects of natural science, be it cosmology or cosmogony, and philosophy can only speculate on them.[64] 'There can be no scientific problems, objections or aids in relation to what Holy Scripture and the Christian Church understand by the divine work of creation.'[65] Philosophy's limitation is well illustrated in Barth's analysis of Descartes' *cogito ergo sum*,[66] where in the context of his discussion of the reality of man's existence he argues that philosophy can never break through the circle of human thinking (*cogitare*) and penetrate to the region of reality (*esse*).[67]

As a theologian Barth is concerned with the problem of whether and, if so, in what manner God and the origin of the universe and of man are related to each other. Hence, his doctrine of creation is wholly theological, being exclusively based on God's Word (above, Ch. II, 2, 6) and, consequently, on God's revelation in Jesus Christ (ibid., 7); and this signifies that it is an article of faith.[68] To the materialist and the atheist this approach may appear to be entirely unrealistic. However, since God has actually revealed Himself to man in Jesus Christ, this revelation confronts man with the supreme Reality and thus with the Source of every other reality. The same revelation also reveals the origin and the purpose of creation. Here we have the immediate point of departure of Barth's doctrine of creation. For with him it is not the First but the Second Article of the Creed which is the key to this doctrine; in other words, with him Jesus Christ is that key. It is in Jesus Christ and through Him that we know

about God as the Creator of heaven and earth and man as
His creature and about the purpose of creation.[69]

Barth argues at length that from every angle Jesus Christ
is the key to the mystery of creation. He claims in particular
that, as in the person of Jesus Christ God and man meet in
that the Son of God assumed human nature in Him, thereby
becoming a creature and calling God His Father, we learn
therefrom that neither God nor man is alone, that there is
a sphere in which God acts and reveals Himself apart from
His own sphere, and that there is someone upon whom and
with whom He acts and to whom and through whom He
reveals Himself; again, that man exists after his own fashion
by the will of God and, consequently, that God is his Creator
and therefore is the Creator of heaven and earth as well. The
person and work of Jesus Christ moreover explain the purpose
for which the world and man were created (see below).

Thus it is in Jesus Christ that God Himself has revealed the
relationship between God, the universe and man and has done
so in the most direct, most effective and most certain manner.
No theologian has criticized Barth more severely on account
of his radical reversion of the traditional teaching according
to which creation is treated separately from and prior to the
person and work of Jesus Christ than G. Wingren.[70] But the
latter is unable to do justice to Barth's teaching on creation
since, on account of his narrower concept of the Gospel as
God's answer to human guilt and bondage,[71] he looks at
creation in separation from the Gospel, whereas Barth views
it in the light of his teaching on God's election of grace in
Jesus Christ (above, par. 2). Moreover, in accusing Barth of
making man and his knowledge the centre of his teaching on
Jesus Christ as the key to creation,[72] Wingren overlooks that
it is God and His revelation in Jesus Christ—and this includes
God's entire work in and through Jesus Christ—which occupies the centre of that teaching, whereas man is but the
recipient of God's revelation.

Barth's teaching on Jesus Christ as the key to the mystery
of creation is most closely connected with his teaching on

election, reconciliation and redemption and cannot be properly understood apart from the latter teaching. For in his view all the works of God *ad extra* are integral parts of the one eternal will and plan of God which took shape in His eternal decree before time (above, par. 2) and was designed to be executed in and through the person of Jesus Christ, the eternal Son of God who in the unity of the Holy Spirit proceeding from the Father and from the Son and for the purpose of the execution of that plan elected Himself from eternity in obedience to the will of His Father to become man in the man Jesus of Nazareth and to suffer and die in the place and for the sake of all other men that they might be saved. All God's works in creation, reconciliation and redemption are thus but the one work of God's free grace in Jesus Christ and in their totality represent the realization of His eternal decree before time. Consequently, creation is rooted in that decree, which is its eternal basis and in which, so to speak, God's future works of creation, reconciliation and redemption are anticipated, namely in God's thought and will. Moreover, as pointed out (above par. 2), they were so anticipated in Jesus Christ as God's original and primal object in His election of grace. In that the eternal Son of God is said to have co-operated with His Father in the aforenamed manner in order that the eternal decree of God be worked out, Barth's doctrine of creation is intrinsically trinitarian in its ontology. It draws in particular a telling analogy (*analogia relationis*) between the creative innertrinitarian relationship in God Himself and God's creative relationship to the world and man, God the Father, on the one hand, pro-creating Himself from eternity in His Son and with His Son being from eternity the origin of Himself in the Holy Spirit and, on the other hand, as the Creator being the Author of every reality that is distinct from Himself.[73]

Again, Barth claims that God's covenant of grace with man and creation are strictly linked to each other in Jesus Christ. This is another striking feature of his teaching on creation which is based on an extensive theological exegesis of the two creation-narratives in Gen. chs. 1 and 2 [74] and can be summed up in the twofold proposition that creation is the external basis of God's covenant of grace with man and that this covenant is the internal basis of creation. [75]

How does he arrive at this startling conclusion which from the perspective of God's eternal decree before time gives His covenant with man, or rather the covenant-idea, precedence over creation, and what is its precise meaning? God willed, we saw, from eternity to become man in Jesus Christ and to have in Him and through Him fellowship with sinful man. To achieve this end, there was needed, first, a place where this history could be enacted and, secondly, a covenant between God and man in the framework of which God's fellowship with man and man's fellowship with God could be actualized in accordance with God's will for man and therefore in conformity with a definite order ordained by God. Consequently, creation sets the stage for the execution of the history of God's covenant of grace with man, which has its eternal beginning in God's eternal decree before time. In other words, creation functions as the external basis of the covenant. The fulfilment of the covenant, on the other hand, is the eternal positive will of God, and the creation of the universe and of man has no other purpose than to serve this end. Hence, the fulfilment of God's covenant of grace with man is the eternal purpose of creation, that is to say, this covenant, its history, its fulfilment, is the internal basis of creation. This latter proposition has far-reaching consequences for Barth's teaching on creation as a divine blessing (below, par. 4).

As the eternal purpose of creation, the fulfilment of the covenant, in other words, its history, is, as pointed out elsewhere (above, Ch. I, 5 (2b)), the essential theme of history, the true history (*Heilsgeschichte*), in and by which all other history is determined. [76] Again, this covenant was instituted and established in Jesus Christ as the eternal thought and will of God before time, as the first and eternal Word of God in His election of grace before time, because in this free act

I

of God's election of grace there is already present, presumed and assumed into unity with His own existence as God the existence of that man whom He intends and loves from the very first and in whom He intends and loves all other men, of that man in whom He wills to bind Himself with all other men and all other men with Himself.[77] In the Triune God's eternal decree before time His covenant of grace with man was instituted and established between the Father and the Son as the One who was to become man in the fulness of time and thus, in intention and by anticipation, in Jesus Christ. He is the One who, because He was without sin, was and is God's one faithful covenant-partner, whereas all other men, because of sin, can be God's covenant-partners only in Jesus Christ and through Him (below, par. 6). Thus only by Jesus Christ and in Him God's covenant of grace with man is fulfilled. Hence, Jesus Christ is not only the Elect of God but also God's one true covenant-partner. The covenant is in fact but another aspect of God's election of grace in that the latter aims at the establishment of fellowship between God and man within the framework of a covenant and does so originally and basically in Jesus Christ. Again, God is not only the Electing God (above, par. 2) but also the covenant-God whose very nature as the One who loves in freedom leads Him, not by any necessity but in the overflow of His love and thus by His own free and gracious will, to elect Himself to partnership with man and man to partnership with Himself.[78] Jesus Christ, on the other hand, is the fulfilment of God's covenant of grace with man in the twofold sense that in Him God and man are united in the most intimate and most perfect fellowship and that He alone, as the true man, is the faithful covenant-partner of God.[79]

4. THE YES OF GOD AND THE NIHIL[80]

In the context of his doctrine of creation and on the basis of his major premiss of Jesus Christ as the key to the understanding of God, the universe and man Barth treats the categories of good and evil and their relationship to each other, in particular the problem of theodicy, in a fresh, original, and concrete way, which also enables him to view certain past and present trends in philosophy from a new angle. With him the key-note not merely of his teaching on election, creation and reconciliation but of his theology in general is God's unrestricted Yes to His good creation, spoken in Jesus Christ, in His person and work. In fact, Barth's entire theological labours are directed towards making this Yes understood and intelligible.

It is true, God's Yes is not without His No, pronounced in Jesus Christ's sacrificial death upon the Cross on everything which is evil. However, this No, Barth teaches,[81] is but the reverse of God's Yes to His good creation in that the latter implies His No to whatsoever is antagonistic to His good creation and for that reason is evil. God's No is therefore spoken not for its own sake but for the sake of His Yes, namely for the sake of the preservation and continuance of His good creation in which that which is evil has no part. Thus His Yes and His No must be viewed together since neither of them can be properly understood apart from the other.

To characterize the forces of evil that are the enemies of God's good creation, such as chaos and darkness, sin and death,[82] Barth coined the term *das Nichtige* = the Nihil.[83] He derived this term from his interpretation of the self-manifestation and self-revelation of the living Christ.[84] In that Jesus Christ, according to the witness of Holy Scripture, is the crucified and risen Lord, He has proved Himself to be the Victor not only in the moral, but also in the physical and cosmic sense. For by His death and resurrection He has triumphed over sin, evil and death and thereby has demonstrated the ultimate powerlessness of the forces of evil, namely their true character as that which has already been finally defeated on the Cross of Golgatha.[85] In the last analysis it is for this reason that Barth calls them *das Nichtige* = that which has been brought to naught. Understood in this sense, the concept of the Nihil also serves to

prove the goodness of the divine creation and to solve the
riddles of theodicy.[86]

Barth's proposition of the goodness of God's creation,
which God Himself has affirmed in Jesus Christ as the true
man, is based on his thesis of the strict connection between
creation and covenant. This latter teaching invests the work
of creation with a very definite character of its own in that
it regards the fulfilment of God's covenant of grace with man
as the eternal purpose of creation. For this purpose characterizes creation as a divine blessing.[87] Since creation serves
the exclusive purpose of setting the stage for the realization
of God's covenant of grace with man in Jesus Christ and
through Him in those other men who, because they believe
in Him, are justified, sanctified and called by Him to be His
witnesses (below, par. 6), and since the fulfilment of that
covenant is the exclusive inner meaning of creation and its
eternal purpose, creation has the indelible character of a
divine blessing. For it is intended to be and actually exists
as the theatre where within the framework of the covenant
God reveals to man His own glory and man on his part is
called to serve in and through his person and work as a
witness to that divine glory.

Anything which is inimical to this sublime purpose of
creation is contrary to God's eternal positive will and purpose
in creation and, consequently, because of its negative and
therefore evil character and purpose is excluded from creation. Having no part in God's good creation, it is confronted
with God's No, with His wrath and judgment. God can only
create what is in conformity with His own nature, His own
reality (above, par. 2) and thus can only create what is good.
Evil He can neither will nor create. This is why Barth deals
with God's Yes to His good creation in his teaching on the
work of creation, whereas the discussion of the Nihil forms
a part of his doctrine of providence.

Since the forces of evil undoubtedly exist, though in Barth's
view, as we shall see, only in a peculiar way, the question
arises of the ground and manner of their existence. Before

we turn to this question, which is closely connected with the problem of the true nature of the Nihil, it must be stated from the outset that Barth does not conceive of the forces of evil as a power that has independent existence, confronting God, as it were, as a sort of anti-god. In his view these forces, neither willed nor created by God, would not exist but for God's work of creation and moreover are not beyond the power of God but are ruled and controlled by Him. There is no dualism in Barth's teaching on the work of creation and on the Nihil respectively, as is made perfectly clear in his rejection of Marcion's teaching on creation as the origin of evil and as the work of an inferior God.[88] Again, Barth holds that the Christian doctrine of creation is distinguished from every world-view in that it claims that the divine creative activity, which is its theme, has the character of a divine blessing.[89] By its very nature as an achievement of the human mind no world-view can assert what the Christian doctrine of creation can do in virtue of the eternal meaning and purpose of creation as revealed by God in Jesus Christ, namely that creation is a divine blessing. This is why Barth rejects not only the pessimistic world-view of Schopenhauer,[90] which is diametrically opposed to his view of creation as a divine blessing, but also the optimistic world-view of Leibniz,[91] which according to the self-assured spirit of the Age of Enlightenment is essentially derived from man's judgment about himself and the surrounding world. Over against this illusive eighteenth-century optimism Barth sets the Christian optimism, the meaning and truth of which he finds in the humiliation and exaltation of Jesus Christ, in His death and resurrection, as the mystery of God's will in creation and of His good-pleasure in the world He has created.[92]

To account equally for the goodness of God's creation and for the phenomenon of the Nihil Barth uses a terminology which is open to misunderstanding unless it is understood as theological language and considered in the context of his theology as a whole.[93] Two definitions deserve special attention which are designed to characterize the true nature of the Nihil, namely the designation of the Nihil as 'the non-real' and as 'the impossible possibility'. God, we saw, can only will and create what is in conformity with His own nature and therefore only what is good. This entails that, as He is the source of every reality outside His own reality, only that can be real in which He has expressed and confirmed His own nature.[94] Hence the Nihil as the antithesis to God's good creation cannot be said to be in this sense real; it can only be the opposite of the real, that is, the non-real. By the latter definition Barth does not mean that the Nihil does not exist,[95] but that it exists only as that which God, because of its evil character and purpose, does not want to exist and thus has excluded from His work of creation. In other words, the Nihil is not something which exists in itself; it exists only relatively, namely in relation to God, in the power of His negation and rejection. In this peculiar way however it does exist in a most terrifying and menacing manner, as is clearly revealed in the reality of the Nihil which God faces in Jesus Christ, above all in the agony of the Cross.[96]

Again, as the One who is omnipotent, God is the source and criterion of all genuine possibilities, that is, of those who accord with His own nature. That which has nothing to do with His reality, that which rebels against it, that which tries to be like God instead of serving Him, is in Barth's view an unreal and demonic reality, and any capacity for it is an unreal and impossible possibility.[97] The definition of the Nihil as the impossible possibility does not signify an existential impossibility and also expresses not merely an ethical but a theological impossibility in that the capacity for evil and thus the possibility of evil is excluded from God's work of creation as the impossible by virtue of what is possible for God as the criterion of every genuine possibility.[98] In other words, seen from the perspective of God's good creation, the Nihil as that which is negated and rejected by God in His work of creation is the impossible possibility in that it lacks any *ratio* that would justify its existence and yet actually exists in its peculiar negative way. This is why Barth also calls it 'the absurd (irrational) possibility of the absurd (irrational)'.[99] Thus the definition of the Nihil as the impossible possibility, which, taken verbally, is a *contradictio in adjecto*, and indeed the very term 'the Nihil' expresses the strongest possible condemnation of the forces of evil, in particular of sin. We shall not understand Barth's teaching on the Nihil unless we discern in this concept the distinctly qualifying note of the Nihil as that which is 'downright abominable, even accursed'.[100]

Barth does not attempt to explain the origin of the Nihil.[101] Its irrational nature defies any such explanation. 'It would not be the Evil if we could explain its reality.'[102] Forming no part of God's good creation, it is in this sense ontologically impossible.[103] The ontic context in which the Nihil is unaccountably actual and active after its own particular fashion is that of God's activity as the latter arises out of His eternal decree before time (above, par. 2).[104] Thus creation as the first work of God *ad extra* involves *de facto* the impossible possibility of evil in the world. This is particularly true of man's opposition to God, made possible by his free will and yet an impossible possibility since man's freedom is his freedom *for* God (above, Ch. II, 7 (4) and below, Ch. IV) and, consequently, his rebellion *against* God is an impossible and incomprehensible abuse of that freedom.

The fact of evil in the world, in particular of man's enmity towards God's grace in Jesus Christ and therefore of sin, Barth argues,[105] does however not imply an imperfection of God's work of creation. As His good creation it inevitably carries with it the negation and rejection of the Nihil and thus the relative negative actuality of the latter. Moreover, man is not required to resist of himself the forces of evil since man as a creature is no match for the Nihil. Created to depend in everything on God's grace, that grace will see him through in his struggle against evil (below, par. 5). For the Nihil is an attack on God Himself, on His good creation, and thus it is God Himself who for the sake of His good creation and of man as His creature in particular fights this battle against the Nihil and has done so in Jesus Christ.[106]

God's power embraces the Nihil which apart from His work of creation would never have had this negative actuality. Ruling over the forces of evil and controlling them as the Lord also over the Nihil, He makes them to serve His positive purpose in creation and in His eternal decree before time has already resolved on their final defeat in Jesus Christ.[107] In the last analysis Barth derives this interpretation of the relation between God and the Nihil from God's eternally fore-ordained triumph over the Nihil in Jesus Christ, from Jesus Christ's victory over sin, evil and death in the miracles He wrought and in His death and resurrection.[108] There the negative actuality and ultimate powerlessness but also the transient dreadful reality and menace of the forces of evil is revealed. In the light of this revelation Barth, in a penetrating analysis of the theories of evil and sin respectively developed by Julius Müller, Leibniz, Schleiermacher, Martin Heidegger and Jean Paul Sartre, rejects all these theories because they ignore, for one reason or another, the true nature of the Nihil as revealed in Jesus Christ and in particular claims that the reality of the Nihil so revealed is more dreadful than even the one envisaged by Sartre.[109]

In answer to the question of why God tolerates the existence of the Nihil, the limitation of His good creation by sin, evil and death, Barth, first of all, refers us to the freedom of God's will in which from eternity He allowed the world and man to exist under these very conditions. Again, God is said by Him temporarily to permit and thus tolerate the existence of the Nihil in order to safeguard man's autonomy and freedom in the interest of man's free obedience to His holy will and of man's free response to His grace in Jesus Christ even though this involves the risk of man's falling away from Him. Above all, God's supreme and truest lovingkindness to His creature is said to be revealed in its full splendour only when the obedience and blessedness of man are not simply his nature but salvation from the edge of an abyss, when in his obedience and blessedness man is constantly reminded of his gracious creation out of nothing and of his gracious preservation from the Nihil by the menacing proximity of the realm of the Nihil, in short, when man's obedience and blessedness are the fruits of faith and thus of God's grace in Jesus Christ.[110] 'If God is greater in the very fact that He is the God who forgives sins and saves from death, we have no right to complain but must praise Him that His will also includes a permitting of sin and death.'[111]

5. THE ELECTED MAN

Barth's doctrine of man[112] is the most consistent one of its kind and is revolutionary in content. The traditional dogmatic way of thinking is here once more radically reversed. He does not start from the phenomena of the human in general as they present themselves to the philosopher or the scientist. He does not begin, as the anthropology of traditional Christian dogmatics usually does, with the problem of the constitution of man's being, of man's existence (*Dasein*) and nature (*Sosein*) in order to proceed from there to the human nature of Jesus Christ in particular. On the contrary, he derives his concept of man, of real man, from the human nature of the one particular man Jesus Christ who, because He is shown to be the revealing Word of God also in respect of the true nature of man, is treated as the source of our knowledge of man as God created him. Moving once more from the particular to the general (above, Ch. I, 5 (1a)), Barth takes the concrete man Jesus as the key to the understanding of man, basing his anthropology on Christology and not contrariwise.[113] Thus his anthropology is both theological and christological. In developing his doctrine of man he constantly turns in the first instance to the nature of man as it confronts us in the person of Jesus and only then—'asking and answering from this place of light'—to the nature of man as that of every man.[114]

This particular approach to the Christian doctrine of man, which to the mind of twentieth-century man may appear to be quite unrealistic but from the perspective of the Christian Faith is more realistic than any existentialist or scientific approach can ever be, is not motivated by any disregard for the study of the phenomena of the human in general, let alone by any disparagement of the exact science of man but by Barth's profound concern to discover man as God willed and created him, that is, real man. On the basis of God's revelation in Jesus Christ he argues that neither the study of the phenomena of the human in general nor the exact science of man in particular encounters that man within their limited fields of research but that he can be found only through Jesus Christ as the revealing Word of God and in Him, that is, in His humanity. For that revelation tells us not only that man is incapable of knowing of himself who and what he is in reality, but that man, because of his sinful human nature, is estranged from his own reality, that his corrupt human nature conceals from his sight the true nature of man as God willed and created it.

To discover real man, Barth therefore turns to the man Jesus who was without sin and by His vicarious sacrificial death upon the Cross has recovered for us our true humanity, namely by our justification and sanctification through faith in Him. In the light of the proposition of his doctrine of God's election of grace that Jesus Christ is the elected man precisely because He, and He alone, lives the perfect life of the true man as God willed and created him, that is, the life of real man, he has every reason to do so.[115] In that God (in His Son) assumed human nature in the man Jesus and as the real man lived in perfect fellowship with God and with His fellow-men, He revealed to us thereby, that is, by His turning to man in Jesus Christ, by His most intimate union with man in the divine-human person of Jesus Christ, and by the latter's devotion of His entire life to the service of God and of His fellow-men (i) that man is God's creature, derived from God, existing with God and thus not without Him, and wholly belonging to God, (ii) that man is willed and created by God as a being existing in fellowship both with God and with his fellow-men, in other words, that the being of man is a being in relationship, in relation namely to God and to other men.[116] Thus man is man, real man, only as he exists in this twofold relationship, in this togetherness of his being both with God and with other men, and this means that the relation to God and to other men is an essential part of man's humanity. The latter is true humanity only as it is directed towards God and our neighbour, only as it is God-related and related to other men (= co-humanity). This is man's true nature, man's reality, as determined by God.

Hence, in the light of this revelation of God in Jesus Christ natural theology's view of man's independent existence[117] is at variance with man's reality; in Jesus Christ we know that man, real man, does not exist in and for himself but in the aforesaid relationship.[118]

Again, since the non-theological anthropologies are developed apart from the Word of God, they can only describe individual features of man, that is, the appearances of real man, but cannot penetrate to real man as one who exists in that twofold relationship. Speculative theories of man in particular can produce only a phantom man since they analyse man apart from God's revelation in Jesus Christ and thus on the basis of the erroneous assumption that man can attain of himself to the truth about himself. The exact science of man, on the other hand, be it human physiology, biology, psychology or sociology, is concerned with man only in so far as he represents one of the phenomena of the cosmos; it can only show *how* man is but not *that* he is and *what* he is, in brief, his reality; the ground and determination of man's being or, to put it more concretely, the fact that man is God's creature and has his very being and reality in *this* fact and, consequently, in his relation to God and to other men is outside the scope of its field of research.[119]

In seeking real man in the human nature of Jesus, Barth makes clear that there can be no question of equating our human nature with that of Jesus and, therefore, that there can be no question of a simple deduction of anthropology from Christology.[120] For, though Jesus has the same nature as we have (above, Ch. II, 7 (3)), He has it in quite a different way. In Him are the peace and clarity which are not in ourselves; His human nature is without the self-contradiction and self-deception which afflict us; above all, in Him human nature is without sin. Though, as the Son of God, He became what we are, He did not do what we do and did what we fail to do. Again, in that He became man, He did not cease to be the Son of God and thus, as man, stands in a unique relation to God. This, however, Barth claims, does not imply that the constitution of the human nature of Jesus is different from ours but only that His human nature operates differently from ours, namely in the way God willed and created it. The latter, therefore, can serve, and is intended to serve, as the source and basis of our knowledge of the true nature of man; on the other hand, that knowledge, for the aforesaid reasons, can only be an indirect one.

Accordingly, Barth uses the several aspects of the human nature of Jesus, whom he shows to be man for God,[121] man for other men,[122] whole man[123] and Lord of time,[124] merely as signposts to our knowledge of real man and as the framework within which that knowledge is to be developed. The man that emerges from this enquiry is one whose being rests upon his election to partnership with God in God's covenant of grace with man in Jesus Christ and consists in the hearing and obeying of God's Word and, consequently, in continual engagement in active responsibility to God and man's neighbour. Again, the being of that man is shown to be expressed in a definite history that takes place between God and man,[125] a history grounded in God's attitude to man in Jesus Christ as resolved in God's eternal decree before time (above, par. 2) and actualized in Jesus Christ's work on earth in the fulness of time. Man's history, therefore, is determined by the divine deliverance enacted in the man Jesus for the benefit of all men and thus is firmly related to and wholly dependent on the latter's history, the history of the man Jesus. Hence, man is real man in that the man Jesus (and in Him God

Himself) moves towards him and in that he moves towards the man Jesus and therefore towards God; as man is engaged in this movement, he is real man; his true being is his being in this history.[126] In a critical analysis of the theories of human nature developed by A. Polanus,[127] J. G. Fichte[128] and K. Jaspers,[129] Barth argues that neither the naturalistic nor the ethical nor the existentialist approach to the problem in question can catch sight of real man as the one who exists in this definite history.

Again, the man that emerges from this enquiry is a being whose entire relationship with God is based on grace, living by the grace of God, under the grace of God, and from the grace of God as manifested in Jesus Christ. This does not mean, as Barth makes perfectly clear,[130] that 'God is everything and man is nothing' but that without the electing, creative, preserving, accompanying and ruling grace of God man would neither exist nor continue to exist nor be able to avoid evil; again, that without the reconciling grace of God man, sinful man, would fall a prey to the Nihil but by virtue of that grace is justified, sanctified and called to live in his place, on his own level and within his own limits, in particular within the span of time given and allotted to him by God,[131] the glorious life of the children of God, lived in true freedom and in active personal responsibility to God and man's neighbour. This leads us to another aspect of real man: the being of real man, Barth teaches, is a being in gratitude, in thanksgiving, to God as the precise creaturely counterpart to God's grace in Jesus Christ. Real man actualizes this gratitude, this thanksgiving, by believing in God and by trusting, obeying and loving Him, responding to God's glory in Jesus Christ by glorifying God in his own life of witness and service.[132]

Living from the grace of God or, to put it differently, depending in everything on that grace, indeed means that man can only *accept* what God has done and is doing for him and to him in Jesus Christ. Barth frequently emphasizes that there can be no question of any positive contribution on

man's part to God's works in election, creation, reconciliation
and redemption and, consequently, no synergism of any
kind.[133] That man accepts God's grace in Jesus Christ and,
therefore, lives from that grace is however said to be the
result of man's own decision, taken, it is true, in faith and
thus in the power of the Holy Spirit and yet being man's own
free and responsible decision. For the Holy Spirit does not
force that decision upon man, let alone replaces man's decision by His decision, but, illuminating, convincing and
guiding him, merely persuades him to take the right decision.[134] God willed and created man as a free being in order
that man may think, will and act in free personal responsibility and, consequently, may offer to God man's free obedience and a personal active response to His grace in Jesus
Christ. Though man's freedom, as a freedom granted to him
by God, is limited—in accordance with its origin and its
responsibility to its Author—in that it is to be exercised only
for God and therefore not against Him,[135] it nevertheless is
within this limitation genuine freedom and in Barth's own
words 'the most profound and the most comprehensive aspect
of real man'.[136]

Actual man, as revealed in God's judgment upon him in
Jesus Christ, does not correspond to this portrait of real
man.[137] His life, because of sin, is continually at variance
with the life of real man as God willed and created it. He
continually rejects God's grace in Jesus Christ, refusing to
live by and from that grace. He is continually at enmity
with that grace and this is his sin. In a telling passage
Barth says:[138] 'when I read Heidegger and Sartre, I ask
myself whether that spirit of defiance in man which despises
grace and therefore lacks grace is not perhaps just as un-
teachably sure of itself as it ever was'.

In accordance with his proposition of the goodness of
God's creation (above, par. 4) he maintains however (1) that
the true nature of man as willed and created by God does
not include any capacity for sin, that human sin, as shown in
the sinless life of Jesus, the real man, who as God's first and

eternal thought and will (above, par. 2) takes precedence over Adam—not chronologically but according to God's eternal plan with man and thus theologically[139]—is but the result of man's inexplicable and impossible[140] abuse of his God-given capacities and endowments; (2) that the true nature of man is indeed altered and distorted by sin but not destroyed, that sinful man is merely alienated from his true human nature as God created it and thus has become a stranger to his own true self. For man, says Barth, cannot create another nature than that which God has given him. Even when he does evil, he still is the creature created good by God which, because God in accordance with His eternal gracious plan with man remains faithful to him in spite of his sin, does not cease to be God's creature, determined to be His partner in His covenant of grace with man and, as fore-ordained in His eternal decree before time, brought back to Him by the work of reconciliation accomplished in and through Jesus Christ.[141]

In Barth's teaching on man the latter's divine determination as God's covenant-partner has its correspondence in the specific character of the humanity that is peculiar to man as a creaturely being.[142] Just as man is shown to be determined for God, so he is shown to be determined for his fellow-men. The basic form of humanity, Barth claims, is co-humanity. Man is a being in encounter-between I and Thou, between man and other men; in that man is engaged in this encounter, he is human. Barth arrives at this conclusion by his study of that aspect of the human nature of Jesus which shows that Jesus—in accordance with His divine mission as resolved in God's eternal decree before time—is in His existence originally, exclusively and totally referred to His fellow-men, that in no sense He exists first for Himself and then for other men but spends His entire life in the service of other men. A man without his fellow-men would therefore be a being that would be fundamentally alien to the man Jesus and, consequently, cannot be man as God willed and created him since Jesus came into this world to share our human nature and to reveal its true character to us.

The statement that every supposed humanity which is not radically and from the very first co-humanity is inhumanity[143] is one of the most pregnant and challenging propositions of Barth's theology. Its message is particularly needed in the present age of discord and hatred as is magnificently illustrated by Barth's trenchant polemic against F. Nietzsche, the prophet of a humanity without the fellow-man and in antithesis to the suffering and dying of the Crucified.[144] In contrast to the inhumanity of Nietzsche's superman Barth expounds[145] the true meaning of man's co-humanity ultimately in terms of the freedom and gladness in which the encounter between man and his fellow-men must take place if it is to reflect man's true humanity.

Again, Barth's notion of humanity as co-humanity is closely related to his concept of the image of God in man as developed in his later theology. The reference to this vital teaching, which passed through several stages before it reached its present form, can be only very brief.[146] Whereas at some point in his earlier teaching[147] the image of God in man signified man's appointment to reflect God's glory in his own existence and, thus conceived, was said to have been totally destroyed and lost as a result of the Fall and restored in the 'new creation' of man in Christ, Barth now finds[148] that image in the mutual relationship between God and man and between man and woman (man and other men) respectively[149] which latter in spite of all dissimilarity is said to have its similarity in the mutual relationship between the Father and the Son within the Being of the Triune God.[150] In other words, he now finds the *Imago Dei* no longer in something which by God's grace takes place in the individual as such but in the I–Thou relationship as the form of life common both to God as the Triune God and (as a copy of the divine form of life) to man as a being in relationship, related to God and created male and female. In short, the *Imago Dei* is now said to consist in an analogy (similarity in spite of all dissimilarity) of relationship (*analogia relationis*) of the aforesaid kind.[151]

Moreover, Barth now holds that because of this character of the *Imago Dei* sin can neither destroy it nor bring about its loss. For God, on account of His eternal purpose for man in Jesus Christ, continues to address man as Thou and to make him responsible as an I, even though or rather because man sins. Again, even as a sinner man does not cease to exist in the togetherness of husband and wife, of man and his fellow-men, and thus in a relationship analogous to the relationship within the inner Being of God.[152]

Again, as a relationship which by its very nature demands to be actualized through intercourse and interaction, the creation of man in the mutual relationship of man and woman (man and other men) and thus in the image of God is designed (1) to prepare man for his covenantal relationship with God by letting him experience the same type of relationship in his own co-existence with others and (2) to reflect the dynamic relationship of mutual love existing within the Being of God between the Father and the Son by the power of the Holy Spirit in the mutual relationship between God and man and between man and woman (man and other men) respectively. Because of man's sin the latter can happen only in faith and thus only by God's grace in Jesus Christ and in the power of the Holy Spirit. Hence, to sum up, with Barth the image of God in man is neither a quality in man nor something which man can seize upon and possess but a relationship which in its structure corresponds to a similar relationship within the inner Being of God and, whenever it reflects the latter qualitatively, has the character of an event of grace.[153]

6. THE RECONCILED MAN

In accordance with the three christological aspects of Jesus Christ as very God, very man and the Godman, Barth develops his massive doctrine of reconciliation along three lines.[154] On the basis of his theological exegesis of the Bible he depicts (1) how in Jesus Christ God is with us and reconciles us with Himself in the self-humiliation and the self-

K

offering of His eternal Son in our stead and for our salvation, thereby revealing to us the true nature of God and His true glory, (2) how in the same Jesus Christ we are with God in the exaltation by God of the Son of Man to eternal fellowship with God, which is also our exaltation and thus the confirmation of our reconciliation with God, thereby revealing to us the true nature and destiny of man and man's true glory in his fellowship with God, and (3) how Jesus Christ in the unity of His person as the true God and the true man, the God-man, is the guarantor and witness of our reconciliation with God.

In this doctrine too, in which Christology, soteriology and ecclesiology are closely interwoven, Christology, or rather Jesus Christ Himself, is the key to the whole doctrine, in particular to the nature, life and work of reconciled man.[155] In it Jesus Christ is presented as the One who in every respect executes the work of reconciliation, be it as the Judge (Son of God) who is judged in our place[156] or as the royal man (Son of Man) who in the freedom of God and in His service lives the perfect life of real man[157] or as the Light of life which lightens our darkness, because His life is light and His reconciling work a prophetic Word, or as the Victor who triumphs over the Nihil.[158] Again, being the Mediator between God and man in the sense that in Him God's reconciling of man with Himself and man's reconciliation with God actually happen, He is presented in it as the living embodiment, the actuality, and thus the truth of man's reconciliation with God and, consequently, because He is the crucified and risen Lord and as such the Living Christ, as its authentic witness who vouchsafes for our future in Jesus Christ.[159]

Again, in this doctrine Jesus Christ is both the continual point of departure and the constantly active primary Subject, be it in His priestly office as the Lord (Son of God) who in obedience to the will of His Father becomes a servant and by His vicarious sacrificial death upon the Cross achieves our justification or in His kingly office as the servant (Son of Man) who in virtue of His exaltation by God places us under

His divine direction and in this way accomplishes our sanctification or in His prophetic office as the Godman who, precisely because He is Himself the reconciling God and the reconciled man and as such the living Christ, guarantees and
testifies to the truth of our reconciliation with God and, consequently, calls and enables us to fulfil our vocation to
witness in the world to man's salvation in Jesus Christ. Thus
in Barth's teaching on reconciliation the threefold office of
Jesus Christ is closely correlated with the aforesaid three
christological aspects; in a sense the former arises out of the
latter and is determined by them. The third christological
aspect, the Godman, is not meant to represent a third element in the nature of Jesus Christ but only views His
history as the Lord who becomes a servant and as the servant
who becomes Lord in its unity and completeness, viewing
Jesus Christ Himself, the Subject of these two movements
from above downwards and from below upwards, in the
unity of His person and work.[160]

Again, on account of Jesus Christ's unique place in Barth's
theology,[161] the latter's doctrine of reconciliation assigns to
the idea of reconciliation a place in theology which in a
startling manner differs from the role played by that idea in
other Christian dogmatics. Though, historically, the reconciliation of the world with God in Jesus Christ undeniably
follows the divine work of creation as well as man's Fall, the
idea of reconciliation, Barth claims, has been in the mind and
will of God from eternity,[162] thus preceding, theologically,
both the creation of the universe and of man and man's
actual opposition to God. In the light of what took place
during the resurrection-period between Easter and Ascension[163] Barth holds that God's positive will for man's salvation has been prior to His will for the creation of the world
and of man, that the ordaining of salvation for man and of
man for salvation is the original and basic will of God, the
ground and purpose of His will as Creator.[164] For the term
'salvation', as here used, connotes in addition to the justification, sanctification and vocation of sinful man or rather

primarily man's participation in the being of God as God's co-worker in His eternal kingdom and in His service.[165] God willed from eternity that this should come to pass in and through Jesus Christ, that in and through Jesus Christ He would have fellowship with man, even with sinful man, both in time and in eternity. This is why with Barth reconciliation has the character of a free act of God's grace in Jesus Christ, decided upon by God in His eternity before time.[166] Thus the idea of reconciliation is implied in that original and basic will of God, and its—logically impossible—priority over God's will as Creator makes sense if, as apparently intended by Barth, it is interpreted in a teleological sense.

To understand this teaching, which completely reverses the traditional sequence of creation—sin—reconciliation, we must recur to Barth's doctrine of God's election of grace (above, par. 2) which decisively determines his teaching on reconciliation. According to that doctrine Jesus Christ was God's first and eternal thought and will, elected by God in His eternal decree before time to carry out His eternal plan with man, God's eternal election of Himself to fellowship with man and of man to fellowship with Himself, and to that end to fulfil God's covenant of grace with man in His own person and work and thereby at the same time to restore the covenant broken by man's Fall. Thus the justification of sinful man in Jesus Christ, the forgiveness of sins, and the sanctification and vocation of the justified sinner are grounded in that eternal decree. The latter has this further meaning that from eternity God has determined upon the acquittal of sinful man at His own cost and upon the exaltation of the justified sinner to existence in covenant with Himself so that man may be enriched, saved and glorified in the living fellowship of that covenant.[167]

This train of thought also shows the close connection between covenant and reconciliation in Barth's teaching and the peculiar character of that connection. Reconciliation is primarily understood in the light of the covenant, that is, as Jesus Christ's fulfilment of the covenant in the face of human

sin and its consequences, and only secondarily in the light
of man's sin, that is, as the restoration of the covenant
broken by sinful man. Since for Barth the fulfilment of the
covenant is the eternal purpose of creation (above, par. 3),
that fulfilment is for him the primary purpose of Jesus
Christ's work of reconciliation. In other words, he regards
the covenant as the presupposition of reconciliation.[168] As
already pointed out,[169] it was the eternally fore-ordained
divine mission of Jesus Christ to fulfil the covenant in His
own person and work and thereby, as very God, to carry into
effect God's promise, 'I will be your God', and, as very man,
to obey God's command, 'Ye shall be my people'. That, in
so doing, He also restored the covenant broken by man's sin,
is in Barth's view of secondary importance because the realization of the original purpose of the covenant, God's fellowship with man and man's fellowship with God, is for him, so
to speak, Jesus Christ's primary task in His work of reconciliation.[170] This view is in harmony with his other teaching
that man's transgression, like the other forces of evil, is
only an episode that is neither willed nor caused by God and
is eternally fore-ordained by God to be overcome by Christ's
triumph over the Nihil in His death upon the Cross.[171]
One may wonder whether it is legitimate to speak of
reconciliation also in so far as the pure fulfilment of the
covenant—apart from man's sin and thus apart from the
need for the restoration of the broken covenant—is in
question.

Other characteristic features of Barth's doctrine of reconciliation are:

(a) The person and the work of Jesus Christ are never
viewed in separation from each other; they mutually interpret and determine each other. The particular fact that, and
the particular way in which, Jesus Christ is very God, very
man and the Godman determines His work of reconciliation,
and He does this work on the basis of the fact, and only on
that basis, that He is this One and not another. Barth
therefore rejects the classical division of Christology into a

doctrine of the Person and a doctrine of the Work of Jesus Christ.[172]

(b) Jesus Christ is never treated in a purely nominalistic way, as a mere formal historical or symbolic sign of the event of reconciliation, or, to use Lessing's phrase, as a 'contingent fact of history', serving as the 'vehicle' of an 'eternal truth of reason'. He is shown to be the One in whom, as the reconciling God and the reconciled man, the event of reconciliation has actually taken place on behalf and for the sake of all men, who therefore is Himself the reality and revelation of the world's reconciliation with God, continually ruling and acting in His threefold work of reconciliation, not only during His lifetime but as our Contemporary.[173] This view of Jesus Christ as the eternally active primary Subject and as the objective reality of man's reconciliation with God, in other words, the view of the historicity of that work in all its aspects, in particular in respect of Jesus Christ's prophetic work throughout the ages,[174] sharply contrasts with Bultmann's attempt to transform Jesus Christ's objective and historical work of reconciliation into existentialist decisions of man which, though made in faith, have the exclusive character of subjective events.[175]

(c) The doctrines of the two Natures of Jesus Christ (His divinity and humanity) and of the two States of Jesus Christ (His humiliation and exaltation) are related to each other in a novel fashion. Firstly, the state of humiliation (of the Son of God) is not followed by the state of exaltation (of the Son of Man) but both these states are represented as two sides or directions or forms of the one indivisible reconciling divine-human action and work of Jesus Christ who, being both God and man, is throughout both humiliated and exalted.[176] Secondly, the doctrine of the two states is interpreted in the light of the doctrine of the two Natures and vice versa since neither of them is autonomous but depends on the other for its true understanding.[177] Thirdly, in Jesus Christ God activates and proves His Deity by subjecting Himself to the limitations and sufferings of the human creature and in the same Jesus

Christ man is the true man who is free in his relation to his (actual) human nature, overcoming it, being its master and not its servant, and is set at the side of God, in short, is exalted by God.[178] The humiliation, therefore, is the humiliation of God in Jesus Christ to supreme glory, demonstrating the wonder and glory of His divine being, and the exaltation is the exaltation of man as the work of God's grace in Jesus Christ, issuing in the restoration of man's true humanity.[179]

(d) In contrast to the one-sided emphasis on justification (Luther) and on sanctification (Calvin) respectively Barth lays equal stress upon the three forms of God's grace in Jesus Christ's reconciling work, that is, upon the justification, sanctification and vocation of sinful man which is God's gracious and victorious answer to human sin. The exclusive principle governing Barth's doctrine of reconciliation is neither justification alone nor sanctification alone nor vocation alone but Jesus Christ who justifies, sanctifies and calls[180] and moreover does so not in stages but in and through one and the same divine-human act of reconciliation. It is only for didactic purposes that the three forms of His reconciling work are expounded one after another.[181] Sanctification and vocation are treated by Barth as integral parts of that work. They are inseparably bound up with Jesus Christ's work of justification and do not represent a second and third action of Jesus Christ alongside this latter work or following it in time but coincide with it. Hence Barth rejects the view of man's self-sanctification after the work of reconciliation has been completed.[182] Again, justification and sanctification are said to have a definite goal which, contrary to a widely held view, is not man's personal salvation but a divine mandate, namely man's vocation to act as God's co-worker and in His service, that is, to be a witness of Jesus Christ. Man's personal salvation is but one of the results of the execution of that vocation.[183]

(e) Barth's vital distinction between the objective and the subjective aspect of Jesus Christ's reconciling work has already been referred to.[184] Just as the Christian revelation

requires for its completeness in addition to its objective
reality in Jesus Christ its subjective reality as the work of the
Holy Spirit in man,[185] so the objective relevance of Jesus
Christ's reconciling work demands its subjective realization,
that is, its acceptance by man.[186] Objectively (*de jure*) all
men are already justified, sanctified and called in Jesus Christ,
in and through what He has done in their stead and for their
sake. In Him, objectively, the old man has already passed
away; in Him, objectively, we are already the new man,
represented as such by Him before God. However, though
the salvation of all men is already objectively accomplished
by Jesus Christ—without them and, as His Cross teaches,
against them—many of them have not yet perceived and
accepted what God has done for them in Jesus Christ.[187]
In order that Jesus Christ's objective reconciling work may
subjectively (*de facto*) bear fruit in the lives of individual
men and through them, as His witnesses, in the lives of other
men, there is still needed as an essential part of the reconciling work of Jesus Christ the subjective apprehension, acceptance, appropriation and application of that work, or rather
of its fruits, by individual men, that is, the existence of
Christians. It is at this point that in Barth's doctrine of
reconciliation the being and work of Jesus Christ becomes
the being and work of the Holy Spirit, the Holy Spirit of the
risen Lord Jesus Christ who, in His prophetic office, achieves
the subjective reality of reconciliation in the life of the community of Jesus Christ and through the latter in the lives of
individual Christians (below, par. 7). The meaning of the
subjective aspect of reconciliation is not that man has to
contribute to Jesus Christ's work of reconciliation which is
already objectively accomplished but that man can only
apprehend and accept the latter and must do so if it is
to bear fruit in his own life and through him in that of
others.

(*f*) The revelatory character of reconciliation, already
pointed out in various contexts, plays a vital part in Barth's
doctrine of reconciliation,[188] especially in Jesus Christ's pro-

phetic office as the true Witness.[189] In and through His
person and work Jesus Christ reveals to us not only that God
is our Creator and we are His creatures but also the true God
and the true man, in particular God as the covenant-God and
man's destiny as God's covenant-partner. Again, He reveals
to us thereby that actual man is fallen man who by his sin
has broken the covenant, that man is flesh, lost and damned
but for God's grace in Jesus Christ, that God says No to
man's sin, which is judged, condemned and rejected in the
death of His Son upon the Cross, but in His grace and mercy
says nevertheless Yes to man by taking upon Himself man's
sin and the rejection resulting therefrom and exalting man
to eternal fellowship with Himself. The revelatory aspect of
reconciliation and thus man's knowledge of the meaning and
content of the latter is however but one element in Barth's
doctrine of reconciliation since with him[190] knowledge implies action.[191] Man's knowledge of what Jesus Christ objectively has done for him and subjectively is doing to him in His
reconciling work is true knowledge only if it issues in man's
grateful active response to God's threefold grace in that work
and thus in man's service as a witness of Jesus Christ. Again,
in Barth's doctrine of reconciliation the revelatory character
of reconciliation is manifested in the fact that he derives his
doctrine of sin from what Jesus Christ's reconciling work
reveals to us regarding man's sin.

Contrary to tradition Barth's doctrine of sin[192] does not
precede his doctrine of reconciliation but arises out of the
latter and is an integral part of it. He argues that just as
there can be no abstract or general idea of sin, so there can
be no abstract or autonomous doctrine of sin.[193] As man's
opposition to the will of God sin has no existence of its own
but, belonging to the realm of the Nihil and sharing its
nature,[194] has only relative existence in that, being neither
willed nor caused by God, it exists only in its antagonism to
God's good creation and thus only in the power of its negation
and rejection by God. In this peculiar relative and negative
fashion sin does however exist in a most realistic and horrifying

way, as is only too clearly demonstrated in the crucifixion of Jesus Christ.

Since God's eternal decree before time and therefore God's free grace in Jesus Christ, resolved in that decree, is the eternal beginning and the eternal basis of all the ways and works of God *ad extra*,[195] grace not only follows but precedes sin in the sense that the latter is man's rebellion against God's eternal grace in Jesus Christ. In Barth's view man's sin is man's opposition to the fulfilment of God's covenant of grace with man which is the goal of God's eternal decree before time and the eternal purpose of creation. In other words, man's sin is man's resistance to God's gracious will to live in fellowship (covenant) with man and to let man live in fellowship (covenant) with Himself, which is His original and basic will in Jesus Christ. We saw already[196] that man does not want to depend on God's grace in Jesus Christ but wants to be his own master. Hence he says No to God's gracious Yes to man in Jesus Christ. He rejects that grace and thus breaks the covenant he is destined to fulfil. The true nature of sin, Barth holds, is therefore man's enmity towards God's grace in Jesus Christ.[197] Man in his sin rebels against the very grace which, being stronger than sin, overcomes that rebellion in the amazing love which God has shown to man in the Cross of Jesus Christ. It is this which makes man's sin so utterly evil. Understood in this sense, sin is an incomprehensible and irrational act on man's part who is God's creature, created good by God. Moreover, it is an impossible possibility since man is elected to fellowship with God and is already objectively justified, sanctified and called by God in Jesus Christ.[198]

Again, understood in this sense, sin is shown to have a quite definite and concrete meaning and direction, being strictly related to God's covenant of grace with man and to Jesus Christ's reconciling work. That sin has this nature, Barth argues,[199] we know however only by virtue of the revelation that has taken place in that work. For it is only through the fulfilment and the restoration of the covenant in the course of that work that we know of this covenant and of the breaking of it by man's sin. Again, it is only in the light of God's gracious Yes to man in Jesus Christ that we know of man's sinful No to God's gracious will towards man in Jesus Christ.

Further, Barth holds that it is only in the light of Jesus Christ's work of reconciliation that the main forms of man's enmity towards God's grace in Jesus Christ and thus of man's sin can be apprehended. In accordance with the three aspects of that work he distinguishes three forms of sin.[200] The humility, obedience, and self-humiliation of the Son of God in His priestly work (the Lord as servant) are contrasted with the *pride* of man who, exalting himself, wants to be like God, to be himself lord, the judge of good and evil, and his own helper. The exaltation and majesty of the Son of man in His kingly work (the servant as Lord) are contrasted with the *sloth* of man who lets himself sink and fall in the morass of his stupidity, inhumanity, dissipation, and anxiety. The self-revelation and the glory of the Mediator (Godman), who in His prophetic work is the Light of life and the Truth, are contrasted with the *falsehood* of man who, though he exists in darkness, thinks he knows better and refuses to hear and obey the truth he encounters in Jesus Christ.[201] Again, Barth argues[202] that man's pride entails his fall, his sloth his misery, his falsehood his perdition.[203]

On the other hand, he offers no doctrine of the original state of man before the Fall as in his opinion there is no scriptural warrant for such a doctrine, no original revelation preceding the one revelation in Jesus Christ. The latter tells us that man has been a sinner from the beginning of history.[204] Again, to him the heart of Jesus Christ's atonement,[205] of His suffering and dying in our place and for our salvation, is neither the punishment of sin nor the satisfaction of the righteous wrath of God against those who are the enemies of His grace but the overcoming of sin,[206] the victory of grace over man's enmity towards grace.[207]

7. Jesus Christ and His Community[208]

Barth developes his doctrine of the Church (as to its structure see above, Ch. I, 4) in so many directions and in so many
diverse contexts that no more can be done by way of introduction than to indicate a few particularly characteristic
features of this teaching.[209] The latter:

(a) is wholly christological in that it asserts that in no
respect, on no account and at no time the Church is to be
thought of apart from Jesus Christ if it is to be the true
Church of Jesus Christ. We saw already [210] that with Barth
the being (*Sein*) of the Church is identical with the being
(*Sein*) of Jesus Christ. This must be understood in its most
comprehensive sense: because Jesus Christ is and in that He
is, the Church is and, on the other hand, the Church is because Jesus Christ is and in that He is.[211] Just as Jesus
Christ is not without His Church which is His body, the
earthly-historical form of His existence, so the Church is not
without Jesus Christ or it is the false Church. He is its
Founder, its Lord, its Head. It is He who continually rules
in the Church and sustains it through the power of the Holy
Spirit, the Holy Spirit of the crucified and risen Lord Jesus
Christ. In other words, the Church lives literally and really
only in and through Jesus Christ as its Head, in and through
the power of His Holy Spirit.[212]

Again, it is Jesus Christ who is the source and criterion of
the Church's identity as the true Church, its only comfort
and hope, and, as the Lord who comes again, its goal. In
His eternal decree before time (above, par. 2) God willed and
planned the covenant between Jesus Christ and His community (Israel and the Church) as the internal basis and the
eternal purpose of creation.[213] Thus Jesus Christ and His
community, on the one hand, have their eternal beginning
in God's original and basic will and plan with man and, on
the other hand, are the eternal goal of that will and plan.
The reality of the Christian Church together with Jesus
Christ as its Head is already the fulfilment of that will and

plan of God, though the final manifestation of that (eschato-logical) reality as the light of the cosmos has to wait for the final *parousia* of Jesus Christ at the end of time.[214]

Again, it is on christological grounds that Barth rejects the exclusion of the question of order and law from the concept of the Church by R. Sohm and E. Brunner who in opposition to the 'organized Church' conceive of the true Church in purely spiritual terms, that is, as the 'Church of love and faith' (R. Sohm) and as the 'pure fellowship of persons' (E. Brunner) respectively. Since Jesus Christ as the Head of His body is the primary acting Subject of the Church, ordering, commanding and controlling His community, whereas the communion of saints is its secondary acting subject, follow-ing and obeying Jesus Christ as the Head of the Church, Barth concludes from this relationship between Jesus Christ and His community as the principle of order and the basic law of the Church that it must express itself in a definite order and law of the Church, taking its form and content from Jesus Christ as the Giver of that order and law. For Him order and law are therefore essential to a christologico-ecclesiological concept of the Church.[215]

(*b*) conceives of the Church in a wholly dynamic fashion. Discussing Barth's actualism[216] his concept of the being of the Church as *actus purus*, as free divine action, has been mentioned. He emphasizes that in respect of the being of the Church being and act cannot be separated from each other, that the very act of the Church is its true being, its status its dynamic, its essence its existence.[217] This too must be under-stood in its most comprehensive sense: not only the being of the Church as such but the life of its members in faith, love and hope is to be regarded as the continually necessary work and achievement of the Holy Spirit of Jesus Christ who by His awakening power gathers the Christian community and creates the faith of the individual Christian, by His life-giving power upbuilds the Christian community and quickens the love of the individual Christian and by His enlightening power sends the Christian community out into the world to

witness to Jesus Christ in the world and imparts to the individual Christian the hope of the future coming of Jesus
Christ in His glory and of eternal life in God's kingdom. Thus
to Barth the Church is not an institution but an event that
by the free grace of God in Jesus Christ and in the power of
His Holy Spirit must continually happen afresh in order that
there may be the true Church of Jesus Christ. The latter
must ever again become the true Church of Jesus Christ in
order to be that Church, and it can become that Church only
by the constantly renewed free divine action of God's grace
in Jesus Christ.[216] In this respect Barth's teaching distinctly
differs from both the static Roman Catholic and the anthropological modernistic concept of the Church.[218]

Again, the Church, as the true Church, is thereby shown to
exist not only in space and time but in a third dimension, the
spiritual dimension created by the work of the Holy Spirit
in the Church. It is this spiritual dimension which in Barth's
view is lacking in Schleiermacher's concept of the Church as
a 'pious society' of a particular kind.[219] For Barth the Church
is the living fellowship of the living Jesus Christ, existing
in a wholly dynamic relationship of its members with
their Lord and Head and with one another. Only if and when
and as long as there is a continually fresh encounter between
God in Jesus Christ and man in the Church in the power of
the Holy Spirit, the Church is the true Church of Jesus Christ.
What has been said of the Church, equally applies to the
individual Christian's faith whereby he is justified, to his
love whereby he is sanctified, and to his hope whereby he is
called to witness to that hope in the world.[220] His existence
in faith, love and hope is indeed his own existence, but is
nevertheless an existence in Jesus Christ by the power of His
Holy Spirit. As one who, though justified by faith, is and
remains a sinner in his actual life,[221] the Christian is in
constant need of that power in order that he may have faith,
love and hope. Hence, it is always an event of God's free
grace in Jesus Christ when he has faith, love and hope. The
latter never become his permanent possession. They are

never something which is at his disposal. They must continually be given to him afresh, and thus he must continually pray for these blessings.[222]

(c) lays stress on the 'Christian community' (*Gemeinde*) rather than on the 'Church' with its implication of an institution and of offices. For the Church, in Barth's view, is not an institution but a particular people set apart by God for a special purpose, being called by God in Jesus Christ to a common life in the Holy Spirit, in obedience to God's Word in Jesus Christ and in faith, love and hope and, above all, to service, serving God and one another as well as those outside the Church.[223] It is the emphasis on the Christian duty of service, modelled on the example of Jesus Christ, the man for God and the man for other men,[224] which in particular explains why Barth shows no interest in any kind of hierarchical system in the Church, be it that of the Roman Catholic Church or that of the Church of England, nor in the Lutheran concept of 'office' (*Amt*) which he wants to be replaced by the service of all for all.[225] He holds that all members of the Christian community are called by Jesus Christ to serve Him in the Church as well as in the world, and it is for this christologico-ecclesiological reason that he rejects the distinction between clergy and laity, between office-bearers and ordinary Christians.[226] 'Strictly, no one has an office; all can and should and may serve; none is ever "off duty".'[227] In this connection it is worth noting that, as a direct reflection of Jesus Christ's life as Saviour, Barth considers man's cooperation in the internal and external service of the Christian community as the supreme and proper form of the active life required of man.[228] Again, the only direct, absolute and material authority in the Church under Jesus Christ as its Head does not belong to the Church, as the Roman Catholic Church teaches, but to Holy Scripture as the Word of God.[229]

(d) gives precedence to the Christian community over the individual Christian since the election of the community is prior to that of the individual (above, par. 2). Moreover, Jesus Christ's divine mission is the reconciliation of the world

with God and only within this larger context the reconciliation of individuals.[230] In the context of his teaching on the
one holy catholic and apostolic Church[231] Barth also claims
that in view of the catholicity of the Church, that is, its
sameness (identity) as the true Church of Jesus Christ
at all times (continuity) and in all places (universality),
the Christian is first a member of the Christian community
and only then and as such this individual Christian in
his particular Christian being and nature. As the body of
Jesus Christ conjoined to its Head, the Christian community has priority over its members not only for the
sake of its Head but also for that of its members.[232] With
this proposition there is closely related Barth's other proposition that to be a Christian *eo ipso* means to be a member
of the Christian community; in other words, there is no
legitimate private Christianity.[233] This conclusion is arrived
at on the basis of his teaching that just as the Church as the
body of Jesus Christ is holy because He, the Head, is holy,
so the corresponding holiness of its individual members,
based on Jesus Christ's relationship with them and their's
with Him, must be equivalent to the fact that they are members of His body and therefore that they are *in* the Church.
Barth, however, is careful to add that this statement is not
identical with the dictum '*extra ecclesiam nulla salus*'. In his
view the latter should read '*extra Christum nulla salus*'.[234]

(*e*) makes witness the centre and the criterion of the life of
both the true Church and the true Christian.[235] Barth emphasizes that the Church is not an end in itself but, as the
provisional representation of the justification, sanctification
and vocation of the whole world, exists for the world in
order that the already accomplished objective reconciliation
of all men with God (above, par. 6) may become a subjective
reality in the lives of all men.[236] The Church has a mission
which is the very raison d'être of its existence; it stands and
falls with it. It is sent out into the world by its living Lord
Jesus Christ in the power of His Holy Spirit to confess Him
before all men and by its witness to call all men to Him,

thereby making known to the whole world that the covenant concluded in Jesus Christ between God and man is the original and ultimate meaning of history and that the future revelation of that covenant at His final coming is their great hope which is already here and now an effective and living hope.[237] Again, witness is the true mark of a Christian. What makes a man a Christian is, in Barth's view, contrary to the classic answer usually given to this question, an answer which he holds is at variance with the teaching of the Bible and with the true nature of Christian existence as service, not the benefits accruing to man from being a Christian, from belonging to the Church of Jesus Christ, but his service as a witness of Jesus Christ within the Church and in the world.[238]

(f) understands the apostolic Church not historically, juridically, sociologically or psychologically but spiritually, namely as the Church which is apostolic because it exists under the normative authority, instruction and direction of the apostles as the direct witnesses of Jesus Christ, listening to them and accepting their message.[239] To be apostolic, the Church must continually hear and accept afresh the apostolic witness as recorded in Holy Scripture. Hence, Barth argues, it is always an event when the Church is apostolic.[240] In accordance with this teaching he rejects all attempts to base the claim of being the true catholic Church on an historically or juridically justified apostolic succession.[241] In his view we can speak of a legitimate apostolic succession, of the existence of a Church in the following of the apostles, only when in the encounter of the Church with the apostolic witness it actually happens that the apostolic witness is heard and obeyed by the Church.[242]

REFERENCES

[1] *Gifford*, pp. 43, 47; CD, II, 1, p. 607; IV, 1, pp. 16 ff., 45, 81, 346; IV, 2, p. 300.
[2] *Systematic Theology*, vol. II, p. 174.

[3] Above, Ch. I, 4.
[4] CD, I, 2, p. 123; see also ibid., p. 883 and II, 2, p. 4.
[5] CD, IV, 3, pp. 38 ff.; this section should be carefully studied as

its extensive argumentation makes clear why Jesus Christ is regarded by Barth as the one Word of God.

⁶ E.g. John Baillie, *The Sense of the Presence of God*, pp. 255 f.; G. Wingren, *Theology in Conflict*, pp. 42, 124 ff.

⁷ Loc. cit.

⁸ *Gifford*, pp. 43, 87 f.; CD, III, 2, pp. 441 ff., espec. 448 ff.; IV, 1, pp. 341, 344; IV, 2, pp. 299 f.

⁹ *Bultmann*, pp. 97 ff., 100 ff., 109 ff.; CD, III, 2, pp. 443 ff., 451 ff.

¹⁰ CD, III, 2, pp. 448 ff.; IV, 1, p. 341.

¹¹ CD, IV, 3, pp. 86 ff.

¹² Ibid., pp. 90 ff.

¹³ Ibid., pp. 106 ff., 122 ff., 158 ff., 179 ff.

¹⁴ CD, II, 1, p. 667.

¹⁵ Ibid.

¹⁶ CD, II, 1, p. 622; II, 2, pp. 94 ff.; IV, 1, pp. 51 ff.; IV, 2, pp. 32 ff.

¹⁷ CD, II, 2, pp. 94 ff.; IV, 2, pp. 33 f.

¹⁸ CD, IV, 1, p. 50.

¹⁹ CD, I, 1, p. 129; I, 2, pp. 45 ff.

²⁰ CD, IV, 2, p. 33.

²¹ CD, II, 1, p. 44.

²² *Gifford*, pp. 14 ff., 21, 25; CD, II, 1, pp. 3 ff., 63 ff., 257 ff.

²³ Above, Ch. II, 7 (1); CD, II, 1, pp. 9 ff., 14 ff., 32 ff., 44 ff., 63 ff., 179 ff.; J. S. Bezzant, *Objections to Christian Belief* (1963), pp. 107 f., overlooks this point in his discussion of the grounds of man's knowledge of God.

²⁴ Above, Ch. I, 3; *The Humanity of God*, loc. cit., pp. 31 ff.; CD, II, 1, pp. 307 ff.; II, 2, pp. 3 ff.; TT, pp. 38 f. The assumption of human nature by the Son of God has of course taken place already at the Incarnation, but He was then not yet the crucified and risen Lord.

²⁵ CD, II, 1, pp. 22 ff., 79 ff., 257 ff.; see also TT, p. 14.

²⁶ CD, II, 1, pp. 79 ff.

²⁷ Ibid., p. 262.

²⁸ Above, Ch. I, 3; *The Humanity of God*, loc. cit., pp. 36 f., 40 ff., 51; IET, pp. 10 ff.

²⁹ CD, II, 1, p. 663; see also CD, IV, 1, pp. 128 ff., 186 f.

³⁰ CD, IV, 1, p. 130.

³¹ *Against the Stream*, pp. 181 ff.

³² *Gifford*, p. 31; CD, IV, 1, pp. 186 f.; IV, 3, pp. 388 ff., 414 ff.; see also IET, pp. 10 f.

³³ CD, IV, 3, pp. 415 f.; Barth's present concept of 'the Wholly Other' is therefore not 'meaningless' as R. Gregor Smith, *The New Man* (1956), p. 66 contends; God's form as the Suffering Servant proves that it does not exclude any relation and knowledge of what is 'wholly' other but, on the contrary, makes them possible. Barth's concept of 'the Wholly Other' has to be understood in a qualified sense.

³⁴ Barth prefers to speak of God's 'perfections' rather than of His 'attributes', see CD, II, 1, p. 322.

³⁵ CD, II, 1, pp. 257 ff.

³⁶ Ibid., pp. 327 ff., 344 ff.

³⁷ *Gifford*, pp. 68 ff., espec. 77; CD, II, 2, pp. 3 ff.

³⁸ CD, II, 2, p. 3.

³⁹ Ibid., pp. 3, 7, 10, 12 ff., 49 ff.

⁴⁰ Ibid., pp. 45 ff.

⁴¹ Ibid., Preface, p. X.

⁴² Regin Prenter, op. cit., p. 34.

⁴³ CD, II, 2, p. 94.

⁴⁴ Ibid., p. 101.

⁴⁵ Ibid., pp. 15 ff., 25 ff., 59 ff., 101 ff., 127 ff., 146 ff.

⁴⁶ Ibid., pp. 94 ff., 195 ff., 306 ff.

⁴⁷ Ibid., p. 59.

⁴⁸ CD, II, 2, pp. 94 ff.

⁴⁹ These arguments are to be found partly in his doctrine of God's election of grace (CD, II, 2, pp. 3 ff., 76 ff., 94 ff.) and partly in

other parts of his *Church Dogmatics* (e.g. CD, IV, 1, pp. 16 ff., 22 ff., 36 ff., 46 ff., 66 f.; IV, 2, pp. 32 ff., 42).

[50] It is at this point that many questions could be raised and some of the implied premisses might be queried; lack of space however forbids such a discussion.

[51] CD, IV, 1, pp. 46 ff.; IV, 2, p. 33.

[52] Z. Th. K., 1951, p. 98.

[53] CD, IV, 1, p. 53.

[54] CD, II, 2, pp. 95 ff., 116 ff.

[55] Ibid., pp. 161 ff.

[56] Ibid., pp. 122 ff., 161 ff., 340 ff., 352 ff.

[57] CD, II, 2, pp. 417 ff.; IV, 3, p. 478.

[58] CD, II, 2, pp. 449 ff.

[59] CD, III, 3, pp. 461 ff.

[60] CD, II, 2, pp. 422 f.

[61] Ibid., pp. 457 ff., 506.

[62] Ibid., p. 320.

[63] Ibid., pp. 126 ff., 180 ff., 340 ff.

[64] Above, Ch. II, 4, 5.

[65] CD, III, 1, p. IX.

[66] René Descartes, *Meditationes de prima philosophia* (1641).

[67] CD, III, 1, pp. 350 ff.

[68] Above, Ch. II, 2; CD, III, 1, pp. 3 ff.

[69] *Gifford*, pp. 15, 37, 43 f.; CD, III, 1, pp. 3, 6, 11, 23 ff.

[70] G. Wingren, *Creation and Law* (1961), pp. 11 ff., 92.

[71] The same, *Theology in Conflict*, p. 82; *Creation and Law*, p. 12; see also above, par. 1.

[72] G. Wingren, *Creation and Law*, p. 11.

[73] CD, III, 1, pp. 11 ff., 49.

[74] Ibid., pp. 87 ff., 99 ff., 119 ff., 135 ff., 158 ff., 171 ff., 191 ff., 219 ff., 239 ff., 276 ff., 324 ff. With regard to Barth's teaching on the creation story as unhistoriographical history and as saga see CD, II, 1, p. 118; III, 1, pp. 14 ff., 42 ff., 59 ff., 76 ff.

[75] CD, III, 1, pp. 42 ff., 94 ff., 228 ff.

[76] Ibid., pp. 59 f.

[77] CD, II, 2, pp. 8 ff., 102; III, 1, pp. 48 ff.; IV, 1, pp. 35 ff., 47 ff., 66.

[78] CD, II, 2, pp. 10 f., 94 ff.; III, 1, pp. 42 ff.; IV, 1, p. 53.

[79] As to Barth's teaching on created time see CD, III, 1, pp. 67 ff.

[80] CD, III, 1, pp. 330 ff.; III, 3, pp. 289 ff.

[81] CD, II, 2, p. 13; III, 1, pp. 257 ff., 330 ff., 375 ff.; IV, 1, pp. 409 ff.

[82] The term 'death' is not used here in the sense of life's natural limitation but in its second sense as eternal death, CD, III, 3, p. 74.

[83] For this translation I am indebted to A. C. Cochrane, who in note 1 on page 187 of O. Weber's, *Karl Barth's Church Dogmatics*, gives the reasons for this translation. The term 'nothingness', used for the translation of *das Nichtige* in CD, III, 3, par. 50 and elsewhere, is much to be regretted as it obscures the grim reality and great temporary power of evil as asserted in Barth's teaching on the Nihil.

[84] CD, III, 3, pp. 302 ff.; IV, 3, pp. 173 ff.

[85] CD, III, 3, pp. 311 f., 354 ff., 362 ff.; IV, 1, pp. 408 ff.; IV, 3, pp. 173 ff.; this teaching is of special importance to preachers.

[86] Comp. Tillich's narrower concept of evil (*Systematic Theology*, vol. II, pp. 52 ff., 70 f.) as the consequences of sin, of estrangement from God, one's self and the world, and as a means of clarifying the concepts related to the problem of theodicy only.

[87] CD, II, 2, p. 122; III, 1, pp. 330 ff., 366 ff., 377 ff.

[88] CD, III, 1, pp. 334 ff., 337 ff.

[89] Ibid., pp. 340 ff.

⁹⁰ CD, III, 1, pp. 334 ff., 337 ff.

⁹¹ Ibid., pp. 388 ff., 406 ff.

⁹² Ibid., p. 412.

⁹³ This appears to be the ultimate explanation of G. Wingren's (*Theology in Conflict*, p. 25, 109, 117) misinterpretation of Barth's teaching on the Nihil.

⁹⁴ CD, II, 1, p. 532.

⁹⁵ See the sub-section 'The Reality of the Nihil', in CD, III, 3, pp. 349 ff., which G. Wingren's assertion (op. cit., p. 25) that 'there is no devil in Barth's theology' seems to ignore; also CD, IV, 3, pp. 176 ff. and TT, p. 17.

⁹⁶ CD, II, 1, pp. 553 ff.; III, 3, p. 332.

⁹⁷ CD, II, 1, p. 532.

⁹⁸ Ibid.

⁹⁹ CD, IV, 3, p. 178.

¹⁰⁰ Barth in a letter referred to by A. C. Cochrane in his footnote, quoted above, note 83.

¹⁰¹ *Credo*, pp. 36 f.; CD, II, 1, pp. 503 f.; 532 ff., 549 ff.; III, 3, p. 354.

¹⁰² CD, IV, 3, p. 177.

¹⁰³ Prof. David Cairn's criticism of this terminology in *A Gospel Without Myth?* (1960), p. 211, as 'an expression of emotion rather than of thought' overlooks this point.

¹⁰⁴ CD, II, 2, pp. 170 ff.; III, 3, p. 351; IV, 3, pp. 178 ff.

¹⁰⁵ CD, II, 1, p. 503; III, 3, pp. 354 ff.

¹⁰⁶ CD, III, 3, pp. 302 ff., 354 ff.

¹⁰⁷ CD, II, 2, p. 172; III, 3, pp. 74 ff., 302 ff.; IV, 1, pp. 407 ff.

¹⁰⁸ CD, II, 2, pp. 170 ff., 291; III, 3, pp. 302 ff., 354 ff.; IV, 1, pp. 408 ff.; TT, pp. 16 f.

¹⁰⁹ CD, III, 3, pp. 312–49.

¹¹⁰ CD, II, 1, pp. 555 ff., 561, 594 ff.; II, 2, p. 172; III, 1, p. 127.

¹¹¹ CD, II, 1, p. 595.

¹¹² CD, III, 2, pp. 1 ff.

¹¹³ *Gifford*, p. 48; *Against the Stream*, pp. 186 ff.; *Christ and Adam*, SJT, Occasional Papers No. 5 (1956), p. 5; CD, I, 2, pp. 296 f.; II, 1, pp. 161 ff.; III, 2, pp. 3 ff., 19 ff., 42 ff., 325 ff.

¹¹⁴ CD, III, 2, p. 46.

¹¹⁵ Above, Chs. II, 7 (3); III, 2.

¹¹⁶ *Against the Stream*, pp. 186 ff.; CD, III, 2, pp. 13 ff., 19 ff., 55 ff., 71 ff.

¹¹⁷ Above, Ch. II, 3.

¹¹⁸ CD, I, 1, p. 197; II, 1, pp. 162 ff.; III, 2, pp. 68 ff., 71 ff.

¹¹⁹ CD, III, 2, pp. 23 ff.

¹²⁰ Ibid., pp. 47 ff.; see further, J. G. Gibbs, *A Secondary Point of Reference in Barth's Anthropology*, SJT, June 1963, pp. 132 ff.

¹²¹ CD, III, 2, pp. 55 ff.

¹²² Ibid., pp. 203 ff.

¹²³ Ibid., pp. 325 ff.

¹²⁴ Ibid., pp. 437 ff.

¹²⁵ Comp. on this point R. Gregor Smith, *The New Man*, pp. 15 ff.

¹²⁶ CD, III, 2, pp. 157 ff.

¹²⁷ Ibid., pp. 76 ff.

¹²⁸ Ibid., pp. 96 ff.

¹²⁹ Ibid., pp. 113 ff.

¹³⁰ CD, IV, 1, p. 89.

¹³¹ Barth's teaching on 'Man in his Time' (CD, III, 2, pp. 437 ff.) is one of the most instructive sections of his *Church Dogmatics* and deserves careful study, especially by preachers.

¹³² CD, II, 1, pp. 211 ff., 667 ff.; III, 2, pp. 166 ff.; IV, 1, pp. 42 f.

¹³³ Above, Chs. I, 5 (3); II, 3, 4.

¹³⁴ CD, II, 2, p. 178; III, 2, pp. 165 ff.; III, 3, pp. 90 ff.

¹³⁵ Above, Ch. II, 7 (4); below, Ch. IV.

¹³⁶ CD, III, 2, pp. 192 ff., espec. 195.

¹³⁷ *Gifford*, pp. 45 ff.; *Against the Stream*, pp. 188 f.; CD, III, 2, pp. 26 ff.

¹³⁸ *Against the Stream*, p. 189.

¹³⁹ *Christ and Adam*, loc. cit., pp. 6 ff.

[140] Impossible from the standpoint of man's election as God's covenant-partner and of his already accomplished objective justification and sanctification in Jesus Christ (below, par. 6).

[141] *Natural Theology*, p. 79; CD, III, 1, pp. 366 ff.; III, 2, pp. 31 ff., 42, 146 ff., 196 ff.; III, 3, pp. 292, 356; IV, 1, pp. 405 ff., 480 ff., 492 ff.

[142] CD, III, 2, pp. 203 ff.

[143] Ibid., p. 228.

[144] Ibid., pp. 231 ff.

[145] Ibid., pp. 250 ff., 265 ff.

[146] See further, CD, III, 1, pp. 182 ff., 288 ff.; III, 2, pp. 219 ff., 323 f.; IV, 1, pp. 203, 492 f.; my essay on '*The Teaching of Karl Barth on the Doctrine of the Imago Dei*', loc. cit.; David Cairns, *The Image of God in Man* (1953), pp. 164 ff.; A. B. Come, *An Introduction to Barth's Dogmatics for Preachers*, pp. 145 ff., 153.

[147] *Credo*, p. 33; *Gifford*, pp. 38, 41 ff., 48 ff.; CD, I, 1, pp. 273, 276; I, 2, pp. 307 f.; II, 1, pp. 188, 673; II, 2, p. 173.

[148] Compare with this the very different teaching of Emil Brunner, *Dogmatics*, vol. II, pp. 55 ff., espec. 77, 123, who, distinguishing between a formal structural and a material *Imago Dei* in the individual man, claims that the latter but not the former is lost through sin.

[149] The decisive importance of man's creation as male and female (Gen. 1:27) for Barth's teaching on the *Imago Dei* cannot be discussed here; what is primarily said of man and woman, however, applies also to man's relation to other men, see CD, III, 1, pp. 184 ff.; TT, pp. 41, 57, 96.

[150] See above, Ch. II, 7 (2).

[151] Above, Ch. II, 4; CD, III, 1, pp. 184 ff.; III, 2, pp. 219 f., 323 f.

[152] CD, III, 1, pp. 189 f., 200;

III, 2, p. 324; IV, 1, pp. 406, 492 f.; TT, p. 41.

[153] As to Barth's teaching on 'Man as Soul and Body', see CD, III, 2, pp. 325 ff., in particular his critical analysis of the scientific materialism of Ernst Haeckel and of the historical materialism of Karl Marx (ibid., pp. 383 ff.).

[154] As regards its magnificent and profound structure see above, Ch. I, 4.

[155] CD, IV, 1, pp. 16 ff., 79 ff., 125 ff.

[156] CD, IV, 1, pp. 211 ff.

[157] CD, IV, 2, pp. 154 ff.

[158] CD, IV, 3, pp. 38 ff., 165 ff.

[159] CD, IV, 1, pp. 122 ff., 135 ff.

[160] Ibid., p. 136; TT, pp. 17 f.

[161] Above, Ch. III, 1, 2.

[162] See above, Ch. III, 2.

[163] See above, Ch. III, 1.

[164] *Gifford*, pp. 73 f.; CD, IV, 1, pp. 7 ff., 46 ff.

[165] CD, IV, 1, pp. 8 ff., 13 ff., 46 ff.

[166] Ibid., pp. 79 ff.

[167] CD, II, 2, pp. 167 ff.

[168] CD, IV, 1, pp. 22 ff., 135 ff.

[169] Above, Ch. III, 2.

[170] CD, IV, 1, pp. 3 ff., 22 ff.

[171] Ibid., p. 36.

[172] Ibid., pp. 125 ff.

[173] CD, II, 2, p. 421; IV, 1, pp. 20 f., 122 ff.

[174] See above, Ch. I, 5 (2); CD, IV, 3, pp. 7 ff.; R. Gregor Smith, *The New Man*, pp. 47 f. makes the same point in respect of the Word of God.

[175] In his Preface to his doctrine of reconciliation (CD, IV, 1, p. ix) Barth says: 'throughout I found myself in an intensive, although for the most part quiet, debate with Rudolf Bultmann'; see also *Bultmann*, p. 99.

[176] CD, IV, 1, pp. 132 f.

[177] Ibid., pp. 133 f.

[178] But not divinized.

[179] CD, IV, 1, pp. 134 f.

[180] CD, IV, 1, pp. 145 ff., 514 ff.; IV, 2, pp. 499 ff.; IV, 3, pp. 481 ff.

[181] CD, IV, 1, pp. 92 ff.; IV, 2, pp. 499 ff.; IV, 3, pp. 3 ff., 481 ff.

[182] CD, IV, 1, p. 101; IV, 2, pp. 499 ff.

[183] CD, IV, 1, pp. 108 ff.; IV, 3, pp. 3 ff., 481 ff., 520 ff., 554 ff.

[184] Above, Ch. I, 5 (2).

[185] Above, Ch. II, 7 (4).

[186] *Christ and Adam*, pp. 2 ff.; CD, III, 1, pp. 386 f.; IV, 1, pp. 20, 89 ff., 92 ff., 147 ff., 643 ff.; IV, 3, pp. 179 ff.; A. B. Come's criticism of 'two unreconciled strains in at least the language if not the thought' of the *Church Dogmatics* about Christ's reconciling work (*An Introduction to Barth's Dogmatics for Preachers*, p. 161) overlooks this important distinction.

[187] CD, III, 2, pp. 298 ff.; IV, 1, pp. 147 ff.

[188] *Against the Stream*, pp. 186 ff., 235 ff.; CD, I, 1, pp. 51, 457 ff., 468, 509; I, 2, pp. 40, 190, 195; IV, 1, pp. 3 ff., 39 ff., 79 ff.

[189] CD, I, 2, pp. 38 ff.; IV, 3, pp. 3 ff., 38 ff.

[190] See above, Ch. I, 5 (1c).

[191] G. Wingren, *Theology in Conflict*, pp. 67, 125, misses this point in his criticism of what he regards as Barth's intellectualist concept of the Gospel.

[192] *Gifford*, pp. 47 ff.; CD, III, 2, pp. 26 ff., 34 ff.; III, 3, pp. 306 ff.; IV, 1, pp. 10 ff., 36, 38 ff., 79 ff., 138 ff., 358 ff.; IV, 2, pp. 378 ff.; IV, 3, pp. 368 ff.

[193] CD, IV, 1, pp. 138 ff.

[194] See above, Ch. III, 4.

[195] Above, Ch. III, 2.

[196] Above, Ch. III, 5.

[197] This concept of sin goes further and is even more concrete than Tillich's notion of sin (*Systematic Theology*, vol. II, pp. 51 ff.) as man's turning away from God, from his own self and from other beings.

[198] CD, I, 1, pp. 175, 509; I, 2, pp. 398 f.; II, 1, pp. 503 f.; II, 2, p. 452; III, 2, p. 146; III, 3, pp. 353 f.; IV, 1, pp. 67 ff., 138 ff.

[199] CD, III, 2, pp. 26 ff., 34 ff.; III, 3, pp. 306 ff., 356; IV, 1, pp. 44 ff., 140 ff.

[200] CD, IV, 1, pp. 142 ff., 358 ff.; IV, 2, pp. 378 ff.; IV, 3, pp. 368 ff.

[201] CD, IV, 3, p. 369.

[202] CD, IV, 1, pp. 478 ff.; IV, 2, pp. 483 ff.; IV, 3, pp. 461 ff.

[203] 'Perdition' renders the meaning of the German term *Verdamnis* more adequately than the word 'condemnation' used in CD, IV, 3, pp. 461 ff.

[204] CD, III, 1, pp. 307 f.; IV, 1, pp. 44 ff., 67 ff.

[205] As to the various doctrines of the Atonement see J. K. Mozley, *The Doctrine of the Atonement* (1915), *passim*.

[206] CD, IV, 1, pp. 252 f.

[207] See the magnificent passage on Jesus Christ's reconciling work in CD, II, 1, pp. 152 f.

[208] For reasons subsequently given, Barth prefers to speak of the Community of Jesus Christ instead of the Church.

[209] Much teaching on this subject-matter will be found in *Credo*, pp. 139 ff.; *Gifford*, pp. 148 ff., 233 ff.; *Against the Stream*, pp. 13 ff.; CD, I, 1, pp. 1 ff., 51 ff.; I, 2, pp. 203 ff., 362 ff., 538 ff., 661 ff., 743 ff.; II, 2, pp. 195 ff., 306 ff.; IV, 1, pp. 643 ff., 650 ff., 740 ff.; IV, 2, pp. 614 ff., 727 ff.; IV, 3, pp. 481 ff., 681 ff., 902 ff.

[210] Above, Ch. I, 5 (3).

[211] CD, IV, 1, p. 661; IV, 2, pp. 650 ff., espec. 655.

[212] *Gifford*, pp. 150 ff.; CD, II, 1, p. 161.

[213] CD, II, 1, p. 622; III, 2, pp. 299 ff.

[214] CD, III, 2, pp. 301 ff.; IV, 1, pp. 725 ff.; IV, 3, pp. 327 ff., 357 ff.

[215] CD, IV, 2, pp. 676 ff.; compare therewith E. Brunner, *The Misunderstanding of the Church* (1952), pp. 10, 17, 84, 110.

[216] Above, Ch. I, 5 (3).

[217] CD, IV, 1, pp. 650 ff.

[218] CD, I, 1, p. 44; IV, 1, pp. 650 ff.

[219] CD, IV, 1, p. 656.

[220] *Against the Stream*, pp. 15 f., 190; CD, IV, 1, pp. 147 ff., 608 ff., 643 ff., 694 ff., 740 ff.; IV, 2, pp. 499 ff., 727 ff.; IV, 3, pp. 481 ff., 902 ff.

[221] CD, IV, 1, pp. 96 ff.

[222] On the meaning of 'to be in Christ' see CD, I, 2, pp. 240, 362 ff.; II, 1, pp. 128 ff., 667 ff.; IV, 1, pp. 92 ff.

[223] *Against the Stream*, pp. 13 ff.; *Gifford*, pp. 150 ff.; IET, p. 37; CD, III, 4, pp. 470 ff., 488 ff.; IV, 1, pp. 650 ff.; IV, 2, pp. 614 ff.; IV, 3, pp. 681 ff.

[224] Above, Ch. III, 5.

[225] CD, III, 4, pp. 488 ff.; IV, 2, pp. 690 ff.

[226] CD, III, 4, p. 489.

[227] Ibid., p. 490.

[228] Ibid., p. 515.

[229] *Gifford*, p. 185; CD, I, 2, pp. 538 ff.

[230] CD, IV, 1, p. 150.

[231] In which burning Church problems of today are dealt with: CD, IV, 1, pp. 668 ff.

[232] Ibid., pp. 705 f.

[233] Ibid., pp. 685 ff.

[234] Ibid., p. 688.

[235] CD, IV, 3, Preface, pp. xi f. and pp. 554 ff., 762 ff., 795 ff., 830 ff.

[236] CD, IV, 1, pp. 725 ff.; IV, 3, pp. 762 ff., 795 ff.

[237] CD, IV, 3, pp. 780 ff.

[238] *Credo*, p. 150; CD, IV, 3, pp. 520 ff., 554 ff., 573 ff.

[239] CD, II, 2, pp. 431 ff.; IV, 1, pp. 712 ff.

[240] This is another example of Barth's actualism.

[241] CD, IV, 1, pp. 715 f.

[242] Ibid., p. 719.

IV.—GOSPEL AND LAW

1. THEOLOGICAL ETHICS[1]

BARTH uses the term 'ethics' not in the abstract and neutral sense in which it is generally used, but in the quite specific and concrete sense it receives from the specific object to which it is applied. For the ethical problem, he argues, is not posed in a vacuum; we are not free to investigate the question of good and evil in human behaviour as if God's revelation in Jesus Christ had never occurred. His ethics arises, as it were, out of man's living encounter in every sphere of his existence with the command of the Living God as the latter is enacted in and through the person and work of the living Lord Jesus Christ.

It is theological ethics in that, as Christian ethics, it takes as its point of departure the Word of God as addressed to man in Jesus Christ and, consequently,[2] Jesus Christ Himself, the incarnate Word of God, who, being both the holy God and the sanctified man who as such has fulfilled the Law by keeping its commandments, is for that very reason the key to the understanding of Christian ethics.[3] The work and revelation of God's grace in Jesus Christ, Barth contends, represent the answer to the ethical problem and on that account constitute the point of departure of theological ethics as the doctrine of God's command. In other words, theological ethics represents the insight that 'what is good' has been said to man in and through that work and revelation.[4] To put the same thought more concretely, the question of good and evil has been decided once for all in God's eternal decree before time[5] when God, electing man for fellowship with Himself, claimed man for Himself and thereby made Himself responsible for man's sanctification.

Again, that question has been decided once for all by the Cross and resurrection of Jesus Christ whereby the justification, sanctification and vocation of sinful man was accomplished in Jesus Christ.[6] For the Cross of Jesus Christ reveals to us, in the light of His resurrection, God's Yes to what is good in His creation and His No to the forces of evil opposing His good creation, including man's sin. Hence, ethics, as theological ethics, can only accept this divine answer and expound it. There is no room for man's independent enquiry into the question of good and evil. Otherwise man would usurp God's place as the sole Judge of good and evil. Moreover, in so doing, man would reject God's gracious decision and revelation of what is good in His sight and thus, contrary to man's true nature as God's creature, elected by God, reconciled with God and called to His service,[7] would refuse to depend on God's grace in this respect. This is why Barth is opposed to making an independent science of morals, in particular moral philosophy, or the abstract idea of good and evil or any so-called natural law the basis and object of Christian ethics.[8]

Again, in the sphere of the Christian Faith knowing (theory) and doing (practice) cannot be separated from each other since the hearing of the Word of God and the doing of it postulate and imply each other. There is no knowledge of God without the service of God and vice versa.[9] Consequently, theological ethics forms an integral part of dogmatics. A separate ethics alongside dogmatics is in Barth's view not only superfluous, but leads to errors since it is exposed to the danger of replacing God's Word in Jesus Christ by the word of man, and moreover separates the Law from the Gospel which, as we shall see, is said by Barth to include the Law. As the doctrine of God's command theological ethics is regarded by him as belonging more particularly to the doctrine of God[10] in that it deals with, and bears witness to, God's grace in Jesus Christ in so far as that grace

is the saving engagement and commitment of man. For, as
a distinct attitude of God, the grace of God in Jesus Christ is
an essential element in the reality of God who is not known
and not knowable except in Jesus Christ (above, Ch. III, 2)
and therefore does not exist without His covenant with man
established and executed in the Godman Jesus Christ.[11] In
that God, as the Electing God,[11] made a covenant with man
in Jesus Christ and thereby made Himself responsible for
man as His covenant-partner, He demanded something from
His covenant-partner.[12] For He is the Lord and man is His
creature and thus, within the framework of the covenant, He
is both the One by whom man will be judged and the One
whom man must take as His model. In other words, God as
the covenant-God, and therefore God in Jesus Christ in
whom that covenant was instituted and fulfilled, is for man
the criterion of the rightness or wrongness of man's being
and acting.[12] This shows that within Barth's doctrine of
God it is God's covenant of grace with man in Jesus Christ
which is the proper setting for his theological ethics. In a
narrower sense the latter starts from, and is governed by, the
covenant. On this basis two major aspects of Barth's theological ethics have been developed to which we must now
turn as they are of vital importance for the true understanding of his teaching on this subject-matter, namely his concepts of theological ethics as an ethics of grace and as an
ethics of freedom.

2. The Precedence of the Gospel

Of the many reversions in Barth's theology of the traditional dogmatic teaching one of the most striking ones is his
theological proposition[13] that the Gospel precedes the Law
and that the Law is the form of the Gospel. This radical
reversal of the customary thought of the Gospel as the antithesis and saving answer to the Law is so much at variance
with everything we have learned in the past about the
relationship between, and the sequence of, Law and Gospel
that it is not surprising that this tenet of Barth's theology

has been widely criticized.[14] However, the primary cause of this controversy, which ultimately rests upon a divergent theological exegesis of the Bible, is of a terminological and teleological nature, namely a different concept of the term 'Gospel' and a different understanding of the purpose of the Law.

As previously pointed out,[15] with Barth the Gospel starts in God's eternity before time when God resolved in His eternal decree[16] to have fellowship with man, even with sinful man, in Jesus Christ. This eternal plan of God with man in Jesus Christ, Barth holds, is already Good News, Gospel, in that it proclaims God's free and sovereign grace towards man in Jesus Christ, God's eternal Yes to man in Jesus Christ, taking upon Himself (in His thought and will) the (future) rejection of man's sin and fore-ordaining man's ultimate salvation in Jesus Christ, man's future participation in the being of God as God's co-worker in His eternal kingdom.[17] Thus God's free and sovereign grace in Jesus Christ, and therefore the Gospel, stands at the beginning of all the ways and works of God *ad extra*; in other words, God's grace, and therefore the Gospel, comes first in God's dealings with man.[18]

On the other hand, the instrument whereby, and the framework within which, that grace, that Gospel, is carried into effect, is God's covenant with man. The origin, object and goal of the latter is therefore the actualization of God's grace in Jesus Christ and thus of the Gospel. In brief, it is a covenant of grace, and everything which is done within this relationship between God and man takes place within the sphere of that divine grace. This means two things: the Gospel both precedes and includes the Law.[19] In His covenant with man God is gracious to man not only in that He binds Himself to man and thereby makes Himself responsible for man's sanctification but also in that He binds man to Himself and thereby makes man responsible to Himself as the Lord and Judge of man. For the claim He lays upon man serves the gracious purpose of guiding and directing man by His commandments in order that, in this way, He may work out man's sanctification. The purpose of the Law, in Barth's view, is therefore not, as E. Brunner[20] assumes, to provide an answer to man's sin by bringing man to a recognition of his sin by means of the Law, but to make man a worthy partner in God's covenant with man.

Again, it is for a definite purpose that in His election of grace (above, Ch. III, par. 2) God elects man as His covenant-partner; for His own as well as for man's sake He wants to commission man for a share in His work, making man a witness of Jesus Christ and thus of God's glory.[21] This gracious purpose, however, cannot be achieved without man's obedience to God's Word in Jesus Christ. Thus God requires man's responsible self-determination in response to his divine predetermination in Jesus Christ. This does not mean that man has to work out his own salvation; all that is demanded from him by God is that in grateful response to God's grace in Jesus Christ, whereby man's salvation (objectively) has already been accomplished in Jesus Christ, he lives by and from that grace, following Jesus Christ and obeying His commandments. To put it differently, the Christian serves God not in order to be saved but because he has been saved in Jesus Christ. He obeys God's Law in recognition and acceptance of God's grace in Jesus Christ.

Thus the Law is in the Gospel, comes from the Gospel and is directed to the Gospel; the Gospel, that is, God's grace in Jesus Christ, manifests itself also as God's gracious claim on man, on his obedience, for the sake of man's sanctification.[22] The grace of God in Jesus Christ is therefore also a demanding and commanding grace, calling man, as Jesus Christ's disciple and witness, to the active service of God and of his fellow-men.[23] This is why this grace, and therefore the Gospel, is said to have the form of the Law. The latter is the instrument whereby, and the form in which, God's grace in Jesus Christ accomplishes its purpose. Consequently, Gospel and Law are not opposed to each other; on the contrary, the former requires the latter for the realization of its purpose and the latter presupposes the former as its source and goal. Barth emphatically rejects the traditional view of the Old Testament as 'the Book of the Law', as the document of a legalistic religion, and of the New Testament as 'the Book of the Gospel', as the document of the reconciling love of Jesus Christ without and in opposition to the Law. He contends that both the Old and the New Testaments bear witness in the first place to God's grace in Jesus Christ and therefore to the Gospel and because of that also to the Law as a means of man's sanctification. Again, this Law is said to be one and the same Law in both of them, a sign of God's grace towards man and of the election of His people, first Israel and then the Church, and a means of grace for the sanctification of God's people. The New Testament witness in particular is characterized as having everywhere the form of the Law, being throughout proclamation of the justifying and sanctifying grace of God.[24]

The traditional order 'Law and Gospel' is in Barth's view[25] legitimate in so far as it is a question of the victory of God's grace in Jesus Christ's death upon the Cross and resurrection, and therefore of the triumph of the Gospel, over man's sinful misuse of God's Law, using the latter to justify himself by the works of the Law. He insists however that for the reasons previously given the Gospel not only follows the Law but, first and foremost, precedes it. He would not agree with Bonhoeffer's dictum[26] that 'it is only when one submits to the Law that one can speak of grace' but claims that we must first know about the Gospel before we can know about the Law since we truly apprehend and obey the Law because we first hear and accept the Gospel.[27]

Again, Gospel and Law cannot be separated from each other. For the Law receives its power of compelling man's obedience from the Gospel and the Gospel requires the Law for its execution. Above all, the one Word of God, Jesus Christ Himself, is both Gospel and Law.[28] In Him Gospel and Law meet in that God's covenant with man, as originally resolved in God's eternal decree before time, became a living reality, and was fulfilled by God and by man, in the person of Jesus

Christ who as the Son of God fulfilled God's promise to have
fellowship with man and as the Son of man fulfilled the Law
by keeping God's commandments. This is why Barth can say[29]
that Christology is the point where the relationship between
Gospel and Law is fixed. Jesus Christ is not only the Electing
God and the elected man in One (above, Ch. III, par. 2), but
He is also the sanctifying God and the sanctified man in One.
In the one image of Jesus Christ we have both the Gospel
which reconciles us with God and enlightens and comforts
us, and the Law which binds and obligates us because He
Himself has fulfilled the Law in our stead and for our salvation. This is the Law, He is the Law, to which theological
ethics clings. The latter is an ethics of grace because it is in
grace, the grace of God in Jesus Christ, that also the command
of God is established and fulfilled. Therefore, to act rightly,
to realize 'the good', means to become obedient to the
revelation of God's grace in Jesus Christ.[30]

As an ethics of grace theological ethics is by necessity an
ethics of freedom. The special importance of the concept of
freedom for Barth's teaching on ethics has already been
stressed.[31] The main theme of his ethics is not the usual one
of morals but the freedom into which God calls man by His
command as a counterpart to His own freedom for man in
Jesus Christ.[32] In His own freedom as the God who loves in
freedom (above, Ch. III, par. 2) God bestows human freedom[33]
in order that man, as a free being,[34] may use this freedom to
respond to God's grace in Jesus Christ by his own free and
responsible decision for God, rendering to God that free
obedience to His Word and command in Jesus Christ which
is required by man's election as the covenant-partner of God
and is necessary for man's sanctification. Thus man's true
freedom is his freedom *for* God.[35] It is not a choice between
alternatives, between God and someone or something else,
as this would mean that God, who is good and the source of
all goodness, could or would allow man to turn to that which
does not originate in God and, belonging on that account to
the Nihil, can only be evil.[36] Hence, man's freedom is the

freedom of obedience to God's command as the sum total of the good and as such is simultaneously his freedom from bondage to the powers of darkness.[37]

The decisive significance attributed to the concept of freedom within the context of Barth's ethics can be inferred from his characterization of the divine gift of freedom as the foundation of Christian ethics and of Christian ethics as the reflection upon what man is required to do in and with the gift of freedom[38] and further from his description, in one of his sermons,[39] of the Bible as a 'book of freedom', namely as the testimony to man's God-given freedom for God. Barth's basic ethical proposition concerning God's command is—and it is at this point that we can discern how in his ethical teaching grace and freedom, man's sanctification as the gracious purpose of the Law and man's freedom as God's gracious gift to man for the purpose of man's sanctification and therefore freedom and obedience concur and postulate each other—that God's command, His claiming and demanding, is actually a gracious offer, a giving and permitting, not a 'must' but a 'may'. For God by His Law, which is 'the law of the spirit of life' (Rom. 8:2), calls man into a marvellous freedom, namely the freedom to rely in everything, including the problem of right human conduct, on God's grace in Jesus Christ, who, as the sanctifying God and the sanctified man, has already answered for us the question of what we ought to do in that He Himself rendered the obedience demanded of us by God.[40] Thus we only need to show our gratitude for what He has done in our stead and for our salvation by confirming His action by our action, responding to His sacrificial love with our thanksgiving, praise and love and using the God-given freedom in which we are placed in Jesus Christ by following His example and direction. In that God commands us to act in this manner, His command assumes the character of a permission rather than an order, of a direction into freedom rather than the imposing of a law.[41] In short, God's command is man's liberation to a life lived in the joyful freedom of the children of God who by the 'totally unmerited and wondrous' gift of freedom are awakened to 'true selfhood and new life'.[42]

3. THE COMMAND OF GOD

Just as Barth's teaching on man is modelled on the humanity of Jesus Christ as the real man (above, Ch. III, par. 5), so his teaching on the nature, form and content of God's command is derived from the knowledge of Jesus Christ as the holy God (Son of God) and the sanctified man in One, who in His relation to God, to His fellow-men and to His own self has rendered perfect obedience to the will of His heavenly Father and thus has fulfilled the Law.[43] With Barth Jesus Christ is the ground, content and form of God's command. What right conduct is for man is determined in Jesus Christ. In Him the holy God has acted rightly towards man and man has acted rightly for his fellow-men. He, and He alone, is the true Christian life because He, and He alone, did not sin but was the obedient doer of God's will. Thus, believing in Him, the Christian, as His disciple and witness, can only look to Him for guidance in the question of his conduct. The latter will be good in God's sight if it is determined by Jesus Christ, by faith in Jesus Christ.[44]

Consequently, the criterion of Christian conduct, and thus the voice to which the Christian is called to listen, is neither 'the Christian self-consciousness', as Schleiermacher taught,[45] nor an 'inner light' in man, 'alleged to be divine',[46] nor man's conscience but Jesus Christ. The human conscience is only the organ through which the living Lord Jesus Christ speaks to man in the power of the Holy Spirit.[47] Thus the command of God is not an independent theme to be dealt with apart from God's grace in Jesus Christ but has its basis, authority and validity in the crucified and risen Jesus Christ in whom the Law has been established and fulfilled.[48] Again, the command of God is the perpetually renewed encounter between the living Lord Jesus Christ and individual men, namely the constant hearing of the Word of God which God in Jesus Christ speaks throughout the ages to individual men in their specific concrete situation. Hence, it is always a single concrete event. It is neither static in essence nor general in character but is always a distinct divine action of a particular character, continually addressed by God to this or that individual in a particular concrete situation.[49] Again, it is God's continual fresh giving and man's continual fresh receiving of the freedom to obey God's will in a particular situation, a freedom which, because of man's sinfulness, has to be created in man ever anew by the power of the Holy Spirit.

This shows how at this point too Barth's actualism[50] is at work, contending that God continually gives fresh commands the definite and specific content of which accords with the particular situation in which they are issued.[51] Consequently, Barth rejects the view of ethics as a fixed set of rules and of God's command as a collection of general precepts the application of which in an individual case would be a matter for man's judgment and action.[52] Such a view, he holds, is at variance with the freedom of God's grace which does not leave to man the final decision of whether in an individual case a command of God is applicable and therefore is to be obeyed by man. In each and every command it is God Himself who actually *gives* the command and in so doing gives Himself to be man's Commander so that man can only obey or disobey the command in question. In the last analysis it is for the same reason that Barth also rejects the Roman Catholic demarcation and synthesis of natural ethics (moral philosophy) and an ethics of grace (moral theology), arguing that grace which from the outset has to share its power with a capacity of nature is no longer God's grace as we know it in Jesus Christ.[53] On the other hand, though there are many particular divine commands, they have their unity in Jesus Christ who is the same yesterday, today and for ever. Again, they serve, all of them, one and the same purpose, namely the actualization of God's eternal decree before time (above, Ch. III, par. 2), in other words, the establishment of fellowship between God and man in Jesus Christ.[54]

Barth's teaching on the nature of God's command as God's

M

claim whereby He claims man for Himself,[55] as His sovereign, definite and good *decision* concerning the character of man's action[56] and as His gracious *judgment* whereby He judges man in Jesus Christ to make man free for eternal life under His Lordship[57] can here only be referred to. This general ethics is to be followed by a special ethics showing in detail how God's command is directed to man in the particular spheres of creation, reconciliation and redemption, in other words, in what manner man is addressed by God's command in his threefold determination as God's creature, as the sinner to whom grace is shown in Jesus Christ, and as the heir of God's kingdom.[58] Though by way of appropriation Barth distinguishes the command of God the Creator (the Father), God the Reconciler (the Son), and God the Redeemer (the Holy Spirit),[59] he holds that in essence it is one and the same command of the one and only God. Its content indeed varies according to the particular spheres in which it is issued, but it nevertheless pursues in every sphere the same purpose of man's sanctification, unifying man by its goodness with God, with his fellow-men and in himself.[60]

So far only the special ethics in the sphere of creation has been published (CD, III, 4). Taking as its starting-point the structure of real man as inferred from the humanity of Jesus Christ—the man for God, the man for other men, the whole man, and the Lord of time (above, Ch. III, 5)[61]—the command of God the Creator is said to grant to His creature a fourfold freedom, namely freedom in relation to God,[62] in relation to his fellow-men,[63] in the conduct of his life as the soul of his body,[64] and in his existence as a finite and temporally limited being bounded by God.[65] This teaching covers a wide field. There is hardly any burning problem of everyday life which is not dealt with therein.[66] Again, its sections on 'The Active Life'[67] with its evaluation of human work in the light of man's primary obligation to serve God in the Christian community and on 'The Unique Opportunity'[68] offered to man within the fixed span of his life deserve special attention.

REFERENCES

[1] GL, pp. 1 ff.; *Gifford*, pp. 124 ff.; CD, I, 2, pp. 362 ff., 782 ff.; II, 2, pp. 509 ff.; III, 4, pp. 3 ff.

[2] See above, Ch. II, 6.

[3] GL, p. 8; *Gifford*, pp. 127, 141 ff.; CD, I, 2, pp. 367 ff.; II, 2, pp. 509, 517 ff., 538 ff.; III, 4, pp. 41 ff.

[4] CD, II, 2, p. 537.

[5] See above, Ch. III, 2.

[6] CD, II, 2, pp. 535 ff.

[7] See above, Ch. III, 5, 6.

[8] CD, II, 2, pp. 522 ff., 535 ff.; TT, p. 7.

[9] See above, Ch. I, 5 (1c); CD, I, 2, pp. 365 ff., 787 ff.

[10] See above, Ch. I, 4.

[11] See above, Ch. III, 2; also CD, II, 2, pp. 509 f.

[12] CD, II, 2, pp. 12 f., 509 ff.

[13] GL, pp. 4, 10, 12, 13; CD, II, 2, pp. 509 ff.

[14] See, e.g. G. Wingren, *Theology in Conflict*, pp. 34 f., 67 ff., 110, 126, 159 f.; the same, *Creation and Law*, pp. 125 f., 128, 156, 173.

[15] Above, Ch. III, 1.

[16] Above, Ch. III, 2.

[17] See above, Ch. III, 6.

[18] GL, pp. 3 ff.; *Dogmatics in Outline* (1949), pp. 19; CD, I, 2, pp. 384, 437 f.; II, 2, pp. 511, 539, 547 ff.; III, 1, p. 219; IV, 3, pp. 369 ff.

[19] As to how ethics (Law) arises out of a response to the Gospel, compare also C. H. Dodd, *Gospel and Law* (1951), pp. 8 ff., 25 ff., 46 ff., 59, 64 ff., 83; see further, TT, p. 7.

[20] *Dogmatics*, vol. II, pp. 118 ff., 222 ff.

[21] CD, II, 2, p. 510.

[22] GL, pp. 3 f.; CD, II, 1, pp. 363 f.; II, 2, pp. 12, 509 ff., 556 ff.

[23] GL, pp. 9 f.; CD, II, 2, pp. 509 ff., 552 ff.; Gollwitzer, op. cit., p. 21.

[24] GL, p. 9; CD, I, 2, pp. 272 ff., 310 ff., 359 ff.; II, 2, pp. 244 f.; IV, 3, pp. 369 ff.

[25] GL, pp. 3, 14 ff., 23 ff.

[26] *Letters and Papers from Prison* (Second Edition), p. 79; likewise E. Brunner, op. cit., p. 229.

[27] *Credo*, p. 58; GL, p. 9; CD, II, 2, pp. 556 ff.; IV, 3, pp. 369 ff.

[28] GL, pp. 8 ff.; *Gifford*, pp. 127 ff., 141 ff.; CD, II, 2, pp. 510 f.; IV, 1, p. 53.

[29] *Dogmatics in Outline*, p. 66.

[30] CD, II, 2, pp. 538 ff.

[31] Above, Ch. II, 7 (4).

[32] GF, pp. 69 ff., 84 ff.; CD, II, 2, pp. 552 ff.; III, 4, pp. 47 ff., 116 ff., 324 ff., 565 ff.; IV, 1, pp. 101 f.

[33] GF, pp. 75 ff.; *Against the Stream*, pp. 239 f.

[34] Above, Ch. III, 5; CD, III, 1, pp. 262 ff.

[35] Above, Chs. II, 7 (4), III, 5; GF, pp. 75 ff.; CD, II, 2, pp. 552 ff.; III, 1, pp. 263 ff.; IV, 1, pp. 43; TT, p. 99.

[36] Above, Ch. III, 4; GF, pp. 76 f.; CD, II, 2, pp. 12, 535 ff., 546 ff.; III, 1, pp. 257 ff.; TT, pp. 37, 99.

[37] GF, pp. 80, 82; CD, I, 2, pp. 364 ff., 408; II, 2, pp. 516 ff., 535 ff., 552 ff.; III, 1, pp. 265 f.

[38] GF, pp. 69, 87, 96; CD, IV, 1, p. 102: 'all the individual directions which have to be unfolded in Christian ethics can only be concretions of the one necessary direction to the freedom given to man'.

[39] *Deliverance to the Captives* (1961), p. 15.

[40] *Gifford*, pp. 130, 141 ff.; CD, I, 2, pp. 274 ff.; II, 2, pp. 539 ff., 552 ff., 566 ff., 583 ff.; IV, 1, pp. 99 ff.

41 GF, pp. 76, 82; *Dogmatics in Outline*, p. 19; CD, II, 2, pp. 552 ff.; III, 4, pp. 647 f.; IV, 1, pp. 99 ff.; IV, 2, pp. 264 ff.

42 GF, pp. 78 ff.; CD, I, 2, pp. 362 ff.; II, 2, pp. 583 ff.

43 *Gifford*, pp. 127 ff., 141 ff.; GL, p. 8; CD, II, 2, pp. 244 ff., 509, 517 ff., 538 ff., 560 ff., 566 ff., 577 ff., 605 f.; IV, 1, pp. 53 ff.

44 *Gifford*, pp. 141 ff.; GL, pp. 12 ff.; CD, II, 2, pp. 566 ff., 605 ff., 632 ff., 778 ff.

45 CD, II, 2, pp. 538, 541.

46 *Gifford*, p. 126.

47 *Gifford*, p. 126; GF, pp. 85 f.; CD, II, 2, pp. 543 ff., 667 f.

48 CD, II, 2, pp. 564 f.

49 Ibid., p. 548.

50 Above, Ch. I, 5 (3).

51 *Gifford*, pp. 126 f.; CD, II, 2, pp. 566 ff., 612 f., 631 ff., 645 ff., 661 ff.; IV, 1, pp. 99 ff.; IV, 2, pp. 264 ff.

52 GF, p. 85; CD, II, 2, pp. 661 ff., 675 ff.

53 CD, II, 2, pp. 527 ff.

54 Ibid., pp. 669 ff., 676 ff.

55 Ibid., pp. 552 ff.

56 Ibid., pp. 631 ff.

57 Ibid., pp. 733 ff.

58 Ibid., pp. 549 f.

59 Above, Ch. II, 7 (2).

60 CD, II, 2, pp. 710 ff.

61 CD, III, 4, pp. 45 f.

62 Ibid., pp. 47 ff.

63 Ibid., pp. 116 ff.

64 Ibid., pp. 324 ff.

65 Ibid., pp. 565 ff.

66 Such as, for instance, questions related to the Lord's Day, to prayer, celibacy, marriage, sexuality, abortion, euthanasia, suicide, capital punishment and war.

67 CD, III, 4, pp. 470 ff.

68 Ibid., pp. 565 ff.

V.—THE GRACE OF GOD

IN a previous chapter[1] an attempt has been made to show that in Barth's theology Jesus Christ is the key to the understanding of God, the universe and man. In a similar way it may be claimed that the grace of God is the light in which we have to understand Barth's theology as a whole as well as every individual part of it, and for that reason must be regarded as the key to the true understanding of his theology.[2] The latter is a theology of grace *par excellence*,[3] not only because a place of the first magnitude is assigned in it to the concept of grace as never before in the history of the Christian doctrine of grace, but because in it, generally speaking, all theological concepts, or rather the actions and realities adumbrated by these concepts, have in the last analysis their origin or motive-power in the grace of God or at least receive from that grace their essential character as a work of grace. Barth's particular concept of grace permeates and dominates his theological themes to such a degree and in such a decisive and characteristic manner that the grace of God can be said to occupy at least virtually the central place in them. We must go even further and maintain that apart from that concept the trend of Barth's theology in general and its theological tenets in particular cannot be accurately understood. These statements are not at variance with the claim previously made that Jesus Christ holds the key-position in Barth's theology since in Barth's view, as will presently be discussed, Jesus Christ Himself and as such is the incarnate grace of God in the most comprehensive sense of that term. Again, it is no exaggeration to state that in a sense God's grace in Jesus Christ or, to put the same thought differently, God's gracious eternal Yea and Amen in Jesus Christ to His creation and, above all, to man (above, Ch. III, 4) is the starting-point and the dominant theme of his theology. This theme played a vital, though rather fragmentary, part already in his early theology.[4] It has been fully developed in the existent twelve volumes of his *Church Dogmatics*.

With Barth the divine grace is not an abstract or general principle on which his theology is based.[5] Again, with him grace has not the character of depersonalized grace. In other words, it is not 'a supernatural something in man coming forth from God' (Thomas Aquinas) which can be detached from the Spirit of the living personal God and, as an impersonal divine 'substance of grace', can be transmitted to man as a per-manent gift of sanctifying power. In particular, it is not a physical or quasi-physical substance endowed with magic power which like a seed can be planted in man or like a fluid can be infused into him to work in man its saving power. In short, it is not a 'third element' between God and the object of His grace but an inner mode of being and self-conduct of God Himself.[6] To quote Barth's own definition of grace:[7] 'grace is the inner being and self-conduct of God which dis-tinguishes His doing directed towards the seeking and creating of fellowship by the fact that it is determined by His own free inclination, favour and benevolence, un-conditioned by any merit or claim in the beloved, but also unhindered by any unworthiness or opposition in the latter —able, on the contrary, to overcome all unworthiness and opposition'.

Rejecting the Roman Catholic teaching on grace as a supernatural gift which is bestowed upon man by God and can be received, possessed and manipulated by man, Barth does not deny that grace is also a gift, and a very supernatural gift indeed, but argues that it is a gift only inasmuch as the Giver Himself, and therefore God Himself, makes *Himself* the gift, entering Himself into fellowship with man and thus proving Himself to the latter to be the One who loves in freedom.[8] Thus God gives grace by giving Himself. His grace signifies the gracious presence of the gracious God in His

Word, in all His actions and works. With Barth the nature and content of grace is therefore determined not by any abstract or general idea of grace, be it of a philosophical, ethical or religious character, but quite specifically and concretely by its Subject, that is, by the person of God who as the Triune God loves in freedom [9] and whose love has the quality of grace in that He seeks and creates fellowship between Himself and man by reason of His own free inclination, favour and benevolence.[10]

Though Barth, in his *Church Dogmatics*, [6] treats grace as one of the perfections of God,[11] it is, like all the other divine perfections, a quality of God's one undivided nature.[11] The Triune God is therefore said to be 'wholly grace' and thus is eternally the gracious God who is constantly gracious in all His decisions and actions, even in judgment.[12] In a remarkable passage [13] Barth argues that the criterion of whether we have found and are worshipping God or an idol is 'whether we have found grace—not grace in general or in any arbitrary sense—but grace before Him and in His very presence'. Thus Barth's doctrine of grace is characterized by a tremendous concentration of the concept of grace on the person of God Himself, and it is for this reason that his concept of grace is purely spiritual, strictly personal, and wholly theocentric. Consequently, he rejects altogether the many Roman Catholic varieties of grace developed in Scholasticism, which he regards as the negation of the unity of grace as God's unique and indivisible grace to man in Jesus Christ,[14] and above all that Roman Catholic division of grace which asserts that the latter is, first of all, God's grace (*gratia increata*), but then also the grace received and possessed by man (*gratia creata*).[15] With him grace is always the particular concrete *event* of God's personal gracious approach to man.[16]

Hence, grace is never static but always dynamic in essence, being always both the ever renewed event of God's personal gracious turning to man in Jesus Christ and an entirely new gift of God's gracious self-giving.[17] Here Barth's actualistic way of thinking is once more exhibited.[18] The Pauline idea

of a 'state of grace' (Rom. 5:2; 6:14 f.; 12:6) is alien to
Barth's concept of grace as it presupposes that man can get,
have, possess and use grace like a talent of his own human
nature. In Barth's view man as a creature and sinner[19] is in
constant need of ever renewed personal gracious acts of God
in order to be able to partake of the benefits of God's grace.
There must always be a fresh movement of God's grace, of
the gracious God Himself, towards man.[20] Man, on the other
hand, must constantly ask for God's grace, for God's gracious
presence in His Word and action. Again, Barth derives from
the Lordship of the one and only God and thus from His
aseity, majesty and freedom as the Lord that His grace is
sovereign and free grace, that is to say, that it is God's own,
condescending, ruling, demanding and all-sufficient grace
and that He grants His grace in His own freedom, owing it to
none and never and yet, in His constancy,[21] being for every
the gracious God.[22]

In speaking of the grace of God Barth thereby always
means, as far as God's relation to someone or something
outside Himself is concerned,[23] quite specifically and concretely 'the grace of the Lord Jesus Christ' (2 Cor. 13:14),
that is, the grace that dwells and is manifest, knowable,
effective and imparted in the person of the Godman Jesus
Christ.[24] This far-reaching proposition, covering God's grace
as witnessed to both in the Old and in the New Testaments,
has its basis in the place which Jesus Christ occupies in Barth's
theology. As previously discussed,[25] Jesus Christ and His
Gospel have their beginning in God's eternal decree before
time. For this pretemporal decision of God is primarily and
directly concerned with the person and work of Jesus Christ
in that God by His own free and gracious will determined
Himself in Jesus Christ from eternity for fellowship with man,
even with sinful man, and man for fellowship with Himself,
taking upon Himself the (future) rejection of sinful man with
all its consequences and electing man to participation in His
own glory.[26] It is therefore an act of pure grace. Hence
God's grace in Jesus Christ, and therefore Jesus Christ

Himself as this grace, is the beginning of all the ways and works of God's grace *ad extra*.

Again, Jesus Christ, in whom and through whom God's eternal gracious plan with man (and that includes the creation of the universe[27]) was, and still is, carried into effect and accomplished, is for that reason Himself 'the one grace of God',[28] the incarnate grace of God, in the most comprehensive sense of that term. As the eternal gracious will of God for man Jesus Christ Himself embodies the free grace of God in its totality, and He does so, above all, because in Him the gracious God Himself united Himself with humanity by an act of His free grace and because, as the risen man, He is the concrete demonstration of the gracious God.[29] Thus it is in and through Jesus Christ that God Himself is acting graciously from eternity to eternity. As the one Word of God[30] He is God's Word of grace in which the gracious God meets man in all His works, in revelation as well as in creation, reconciliation and redemption. There is therefore no grace of God which is not His grace in Jesus Christ and, consequently, which is not the grace of the Lord Jesus Christ Himself.

To corroborate what has been affirmed about the place of God's grace in Barth's theology each and all of his theological propositions would have to be examined under this aspect. This task cannot be undertaken within the limited scope of this volume. The pre-eminence of grace in Barth's theology and the way in which his concept of grace helps to explain the latter may however at least be illustrated by examples taken from various sections of his teaching. In general, his particular concept of grace as God's grace in Jesus Christ explains the movement of his thought from the particular to the general, from reality to possibility, from thought to action.[31] It explains his objectivism, historicism, and above all, because of the dynamic quality of grace, its actualism.[32] Again, it explains the concrete form and content of his teaching, his exclusive emphasis on revelation as the revelation of God's grace in Jesus Christ,[33] the wholly christological character of his theology,[34] the pre-eminence given in his *Church*

Dogmatics to the doctrine of the Trinity,[35] his opposition to any kind of man-made or man-owned religion as well as his teaching on true religion as the work of God's grace,[36] and the uncompromising rejection of natural theology,[37] leaving no room for any kind of synergism,[38] for any operation of grace alongside nature,[39] making, on the contrary, 'not nature but grace' the leit-motiv of his theology.[37] In this latter context it has already been pointed out that no theology has worked out the Reformation principle of *sola gratia* more comprehensively than that of Barth.[37] Further, it is on account of God's grace that in Barth's theology the initiative is always with God, that it is always God who in Jesus Christ acts first in virtue of His grace, be it in election, revelation, creation, reconciliation or redemption, so that man can always only acknowledge and accept what God has done, and is still doing, for him and to him in Jesus Christ and therefore can only show his gratitude to God in praise and thanksgiving and by his obedience to God's command.

Turning to particular features of Barth's teaching, we have already seen that with him God's grace in Jesus Christ is the beginning of all the ways and works of God *ad extra*, that that grace is the Alpha and Omega of his doctrine of God's election of grace[40] in which, to repeat what has been stressed before, the heart of Barth's theology beats, in which his teaching on the divine Providence is grounded,[41] and the function of which, as defined by Barth, is the testimony to the eternal, free and unchanging grace of God as the beginning of all His ways and works.[42] Further, in Barth's view the Word of God is the Word of grace also (see above) for this reason that it speaks to us in its very wordliness,[43] and it is ever again a work of grace when the Bible becomes for man the Word of God[44] and when the Word of God, and not the word of man, is proclaimed and heard in the Church.[45] This becoming, proclaiming, hearing is the work of the Holy Spirit in man, and, consequently, the work of God's grace in Jesus Christ since the Holy Spirit, who does this work, is said to be the Spirit of the crucified and risen Lord Jesus Christ.[46]

Again, it is precisely because God is 'wholly grace' that, as the Triune God, He is the God who in Jesus Christ is 'for us' and 'with us'. Thus the humanity of God[47] is itself an expression of God's grace, of His gracious nature, in that in virtue of His free inclination, favour and benevolence He directs His love to man and seeks and creates fellowship with him in spite of man's unworthiness and resistance to His grace. Again, man's knowledge of the Word of God and his capacity for knowing it,[48] man's knowledge of God Himself and the knowability of God,[49] the event of revelation as God's continually renewed gift to man,[50] the creation of the universe and of man,[51] man's reconciliation with God[52] and man's redemption,[53] human faith, love and hope[54] are altogether treated by Barth as the works of God's sovereign and free grace in Jesus Christ. To this may be added Barth's concepts of God's covenant with man as a covenant of grace[55] and of human existence as an existence under grace, man's destiny as willed by God being to live exclusively by and from God's grace in Jesus Christ, that is, to be utterly dependent on that grace in every sphere of life.[56] 'Man is righteous and holy before God and on the way to eternal life to the degree that he lives by the grace of God and therefore for the grace of God, for its glorification in his creaturely existence.'[57]

In this connection Barth's teaching on the grace of the Lord Jesus Christ as the first and last word about the true Christian life,[58] on the dependence of our actual progress in Christian living on our growing realization of our absolute dependence on God's grace in Jesus Christ[59] and on human freedom as a freedom of grace, under grace, and for grace[60] is of special importance. The startling question put into the mouth of Jesus Christ at His final coming as the Judge,[61] 'Did you live by grace or did you set up gods for yourself and perhaps want to become one yourself?' indicates the centrality of grace in Barth's thought. The same applies to his concepts of the Nihil as that which is opposed to the grace of God[62] as 'the basis and norm of all being, the source and criterion of all good'[63] and of sin as man's enmity towards

God's grace; [64] it is true also of his view of God's grace in Jesus Christ as the over-ruling factor in the events of world history. [65]

Again, Barth's particular concept of grace as God's grace in Jesus Christ is the starting-point and the life-blood of his doctrine of the Church. [66] In this doctrine, which has its ultimate root in Barth's doctrine of God's election of grace, [67] God's grace in Jesus Christ occupies a place of such pre-eminence that the Church as conceived by Barth may be said to be the Church of grace. [68] His concept of the Church will be understood best if we use the simile of one of those mediae-val Gothic cathedrals the lofty pillars of which soar to the heavens, but with the difference that the foundations, walls, pillars and spire of that cathedral are constructed of grace and that the whole edifice is built from above and not from below, by God and not by man. In a similar way the power of the Holy Spirit of the crucified and risen Lord Jesus Christ as the Founder and Head of His Church, which is His body, and, therefore, God's grace as manifested and operative in the living Christ gathers and builds up the Church and simul-taneously creates and continually renews the faith, love and hope of its members. [69] In view of what has been said about 'Jesus Christ and His Community' (Ch. III, 7) it may suffice in the present context to refer to Barth's teaching on the true Church as the Church where God's grace in Jesus Christ rules, [70] on the life of the Church as a life that is wholly dependent on grace, [71] and on the Church as the sphere in which men live by grace from grace. [72] Last but not least, in the chapter on 'Gospel and Law' (Ch. IV) it has been shown that the grace of God in Jesus Christ is also the light in which we have to understand Barth's ethics, that that grace is considered by him to be the answer to the ethical problem and, consequently, that his theological ethics is throughout an ethics of grace. [73]

In conclusion the question arises how Barth arrived at his tremendous and all-embracing concept of grace which domin-ates his whole theology. Since for him Jesus Christ is the incarnate grace of God in the comprehensive sense as previously indicated, this question is actually identical with the enquiry into the reasons for the key-position of Jesus Christ in Barth's theology [74] and thus is bound to receive the same answer. We must therefore once more [74] turn to the resurrection-period after Easter when the crucified and risen man Jesus Christ revealed Himself to His disciples in the glory of His Godhead and made them see that by the grace of God the reconciliation of the world with God and the salvation of mankind had not only been (objectively) accomplished by Him but had been planned by God in His grace from eternity. This is why Barth says, 'By the perception of grace at the end of the ways of God we have been led to the perception of grace at their beginning, as the presupposition of all His ways', [75] arguing that we can draw this inference only by looking upon Jesus Christ as our one and only source. Hence, his singular concept of grace is not the result of any speculation on his part but is based on his theological exegesis of God's revelation in Jesus Christ as attested in Holy Scripture.

REFERENCES

[1] Above, Ch. III.

[2] This proposition has been more fully developed in my unpublished thesis (available in Bodley, Oxford) on *Karl Barth's Conception of Grace and Its Place in His Theology* (1944); see now also G. C. Berkouwer, *The Triumph of Grace in the Theology of Karl Barth* (ET 1956).

[3] Thus my article on *Karl Barth* in the second edition (1950) of Chambers's Encyclopaedia.

[4] E.g. *Romans*, pp. 31, 59, 102 f., 150 ff., 167 ff., 172 ff., 187 ff., 200 ff., 206 ff., 213, 219 ff., 225, 239, 384 ff., 393 ff., 437; *The Word of God and the Word of Man*, p. 178; *Philippians*, pp. 12, 18 f., 22 f., 35, 39, 49, 56 f., 68, 73 f., 76; *Credo*, pp. 13, 16, 25, 37, 43 ff., 56,

66 ff., 70 ff., 90, 102 ff., 125, 131 ff., 150 ff., 165, 172, 201 ff.; *Gifford*, pp. 3 ff., 38, 43, 45 ff., 52 ff., 58, 63, 71 ff., 80 ff., 95, 118 ff., 125 ff., 140 ff., 145 ff., 169, 191 f.; see also *Theology and Church*, pp. 280 ff., 341 ff.

[5] This is his main objection to the title of G. C. Berkouwer's book (above, note 2) which seems to make the triumph of grace the basic principle of Barth's theology; see CD, IV, 3, p. 173.

[6] CD, II, 1, pp. 74, 351 ff.; II, 2, pp. 91 ff.

[7] CD, II, 1, p. 353.

[8] Ibid., p. 354.

[9] Above, Chs. II, 7, III, 2.

[10] CD, II, 1, p. 353.

[11] See above, Ch. III, 2.

[12] CD, II, 1, p. 358; II, 2, p. 92.

[13] CD, II, 1, p. 357.

[14] See further, CD, IV, 1, pp. 84 ff.

[15] Ibid., p. 84.

[16] CD, I, 1, p. 44.

[17] Above, Ch. I, 5 (3); CD, I, 1, p. 44; II, 1, p. 207, 354; TT, p. 93.

[18] Above, Ch. I, 5 (3).

[19] Above, Ch. III, 5, 6.

[20] CD, I, 1, pp. 19, 44, 75 ff., 123, 132, 159, 259, 426, 468, 481; I, 2, pp. 3, 157, 216, 224, 249, 280, 338, 344, 393, 504, 720, 755, 855; II, 1, pp. 23, 69 ff., 85, 207, 209; II, 2, pp. 3 ff., 193 f.; III, 1, p. 365; III, 2, pp. 164 ff.; IV, 1, pp. 81 ff.; IV, 3, pp. 756 ff.

[21] CD, II, 1, pp. 491 ff.

[22] CD, II, 1, pp. 354 ff.; II, 2, pp. 509 ff., 552 ff.

[23] Barth's characterization of the innertrinitarian relationship between the Father and the Son through the Holy Spirit as being also 'grace' (CD, II, 1, p. 358) seems to me to stretch the term 'grace' unduly.

[24] GL, p. 6; Dogmatics in Outline, pp. 16 ff., 57 f.; CD, II, 1, pp. 251, 353, 518 f.; II, 2, pp. 3 ff., 9 ff., 91 ff., 94 ff., 193 f.; III, 2, p. 440; IV, 1, pp. 44 f., 86.

[25] Above, Ch. III, 1, 2.

[26] Above, Ch. III, 2; CD, II, 2, pp. 94 ff.

[27] See above, Ch. III, 3.

[28] CD, IV, 1, p. 86.

[29] CD, III, 2, p. 450.

[30] Above, Ch. II, 6.

[31] Above, Ch. I, 5.

[32] Above, Ch. I, 5 (2, 3).

[33] Above, Ch. II, 6, 7.

[34] Above, Chs. I, 4; II, 6, 7; III, 1–7.

[35] Above, Chs. I, 4; II, 7.

[36] Above, Ch. II, 8.

[37] Above, Ch. II, 3.

[38] But see Ch. III, 5, espec. at note 130.

[39] CD, II, 1, p. 139.

[40] Above, Ch. III, 2.

[41] CD, III, 3, pp. 3 ff., 33 ff.

[42] CD, II, 2, p. 3.

[43] Above, Ch. II, 6; CD, I, 1, p. 193.

[44] CD, I, 1, p. 123; I, 2, p. 504.

[45] CD, I, 2, pp. 249, 504.

[46] Above, Chs. II, 7; III, 6.

[47] Above, Ch. III, 2.

[48] CD, I, 1, pp. 259, 468.

[49] CD, II, 1, pp. 20 ff., 69 ff., 74, 85 ff., 128 ff., 199, 205 ff.

[50] Above, Chs. I, 5 (3); II, 7; CD, I, 1, p. 132; II, 1, pp. 199, 205 ff.

[51] CD, III, 1, pp. 18 ff., 26 ff., 39 ff., 66 ff., 95, 118 f., 218 f., 228 ff.

[52] Above Ch. III, 6; Dogmatics in Outline, p. 115; CD, I, 1, pp. 469 ff.; IV, 1, pp. 79 ff.

[53] Credo, p. 166; Dogmatics in Outline, pp. 129 ff., 153 ff.; CD, I, 2, pp. 882 f.; IV, 3, pp. 902 ff.

[54] Above, Ch. III, 7b; CD, II, 2, p. 349; III, 3, p. 286.

[55] Above, Ch. III, 3; CD, II, 2, p. 9; IV, 1, pp. 39 ff.

[56] Above, Ch. III, 5; CD, I, 2, pp. 157, 393; II, 2, pp. 575 ff.; III, 1, pp. 363 ff.; III, 2, pp. 164 ff.; IV, 1, pp. 83 f.

[57] CD, II, 2, p. 576.

[58] Gifford, p. 147.

[59] Credo, pp. 125, 201 ff.

[60] Above, Ch. IV, 2; CD, I, 1, pp. 478 f.; II, 1, p. 585; III, 1, pp. 363 ff.; Deliverance to the Captives, p. 40.

[61] Dogmatics in Outline, p. 152.

[62] Above, Ch. III, 4; CD, III, 3, pp. 331, 353.

[63] CD, III, 3, p. 354.

[64] Above, Ch. III, 6; Credo, p. 44; CD, II, 1, pp. 152 f., 357; III, 2, pp. 26 ff., 41 ff.; IV, 1, pp. 67 ff.

[65] CD, IV, 3, pp. 706 ff.

[66] Above, Ch. III, 7.

[67] Ibid., 7a.

[68] Barth himself does not use

this phrase but the latter is implicit in all his teaching on the Church.

[69] Above, Ch. III, 7, espec. 7b.; CD, IV, 1, pp. 643 ff., 740 ff.; IV, 2, pp. 614 ff., 727 ff.; IV, 3, pp. 681 ff., 902 ff.

[70] CD, I, 2, pp. 215 ff., 338 ff.; IV, 2, pp. 614 ff.

[71] CD, I, 2, pp. 344 ff.; IV, 3, pp. 758 ff.; TT, pp. 98 f.

[72] CD, I, 2, pp. 344 ff.

[73] Above, Ch. IV, 2; CD, II, 2, pp. 509 ff., 513 ff., 538 f.; III, 4, pp. 575 ff., 647 ff.

[74] Above, Ch. III, 1.

[75] CD, IV, 1, p. 44; see also ibid., pp. 79 ff.

VI.—THE SIGNIFICANCE OF BARTH'S THEOLOGY

THE time has not yet come for a final assessment of the place of Barth's theology in the history of Christian thought. We are still in the midst of passionate controversies about the respective merits of the theologies of Barth, Bonhoeffer, Bultmann and Tillich, to mention but these eminent teachers who have influenced contemporary theological thinking more deeply than any other living theologian. However, since the theological work of Barth is now virtually complete[1] and no major changes in his present thought are to be expected, it is possible to attempt a critical estimation of his teaching.

Much has been written about the significance of Barth's theology at a time when only his early theology existed, dealing with the latter mainly as presented in *Romans* and in the first and only volume of *Christian Dogmatics*.[2] H. R. Mackintosh[3] was able to base his still useful account of Barth's teaching also on the first half-volume of *Church Dogmatics* (CD, I, 1) as well as on *Credo*. Then different labels were attached to Barth's theology, some of which are no longer valid such as 'theology on the wing',[4] 'the dialectical theology',[5] 'the theology of crisis';[6] others characterize only one aspect of it as, for instance, 'the theology of the Word of God'[7] and *'theologia viatorum'*.[8] Only a few books contain an analysis as well as a critical evaluation of Barth's mature theology, and these have come almost exclusively from the pen of Roman Catholic writers.[9] Professor T. F. Torrance's chapter on 'Barth's Place in Modern Theology'[10] is written in the light of the existent *Church Dogmatics*.[11]

Barth's immense theological work exhibits such a wealth

of diverse aspects that a truly balanced assessment of the significance of his theology would demand a critical examination of each one of them before a final verdict could be arrived at. Such a thorough investigation would seem even more necessary in view of the fact, already referred to (above, Ch. I, 1), that many of these aspects are under fierce attack from various quarters.[12] This would however require another volume. For the purpose of the present volume to introduce the reader to Barth's theology it may suffice to point out some of its major achievements and those aspects of it which lay themselves open to criticism.

There is no division of opinion even among his critics as to the greatness of Barth as a theologian.[13] Professor T. F. Torrance calls him 'the greatest theological genius that has appeared on the scene for centuries'[14] and accords him 'an honoured position among the greatest theologians of the Church—Athanasius, Augustine, Anselm, Aquinas, Luther and Calvin'.[15] Anyone who studies Barth's writings thoroughly and objectively can but agree with this verdict, no matter whether or not one's own theological convictions allow one to accept his basic theological propositions. For, as anticipated in the first chapter, Barth's theology represents a Copernican turn in the history of human thought about God, the universe and man, accomplishing such a complete change of the theological scene that it is not too much to say that a new theological epoch has been initiated by it. Though his theology did not emerge from a vacuum but can be understood only in the light of the entire history of Christian thought, many of the best insights of which are incorporated in Barth's own teaching, the originality of the latter, radically changing many traditional beliefs adhered to for centuries and compelling everyone to think afresh about such basic issues as, for instance, the relation between faith and reason, theology and philosophy, revelation and natural theology, Gospel and Law and, to mention but these, the doctrines of predestination and of man, has nevertheless influenced the theological situation of his time so profoundly that since then theologians everywhere had to take cognizance of it. Just as the fundamental theological problems raised by Barth's theology are playing a vital part in the discussions to be found in contemporary theological writings, so future theologians, Protestant and Roman Catholic alike, will not be able to by-pass them if they want their own teaching to be taken seriously.[16]

A comparison of the teaching of P. T. Forsyth[17] with that of Barth shows that, though certain affinities exist between some of the thoughts of these two theologians, it goes too far to say that 'very much of what is of special value in the work of Barth was anticipated by P. T. Forsyth'[18] and to style the latter as 'a Barthian before Barth'.[19] For whereas for Forsyth the Cross is central in his teaching and God's grace in Jesus Christ is understood in the narrower sense of God's gracious answer to human sin,[20] Barth, as we have seen,[21] emphasizes the Incarnation and the Resurrection of Jesus Christ at least as much as His Cross and conceives of God's grace in a much wider sense,[22] making God's eternal decree before time[23] the beginning of all the ways and works of God's grace *ad extra*. And there are many other fundamental differences between their respective theologies which cannot be discussed here.

Barth has restored to theology its place in the Church[24] and thereby has saved it from remaining, as in the last two or three centuries, a science cut off from the life of the Church and thus in danger of losing sight of its proper object, 'the one true God in His union with the one true man Jesus Christ', in other words, 'the history of the fulfilment of God's covenant with man'.[25] Making theology once more a function of the Church, he transformed it into a powerful instrument of the Church which on account of the constant mutual relationship between Church and theology will vitalize both of them and enable them to be open to continual reformation.

Again, he has revolutionized the theological climate that prevailed since the Reformation by making once more God and not man the starting-point, centre and goal of theological

thought. Whatever we may think of Barth's particular theological propositions, this radical reversal of man's way of
thinking is his foremost and, from the purely theological
point of view, his greatest contribution to the theology of his
time. Turning, as previously affirmed,[26] the helm through an
angle of 180 degrees, he does not express in his theology, as
was hitherto done, man's own thoughts about God, the
universe and man but restates and expounds what God has
said to man in that respect, and is continually saying to him,
in Jesus Christ and through Him. Thus theology has once
more been established on the firm foundation of the Word
of God, thereby enabling the preacher to proclaim this Word
and not his own; and this means that the attention of theology
has once more been focused on the Bible as the witness to
that Word. At the same time philosophy has thereby been
removed from the judgment-seat usurped by it and assigned
the relative position of a help-mate of theology.[27]

This Word of God as conceived by Barth is however not
the word of a *Deus ex machina* but is mediated by Jesus Christ
who is not only very God but also very man and Himself this
Word.[28] Again, it is the Word that is attested in the Bible
and thus in a human document.[29] Hence, the accusation
levelled against Barth of 'heteronomic thinking'[30] in the
sense of imposing an 'alien law' on man's mind,[31] and of giving,
in his *Church Dogmatics*, the impression of a 'gnosis fallen
from heaven'[32] has no basis in his teaching. On the contrary,
by deriving his entire theology from the divine revelation
that has actually taken place in the person and work of Jesus
Christ and is attested in the Bible, he has based it on what
has happened, and is still happening, in *this* world and in the
lives of individual men. His theology is but the account and
scientific interpretation of the history of God's covenant
with man in Jesus Christ,[33] and it is precisely for this reason
that it has developed that concreteness of thought[34] which is
another significant contribution of Barth to theology. For
he has thereby delivered theology from the shackles of rigidly
defined abstract and neutral philosophical concepts which

for so long had prevented it from reflecting as accurately as humanly possible God's revelation in Jesus Christ as attested in the Bible.[35]

The concreteness of Barth's thought has found its most potent expression in his concrete concept of God as the living personal God who as the Triune God constantly takes the lead and moves first in the world of man.[36] Barth's emphasis on God's continual active initiative in the affairs of men, working out His purpose for man in the very midst of mankind by the power of the Holy Spirit,[37] is one of the most vital aspects of his theology, invalidating criticisms of what has been regarded as Barth's purely transcendental concept of God.[38] At this juncture in the history of human thought when, disregarding God's self-revelation in Jesus Christ, once more the attempt is made to conceive of God in purely abstract formulas such as 'being itself' and 'the depth and ground of all being'[39] or 'ultimate reality',[40] it is of the utmost importance that Barth asks us to seek God nowhere else than in Jesus Christ.[41] His wholly christological teaching, assigning to Jesus Christ a unique place in theology,[42] only draws to the fullest possible extent and in accordance with the testimony of the Bible the necessary conclusions from the historical fact that in Jesus Christ God Himself has assumed human nature. The meaning of the Incarnation has been expounded by him in a manner which in respect of its comprehensiveness and profundity has no equal in the history of Christian dogmatics.

Again, as regards the doctrine of man Barth's teaching on man's utter dependence in everything on God's sovereign and free grace in Jesus Christ and on the perfect sufficiency of that grace for man[43] contains, besides his fundamental theme of God's eternal Yes to His creation and to man in particular,[44] the most powerful and most timely prophetic message of his theology. In a world which in its arrogance, to use Barth's pertinent comment on Bonhoeffer's familiar phrase, 'thinks' that it has 'come of age',[45] man's need of this message is perhaps even greater than it was ever before. The thorough demythologization of the human ego in Barth's theological anthropology, though reducing man to his proper size, is nevertheless balanced by his teaching on man's God-given freedom, allowing man full scope for free and responsible decisions and actions within the limitation of that freedom.[46] In making this freedom the foundation of his theological ethics Barth has thereby opened up a new vista in this field of dogmatics which will prove fruitful in future studies of this subject-matter. It should be viewed together with his teaching on humanity as co-humanity[47] in order that the full implications of these two basic principles of his theology may be grasped. Again, the conception of the freedom into which man is called by God in Jesus Christ and the manner in which this concept has been worked out in the special ethics of the command of God the Creator[48] prove, together with the concept of humanity as co-humanity and with Barth's teaching on the Church and its mission in the world,[49] that the criticism of the remoteness of his theology from the world in which we live is unjustified.

Another major achievement of Barth's theology is its clear distinction between religion and faith and its rejection of all man-made and man-owned religion, which prepared the way for Bonhoeffer's concept of 'religionless Christianity'.[50] Barth thereby recovered the New Testament truth that religion which is not the result and reflection of a living faith and does not issue in an active life of service and witness is not true religion.[51] Finally, reference must be made to the catholicity of Barth's theology. Having drawn on the treasure of Christian wisdom throughout the ages,[52] his searching questions addressed to patristic, mediaeval, Lutheran and Reformed theologians alike, together with his penetrating criticism of much controversial teaching of Roman Catholicism, will be of great value in future efforts in the ecumenical field to achieve Christian unity. His doctrine of the Church in particular[53] contains much fresh thought which future endeavours to reform the Church could disregard only to their own detriment.

On the other hand, the following major aspects of his theology are open to criticism:

(1) In the course of the exposition of the epistemological foundation of Barth's theology [54] the rejection of apologetics as part of dogmatics has been queried. This rejection is one of the vulnerable points of his teaching as it is difficult to see how the mind of modern man who, generally speaking, is no longer interested in religion can be reached by his teaching and how in particular agnostics and atheists who reject the premiss of faith can be convinced of the truth of the Gospel. Barth's so far negative attitude also bars the way to a fruitful conversation with other religions starting from a different presupposition. His reference, in answer to such objections, to the power of the Holy Spirit to work the miracle of faith wrongly excludes the possibility, admitted by himself, [55] that Jesus Christ as the Lord of the cosmos may speak God's Word in the world through the agency of the Holy Spirit also in a purely secular fashion and thereby may pave the way for the recognition and acceptance of the truth of the Gospel. In other words, it wrongly excludes the possibility that an apologetics informed and enlightened by the Holy Spirit may work in this way and achieve this end. His further argument of the inner consistency of the *intellectus fidei* [56] breaks down where the premiss of faith is denied since the inner consistency of a series of theological propositions does not necessarily imply the vindication of their premiss. Again, his disparaging view of the problem of communication [57] underestimates the value of an intellectual approach to the unbeliever which refrains from making the Christian Faith the starting-point of the conversation.

(2) Though Barth is right in what he is fighting for in his battle against the *analogia entis*, [58] he is wrong in his understanding of that term as used by Thomas Aquinas. The *analogia entis* as understood by the latter is not, or at least not primarily, concerned with two separate kinds of being and their mutual properties but with a distinct predication about the being of one and the same being. 'Being,' writes G. B.

Phelan is his study on 'St. Thomas and Analogy',[59] 'belongs intrinsically to all that is and to each and everything analogically, that is, in proportion to its nature'; in other words, 'being as such is intrinsically analogical'.[60] Hence, the *analogia entis* predicates that each thing possesses being in proportion to its nature and that each being exercises the act of existence in proportion to its essence. Thus understood, the thomistic analogy of being is not at variance with Barth's teaching on God and on man respectively.[61]

(3) Barth makes no distinction between the Son of God as the *designate* Godman Jesus Christ and Jesus Christ as very God *and* very man. He treats the latter as if He too existed from eternity,[62] though He can properly thus be styled only after His birth. In speaking throughout of 'Jesus Christ', Barth obviously wants to stress the continuity between the Son of God and Jesus Christ and, in a sense, their identity; but the language used by him to that end is, theologically, open to question since according to his own teaching[63] Jesus Christ, in contrast to the Son of God, existed before the Incarnation only in the form of God's thought and will.

(4) The proposition that the Son of God is the Subject of the person of Jesus Christ[64] casts a doubt upon the true humanity of Jesus Christ. On the basis of the doctrine of the two Natures of Jesus Christ hardly anyone will object to the principle that priority must be given to the divine nature over the human nature.[65] It is, however, quite a different matter to assert the exclusively divine nature of the Subject of the being of Jesus Christ. Barth's argument that individuality but not Person is necessary to human nature, that humanity means the nature or essence of man whereas personality means the existence of a man,[66] and that the latter but not the former is determined and expressed by the Subject, disregards the fact that the ego, that is, the subject of a human being, is an integral element in both his humanity and his personality. There is not such a thing as an abstract human nature. The latter always requires an ego to make it

what is is, that is, man. Though J. S. Bezzant's solution[67] that in Christ 'two subjects were combined in synthetic activities' is not acceptable as it implies the self-contradictory conception of two egos in one and the same person,[68] it is not impossible to think of the Subject of the person of Jesus Christ as being from the beginning both divine and human without falling either into the Nestorian heresy of dividing Jesus Christ into two persons or into the heresy of Adoptianism, the Spirit of God (Jn. 4:24) blending at the Incarnation and in a manner we cannot comprehend with the human centre of consciousness, the human ego.[69]

(5) The proposition that man's acknowledgement and acceptance of God's grace in Jesus Christ is man's own free and responsible decision and action inplies, contrary to Barth's teaching,[70] a co-operation of some sort on the part of man. In his legitimate endeavour to make quite clear that in the relationship between God and man God works everything and man can add nothing to it, Barth goes too far in denying any co-operation on man's part. If, for instance, the subjective revelation and the subjective reconciliation require for their completion man's acknowledgement and acceptance and if the latter are man's own free and responsible decision and action,[71] man does co-operate at least to this extent even though, paradoxically, his co-operation is the work of God's grace. To deny this, is to deny man's free and responsible decision and action.

(6) Barth has no satisfactory answer to the question why some hear the Word of God and believe whilst other fail to do so.[72] If the rejection of God's Word is the impossible and inexplicable behaviour on the part of some men, there must be something in those who accept it by virtue of their own free choice and decision which constrains them to act in this way; in other words, there must be in them a will to good.[73] To counter this by saying that man's faith is the exclusive work of the Holy Spirit in man is begging the question since in that case the question arises: why then do not all men believe? To assume that God gives faith to some but not to

others contradicts the truth of His love to all men. Since man is created good, [74] may it not be that, though he is a sinner, there is some will to good in this or that man which causes him to respond to God's Word in Jesus Christ? If we deny this, as Barth does, we are left with a riddle. On the other hand, that will to good, in the last analysis, would still be the work of God's grace.

(7) Barth's vital teaching on the objective and subjective aspects of reconciliation [75] fails to clarify the relation between these two aspects. If Jesus Christ has already objectively accomplished man's reconciliation with God by His own reconciling work, in other words, if all men are already objectively justified, sanctified and called in Jesus Christ, the question arises why in this case the subjective reconciliation is needed to 'complete' the work of reconciliation. Are not in this case all men already reconciled with God in Jesus Christ as the representative of all men so that nothing further is required in that respect? On the other hand, if the subjective reconciliation is still necessary for the completion of the work of reconciliation, what is the meaning of the objective completeness of the work of reconciliation, in particular with regard to those who refuse to acknowledge and accept their reconciliation with God? These questions remain unanswered in Barth's doctrine of reconciliation. He has however probably done what we frequently find in his theology: to drive an argument home, he may have expressed one truth without qualifying it at the same time by another truth. In distinguishing between the objective and the subjective aspect of reconciliation he may only mean to emphasize the twofold truth that the work of reconciliation has been accomplished by Jesus Christ to the extent that man cannot and need not do anything more in that respect than acknowledge and accept this saving fact but, on the other hand, must do so if he wants to partake of the fruits of that work. If this is the case, the meaning of the objective reconciliation is qualified and limited by the meaning of the subjective reconciliation.

In conclusion, these criticisms can in no wise detract from

N

the achievements of Barth's theology. The beauty, profundity and universality of the latter is not rivalled by any of the other theologies that have appeared since the Reformation. For the rest, Barth himself would be the first to admit that what ultimately matters is not whether he or Tillich, Bonhoeffer or Bultmann, will be the theologian who will be listened to by future generations but that Jesus Christ is heard and obeyed as the crucified and risen Lord of all men, as the Victor over the Nihil whose final triumph over sin and death will be revealed to the whole cosmos at His final coming, and as the One who is 'the ground, the theme and the goal' of the Christian hope.[76] To the presentation, interpretation and glorification of God's all-embracing and eternal action in Jesus Christ, above all to the proclamation of God's gracious, victorious and joyful Yes to His creation in Jesus Christ, Barth's mature theological work is devoted, and it will be for this reason, if not for any others, that his theology will occupy a pre-eminent and lasting place in the history of Christian thought.

REFERENCES

[1] See above, Ch. I, 4; a brief outline of Barth's doctrine of redemption will be found in his *Dogmatics in Outline*, pp. 129 ff., 153 ff.; see also *Credo*, pp. 166 ff.; CD, I, 1, pp. 513 ff.; I, 2, pp. 875 ff., 882 f.; II, 1, pp. 629 ff.; IV, 1, pp. 110 ff., 116 ff.; IV, 3, pp. 902 ff.

[2] See above, Ch. I, 3; further, John McConnachie, *The Significance of Karl Barth* (1931); the same, *The Barthian Theology* (1933); A. Birch Hoyle, *The Teaching of Karl Barth* (1930).

[3] *Types of Modern Theology* (1937), pp. 263 ff.

[4] Because his thought then 'moved' and did not 'crystallize'; H. R. Mackintosh, op. cit., p. 264.

[5] Above, Ch. I, 3; H. R. Mackintosh, op. cit., pp. 266 ff.; John McConnachie, *The Significance of Karl Barth*, pp. 78 ff.

[6] Above, Ch. I, 3; H. R. Mackintosh, op. cit., p. 265; John McConnachie, op. cit., pp. 45, 73 f., 242 ff.

[7] This is how H. R. Mackintosh, op. cit., p. 263, calls it; see also John McConnachie, op. cit., pp. 93 ff., 266 f.

[8] Above, Ch. I, 5; John McConnachie, op. cit., p. 18.

[9] See Grover E. Foley's valuable paper, 'The Catholic Critics of Karl Barth', SJT, vol. 14, no. 2., pp. 136 ff., giving both an outline and analysis of their writings and the reasons for this striking phenomenon.

[10] In *Karl Barth: An Introduc-*

tion to his Early Theology 1910–1931 (1962), pp. 199 ff.

[11] See now also A. B. Come's book, *An Introduction to Barth's Dogmatics For Preachers* (1963), the title of which indicates its limited purpose.

[12] Some of these criticisms have been dealt with in the course of this study and others are referred to in this chapter.

[13] John Baillie, *The Sense of the Presence of God*, p. 254; A. B. Come, op. cit., p. 21; H. R. Mackintosh, op. cit., p. 319; R. Gregor Smith in his Foreword to *Against the Stream*, pp. 7 ff.; G. C. Berkouwer, *The Triumph of Grace in the Theology of Karl Barth*, pp. 9 ff.

[14] Introduction to *Theology and Church*, p. 7.

[15] *Karl Barth: An Introduction to His Early Theology 1910–1931*, p. 15.

[16] Likewise John Baillie, op. cit., pp. 254 f.; John Marsh, Preface to *Deliverance to the Captives*, p. 7.

[17] W. L. Bradley, *P. T. Forsyth* (1952), pp. 64 ff., 113 ff.; Gwilym O. Griffith, *The Theology of P. T. Forsyth* (1948).

[18] J. K. Mozley, as quoted by Griffith, op. cit., pp. 18 f.

[19] John McConnachie, as quoted by Bradley, op. cit., pp. 259, 268.

[20] Griffith, op. cit., pp. 28, 93 f.; Bradley, op. cit., pp. 252 ff., 273 ff.

[21] Above, Chs. II, 1, 7; III, 1.

[22] Above, Ch. V.

[23] Above, Ch. III, 2.

[24] Above, Ch. II, 1.

[25] IET, p. 202.

[26] Above, Ch. I, 1.

[27] Above, Ch. II, 4.

[28] Above, Ch. II, 6.

[29] Ibid.

[30] Tillich, *The Protestant Era* (ET 1951), pp. 52, 61 f., 95; R. Gregor Smith, *The New Man*, pp. 54 ff.

[31] It may be alien to the mind of sinful man but not to the eyes of faith.

[32] A. B. Come, op. cit., p. 140.

[33] Above, Ch. I, 4, 5 (2b).

[34] Above, Ch. I, 5 (1a).

[35] Above, Chs. I, 5 (1a); II, 4.

[36] Above, Chs. II, 7; III, 2.

[37] Above, Chs. I, 5 (2a); II, 7 (4); see also his address on *Das Christentum und die Religion*, Junge Kirche 8/1963, pp. 436 ff.; D. Jenkins, *Beyond Religion*, pp. 14 ff.

[38] E. Bethge, op. cit., p. 8; R. Gregor Smith, op. cit., pp. 56, 76, 88.

[39] Tillich, *Systematic Theology*, vols. I, pp. 261 ff., II, pp. 8 ff.; the same, *The Shaking of the Foundations* (1949), p. 57.

[40] John A. T. Robinson, *Honest to God* (1963), pp. 29, 55, 226.

[41] And so does Bonhoeffer, see E. Bethge, op. cit., p. 8.

[42] Above, Ch. III, 1.

[43] Above, Chs. III, 5; V.

[44] Above, Ch. III, 4.

[45] *The Humanity of God*, loc. cit., p. 47.

[46] Above, Chs. III, 5; IV, 2.

[47] Above, Ch. III, 5.

[48] Above, Ch. IV, 2, 3.

[49] Above, Ch. III, 7.

[50] Above, Ch. II, 8; Daniel Jenkins, op. cit., pp. 12, 15 f.

[51] Above, Chs. II, 8; III, 7.

[52] See above, Ch. I, 4.

[53] Above, Ch. III, 7.

[54] Above, Ch. II, 2.

[55] Above, Ch. II, 6.

[56] Above, Ch. II, 2.

[57] *The Humanity of God*, loc. cit., pp. 46 f.

[58] Above, Ch. II, 3.

[59] The Aquinas Lectures 1941 of the Aristotelian Society of Marquette University, Milwaukee, Wisconsin, U.S.A., p. 8.

[60] Ibid., pp. 2, 7.

[61] See further, H. U. von Balthasar, *Karl Barth, Darstellung und Deutung seiner Theologie*, pp. 93 ff.; A. B. Come, op. cit., p. 142 ff.

[62] 'There is no *Logos asarkos*, but only *ensarkos*', TT, p. 49; see also ibid., p. 52.

[63] Above, Chs. II, 7 (3); III, 1, 2.

[64] Above, Ch. II, 7 (3).

[65] Above, Ch. II, 7 (3); TT, p. 25.

[66] TT, p. 49.

[67] *Objections to Christian Belief*, pp. 101 f.

[68] But see Nels F. S. Ferré, *Christ and the Christian* (1958), pp. 79 f., 191, 198, who, though denying that there were two egos in Jesus, yet claims that in Him God was the consummating co-Subject along with an accepting human subject within a truly united and genuine personality.

[69] See D. M. Baillie, *God was in Christ*, p. 91 and N. Micklem, *Ultimate Questions* (1955), pp. 96 ff., espec. 102 f.

[70] Above, Chs. I, 5 (3); II, 7 (4); III, 5, 6; V.

[71] Above, Ch. II, 7 (4); III, 6.

[72] Above, Ch. II, 7 (4).

[73] See further, J. S. Bezzant, op. cit., p. 99.

[74] Above, Ch. III, 4.

[75] Above, Ch. III, 6.

[76] CD, IV, 3, p. 915.

SHORT BIBLIOGRAPHY

THIS is only a small selection from the multitude of Barth's own writings and from works dealing with Barth's theology either exclusively or in part. Only writings in English, particularly useful to students, have been included in this brief list. For further studies consult the *Selected Bibliography* in Professor T. F. Torrance's book on *Karl Barth, An Introduction to His Early Theology 1910–1931*, pp. 219 ff. and the more comprehensive bibliography in Karl Barth's, *The Faith of the Church*, Fontana Books, 1960, pp. 147 ff.

I. WORKS BY KARL BARTH

The Epistle to the Romans (1919), 6th edition, translated by Sir Edwyn C. Hoskyns (1933).

The Word of God and the Word of Man (1924), translated by Douglas Horton (1928).

The Epistle to the Philippians (1928), 6th edition, translated by J. W. Leitch (1962).

Theology and Church, Shorter Writings 1920–8, translated by L. P. Smith, with an Introduction (1962) by T. F. Torrance.

Anselm: Fides quaerens intellectum (1931), translated from the second edition (1958) by I. W. Robertson (1960).

Natural Theology (1934), comprising 'Nature and Grace' by E. Brunner and the reply 'No!' by Karl Barth, translated by P. Fraenkel (1946).

Credo (1935), translated by J. Strathearn McNab (1936).

The Knowledge of God and the Service of God, Gifford Lectures 1937/38, translated by J. L. M. Haire and I. Henderson (1938).

Dogmatics in Outline (1947), translated by G. T. Thomson (1949).

Church Dogmatics, edited by G. W. Bromiley and T. F. Torrance (1956–62).

I, 1, The Doctrine of the Word of God, Prolegomena Part 1 (1932), ET 1936.

I, 2, The Doctrine of the Word of God, Prolegomena Part 2 (1938), ET 1956.

II, 1, The Doctrine of God, Part 1 (1940), ET 1957.

II, 2, The Doctrine of God, Part 2 (1942), ET 1957.

III, 1–4, The Doctrine of Creation (1945–51), ET Part 1 (1958), 2 (1960), 3 (1961), 4 (1961).

IV, 1–3, The Doctrine of Reconciliation (1953–59), ET Part 1 (1956), 2 (1958), 3, vols. 1 and 2 (1961 and 1962).

From Rousseau to Ritschl, being the translation (1959) by B. Cozens and H. Hartwell of eleven chapters of *Die Protestantische Theologie im 19. Jahrhundert* (1947).

Christ and Adam, Man and Humanity in Romans 5 (1952), translated by T. A. Small, SJT, Occasional Papers No. 5 (1956).

Against the Stream, Shorter Post-War Writings 1946–52, edited by R. Gregor Smith (1954).

Shorter Commentary on Romans (1956), translated by D. H. van Daalen (1959).

God, Grace and Gospel, comprising 'Gospel and Law' (1956), 'The Humanity of God' (1956) and 'Evangelical Theology in the 19th Century' (1957), translated by J. Strathearn McNab, SJT, Occasional Papers No. 8 (1959).

Karl Barth's Table Talk, recorded and edited by J. D. Godsey, SJT, Occasional Papers No. 10 (1963).

Deliverance to the Captives (1959), a collection of sermons, translated by M. Wieser (1961), with a Preface by John Marsh.

Church Dogmatics, A Selection with Introduction by H. Gollwitzer (1957), translated and edited by G. W. Bromiley (1961).

The Humanity of God, containing, besides two essays translated in 'God, Grace and Gospel', 'The Gift of Freedom'
(1953), translated by J. N. Thomas and T. Wieser (1961).

Evangelical Theology: An Introduction (1963), ET by Grover
Foley of *Einführung in die evangelische Theologie* (1962).

II. Works on Karl Barth

H. R. Mackintosh, *Types of Modern Theology* (1937), pp.
263 ff.

O. Weber, *Karl Barth's Church Dogmatics*, An Introductory
Report on Vols, I, 1, to III, 4 (1950), ET by A. C.
Cochrane (1953).

T. F. Torrance, *Karl Barth, An Introduction to His Early
Theology 1910–1931* (1962).

A. B. Come, *An Introduction to Barth's Dogmatics for Preachers*
(1963).

G. C. Berkouwer, *The Triumph of Grace in the Theology of
Karl Barth*, translated from the Dutch by H. R. Boer
(1956).

G. Wingren, *Theology in Conflict: Nygren–Barth–Bultmann*,
translated from the Swedish by E. H. Wahlstrom (1958).

J. Brown, *Subject and Object in Modern Theology* (1955),
ch. VI. (pp. 140 ff.): God, 'Indissolubly Subject': Karl
Barth.

T. H. L. Parker, 'Karl Barth and the Fourth Gospel' in
Studies in the Fourth Gospel, edited by F. L. Cross (1957),
pp. 52 ff.

R. S. Franks, *The Doctrine of the Trinity* (1953), pp. 177 ff.:
Barth.

D. Cairns, *The Image of God in Man* (1953), pp. 164 ff.: The
Image of God in Karl Barth.

INDEX OF PERSONS

195

INDEX OF SUBJECTS

THE THEOLOGY OF KARL BARTH